To HERM
Jackso
Fred McDavit
+ Etta

Close Calls & Happy Landings

Fred McCarthy

Close Calls & Happy Landings

ADVENTURES IN BOATBUILDING, FLYING, AND LIFE

And so on...
BOOKS

Copyright© 2010 by Fredric McCarthy

All rights reserved. No part of this book may be reproduced or transmitted in any form or by any means, electronic or mechanical, including photocopy, recording, or any information storage and retrieval system, without permission in writing from the publishers.

For permission to make copies of any part of this work, contact:
Fredric McCarthy, P.O., Box 202, Lumberton, NJ 08048

This book is available for purchase at www.booksurge.com

ISBN: 1-4392-6440-6

First edition
Printed in the United States of America

For Etta

Acknowledgements

Etta and I wish to thank Rita Myers and Sarah McElwain for their guidance and help in putting this book together. We would also like to thank our nephew, Michael Piazza, and our neice, Michele Quinones, for all their help.

It was *not* a piece of cake!

Contents

Foreword — 1

Early Years

MY FAMILY AND FRIENDS
Chicago And Oaklyn — 3
A Night To Remember — 8
The Forgotten Shop Teacher — 12
New York Shipyard — 14
Sun Shipyard — 17
The Lifeboat — 20
The Lifeboat Engine — 22
Meeting The Clowers — 23
A Great Day — 27

WORK AFTER THE WAR
My First Job After WWII — 29
My Second Job After WWII — 30
The Big One That Got Away — 32
The Paper Trail — 33
The Savannah Tow — 34

AMERICAN DREDGING COMPANY
The Dredge *Pennsylvania* — 38
The Condenser — 41
Gus Tatman — 42
Payday — 43
Harry Austin And The Whirly Crane — 44
Harry Austin And The Stiff Leg Crane — 45
Harry Austin And The "A" Bar — 46
Harry Austin And The Straw — 47
The Golden Gloves — 47
The C&D Canal — 48
Collision On The C&D — 49
Eddy Bennett — 49
Eddy Bennett And Fort Delaware — 55
The New Dredge — 56
Bad Union Representative — 58
Tugboat Shaker — 59

PLANES
Flying School — 61
Navy N2T, Clementon Airport — 62
Navy N2T, Camden Airport — 66
The Clowers Of Pennington — 67
Navy N2T Comes To An End — 71
The Bird — 72
The Bird, New York Trip — 77
The Bird, Final Trip — 79
The Porterfield — 80

LOVE AND THE SAND PLANT
The Sand Plant — 81
Donuts And Conveyers — 84
Our First Date — 85
The Conveyor — 87
The Black Dress — 89
The Big Wedding — 90
The Honeymoon — 91
The *Etta* — 96

Partnerships

LIFE BEGINS WITH ETTA
Our First Apartment — 101
The Ordeal — 102
The Bishop — 104
The Cinnaminson House — 106
An Afternoon On The Front Porch In Cinnaminson — 107
Etta's First Flight — 109
Navion Flights To Lewes, Delaware — 111

FLYING FARMERS
Flying To Florida — 116
Flying To The Bahamas — 117
Bahamas' West End — 120
Flying Farmers Going Home — 124

SEA MAC

Bottom Design	128
The Ice House	132
The Cherubini Family	137
Mike Chaccio The Crook	139
The Seafarers	140
The Painter Is Sick	142
The Warehouse	146
The Beginning Of The End	149
The End Of Sea Mac	150

JERSEY BOAT WORKS / JERSEY YACHTS

Gordon Keenan, Norwalk Boats	154
The Partnership	155
The Pond	157
Wood To Fiberglass	158
How The Jersey Boats Exhaust System Was Born	161
The First Jersey 40'	163
Diesel 31' Fuel Coolers	166
The Break-Up	170
My Son Freddy	171
Don't Turn Your Back	174
The Big Boss	176
The New Line	178
The Buy-Out	180
The Changing Of The Guard	182
Their True Colors	186

MY FRIEND RUSS

Russ The Photographer	188
The *Miss Terri*	191
Our First Fishing Tournament	193
A Photo Trip	196
The Haddonfield Fishing Club	198
Haddonfield Fishing Club, Cabo San Lucas	200
Mark Homan	203

MORE PLANES

Piper Apache	205
Paul Prince, Camden Airport Flying School	210
The 303	211
Gene Giehl	212
You Gotta Have Balance	216

A New Life

OUR HOME IN LUMBERTON

Looking Around	219
The Right Spot	221
Making Plans	222
The Easement	223
The Boy Scouts	224
The Old Adze	226
The Stairs	228
The Machine Shop	230
Powering The Shop	234
George Homan	238
FHMC	239

TRAINS

The 4-4-0 Locomotive Comes To Life	241
The Maine Two Footer	242
The Colorado Trip	245
The Big Train	247
The State Of New Jersey Undermines Santa Claus	249

WE ALL MAKE MISTAKES

January 24, 2009	254
Afterword	257

Foreword

"Ta-da! Piece of cake."
— Fred McCarthy

Fred doesn't brag and isn't flashy. He always tries to make the hard things seem easy, and he downplays his success as a "piece of cake" and a stroke of luck. So when Fred told me that he wanted to write a book, I grabbed a pad and pen right away and said, "Start talking." I was excited that everyone would be able to read the entertaining stories of a man who did everything he set out to do—someone who never saw problems, only solutions. A person we can all learn from.

When I first met Fred and he showed me the boat he had built in his parents' yard, I knew he was special. He was handsome, for sure—he reminded me of a cross between Alan Ladd and Dennis O'Keefe—but what stood out most was his kindness. He was a gentleman, and my mother approved of him immediately. She never enforced my curfew of 11:00 p.m. In the years since, Fred would prove over and over that he had not only hands of gold, but also a heart of gold.

I want people to remember him for what he is: a wonderful, creative, dedicated, trustworthy, and caring man. Through his generosity, he opened the doors to different worlds and privately helped many in need. Whether cruising to the Bahamas, flying through the Bermuda Triangle, or riding a steam locomotive around Train Tree Plantation, my life with Fred has been a fun and amazing ride. We will be partners forever, and I can't imagine life without him.

I am so proud and grateful to be his co-pilot. I hope you enjoy reading these stories as much as we enjoyed living them.

— Etta McCarthy

Early Years

My Family and Friends

CHICAGO AND OAKLYN

In the summer of 1931, when I was five, we visited Aunt Mercedes and Uncle Danny. At the time, they didn't have any children. Aunt Dee Dee loved me and treated me like her own child. They lived on the first floor of a flat in Chicago. Their neighbors, the Staubes, always offered me ginger ale, which I was dying for, but we were taught never to accept offerings like this.

On this particular visit, my Aunt Mercedes gave me a flint gun that looked like a toy gun. It shot sparks that were created by a little wheel that rubbed on the flint. During the Depression, people stole automobiles, then drove them to some back alley where they would steal the battery, tires, and whatever else they could sell. We called them "alley pickers." On this day one of these cars was in the alley behind my aunt's apartment, and a white man was picking over what had been left by the car thief. He had a black man helping him strip the car.

I can't remember what the black man was wearing,

but the white man wore a World War I army overcoat that came down to his high-top shoes. I was playing cops and robbers with a couple of kids in the neighborhood and thought the stripped automobile would make a great hiding place. I was hiding under the car when I saw this neat little hole over my head. What a great place to shoot my flint gun! Well, you can imagine what happened when the flint gun shot into the gas tank.

My aunt was talking to my mother when they heard this terrific explosion, which could be heard for quite a distance. The first words out of my Aunt Mercedes' mouth were, "Oh my God! What has he done now?"

The white man was leaning over the fence. His World War I army coat was on fire. The black man was beating the army coat to put out the fire. The white man was calling out at the top of his lungs, "You little son of a bitch! Son of a bitch!"

I kept hearing those words until I got out of sight. No one was seriously injured. Fortunately, the crooks had stolen almost all of the gasoline in the tank. The smell of burning hair always makes me think of that day.

Chicago in the middle and late thirties was quite a place. I had two close friends: Conrad Rother and Joey Bosco. Conrad's family ran a little candy store, and Joey's father had a six-lane bowling alley. Conrad's father would go back to Germany every summer for a month. He would bring back small toy soldiers dressed in SS uniforms, carrying flags with the swastika emblem. I used to hear my parents talking, and they were under the impression that Conrad's father was a German spy. Who could afford to go back to Germany during the deep Depression? We moved in 1939, so we never knew what happened to the Rothers.

One night I was lying in bed when the whole house shook from a big explosion. We found out the next day that someone blew up Joe's father's bowling alley, which was half a block from our house. Joe's father wouldn't pay protection money.

When it was time to get a haircut, my mother would give me fifteen cents and I would walk four or five blocks to this big fat lady's house. She wore a housedress and had a Dutch boy haircut, and cut hair for fifteen cents in the living room. The last time I went for a fifteen-cent haircut, her husband was sitting on the steps smoking a cigarette when this car drove up, and blew him away with a gun. Apparently, they wouldn't kick back a percent of their fifteen-cent haircut charge.

As far as I can remember, I only took one walk with my father. We were walking by our local gas station, the kind where the attendant pumped gas by hand. There was a glass container on top of the pump marked 1 to 10 gallons. He put the hose in your tank and the gasoline would gravity-feed into your car. My father would always say, "Give me a buck's worth," which kept the old Model A going for a long time.

A car drove up to the gas pump. We heard several gun shots and the attendant fell to the ground. I wanted to run over to see what was happening, but I remember till this day my father grabbing my hand and almost jerking my arm off to get away from this terrible scene.

We only lived a block from Chicago's North Western Railroad tracks. It was during the Great Depression and men called hobos would ride the rails begging for food wherever they could. They went from town to town looking for work. They were good people, just down on their luck. My mother said to my dad one day, "Why do the hobos only stop at our house asking for something to eat and skip all the other houses?"

"I don't know," Dad said.

"I know why," I said.

"Why?" she asked.

"I'll show you." I went out the front door and walked down to the street curb. "Mom, do you see the letter 'E' in yellow chalk?" "Yes," she said.

"If that was an 'H,' like next door, it would mean 'here you will go hungry.' You have the letter 'E' that means 'here you will get something to eat.' If you change the 'E' to an 'H,' the hobos won't stop here anymore."

As my mother started walking back to the house, she turned and said, "Leave the 'E' alone."

When I was almost 10, my father came home one evening and told my mother, my brother, and me that he had been asked to move to Camden, NJ to start a service company for RCA Victor. My mother asked, "Where is it?"

My dad answered, "It's a little town across the river from Philadelphia, PA, and it's about 55 miles from the Atlantic Ocean."

When I heard the words "Atlantic Ocean," I couldn't wait to move. We all thought it would be a great adventure. My father was to move first, and we would follow about 30 days later. Just before he headed to Camden in his 1931, two-door Model A Ford he took me aside and said that I was now the man of the house and should take care of my mother and younger brother. This meant banking the coal-burning heater, cleaning the basement, selling whatever I could and packing up the house for moving.

The first thing I did was put some electric motors that my father had accumulated into my American Flyer red wagon to see them. After many stops, the man at the tin shop said he would give me a quarter for each electric motor. Success at last! The next step was to clean up the basement. To this day, it's a job I still hate.

My father was a very inquisitive man and was always working on some project. Anything he couldn't use that would burn went into the coal bin. In one section of his cluttered workshop there were several glass containers. I really didn't know what to do with the contents, so I emptied them out in the coal bin. The cheapest coal at the time was soft, or "bituminous" coal It burns very rapidly, so to keep the furnace going all night, you had to bank the fire.

This was a very simple procedure. First, you shook the fire down so the ashes fell into the bottom of the furnace, which was called the ash pit. The second step was to put in enough coal to last the night. Finally, you shoveled the ashes out of the pit and covered the coal completely. The ashes retarded the burning rate of the coal, so the fire lasted all night.

One night, I was sound asleep when I woke up and heard my mother screaming, "Freddy, Freddy! Get up!" When I got up, I could feel the floor shaking. The house was very hot and my mother was hysterical. Then there was a big boom. I ran downstairs to the basement and found the fire and ash pit doors of the furnace blown wide open and flames bulging out of the door. I was scared to death. The smoke pipe had blown off the back of the furnace and the basement was beginning to fill up with smoke.

I didn't know what to do, so I didn't do anything. I couldn't call the fire department, because we didn't have a telephone; in those days, no one could afford one. Now that I think back, I have no idea where the nearest fire station was.

After about five minutes, which seemed like an eternity, the fire died down. I closed the doors and put the smoke pipe back up. We opened the windows to let the smoke out. It was bitter cold that night, and by the time the smoke cleared the fire was almost out, and the house was very cold.

When we finally moved to New Jersey to meet my dad, I told him what had happened. He told me one of the jars that I emptied into the coal bin contained gun cotton, out of which they make gunpowder. That old furnace really rumbled and roared.

I found a wooden barrel and brought it home. It was time to pack the dishes for our journey to New Jersey. The dishes were from our local movie house. Every time we went to the movies, it cost 10 cents. You got whatever they gave away that night: a cup, saucer, whatever. I went around the neighborhood with my little red wagon and loaded it up with all the newspapers I could find. My mother and I wrapped each piece of the special china in newspaper. I very carefully packed everything in the barrel, nailed the lid on, and it was ready to go.

My dad drove to Camden, NJ in his 1931 Model A Ford. My mother, brother, and I went by Greyhound bus a month later. I can still remember the bus ride. It took two days from start to finish, from Chicago to Camden. There were no turnpikes or expressways in those days.

Route 30 ran town to town, from California to Atlantic City, NJ. The route went through every town and every red light. One night in the pouring rain, we stopped on the top of a mountain in Pennsylvania for dinner. I can still see the bus in the pouring rain, and hear the bus driver calling my younger brother Bob, "Whitey." Bob had bright blond hair.

This took place over seventy years ago, but it feels like yesterday.

My father had been living in a boarding house on Cooper Street in Camden. We moved in with him. It had one room, with a bathroom down the hall, but it wasn't that bad. To pass the time, I made small airplane models on the windowsill. But we needed to find a bigger place to stay.

The first house we found was in Parkside, NJ. I started school, but we only stayed in that house for three weeks. For some unknown reason, we moved again to Fairview, NJ where I started school for the second time. It was a row home, which was quite different for us, because in the Chicago area there were no such things. We had been there about a month when my mother turned on the kitchen light one night and saw the floor covered with black water roaches. This was something we had never seen before.

Within a couple of days, my parents found a little house on Oaklawn Avenue, number 521, Oaklyn, NJ. I remember them talking about the FHA loan the got. The selling price was $2,800.

My mother and father went to the furniture store and purchased a dining room set that consisted of a table, four chairs, a sideboard, and a china cabinet. The furniture arrived, but the dishes were still packed away in the barrel, which was sitting in the living room.

My mother took out all the dishes and washed them and stored them in their proper place in the china cabinet. There wasn't a broken plate, cup, or saucer in the entire barrel! Not bad for a kid not quite 11 years old.

One night, a short time later, my mother and father were awakened with this awful crash sound. All three shelves in the cabinet and the china had crashed through the glass door and onto the floor. Everything was broken. Nothing survived the crash, absolutely no pieces at all was saved. Fate works in strange ways.

In Oaklyn, we lived on the edge of Newton Creek. When I was twelve, I would lie in bed in the summertime and hear the frogs croaking. We had a great gang of kids in our circle, about twelve to fifteen of us. Every night during warm weather, we would get together on someone's porch or yard and do whatever we wanted to. How things have changed since World War II. All through our early teens, no one in our gang smoked, drank or had sex. We were just innocent young people. In 2006, we celebrated our 50th class reunion.

Living on the lake, I wanted a motorboat in the worst way. I bugged my father about it. Finally he said, "You build the boat. I'll buy the motor." I didn't have any tools, plans, or experience, so I guess he figured he had a safe bet. I went to Mr. Noise, my woodshop teacher, and asked him if he would help me build a boat. He said yes, but I would have to buy all the materials.

I was making 56 cents a week on my paper route, which my parents let me keep. The materials would cost a little over eight dollars, so it was a go. By the end of the school year, there was my 10', beautifully painted green-gray-and-white rowboat—just waiting for an outboard motor.

My father kept his end of the bargain. That June he took me to Sears, Roebuck and bought me a three-quarter horsepower Waterwitch reconditioned outboard motor for $19. Now, $19 doesn't sound like a lot of money, but in 1939, $12 was a weekly living wage.

A NIGHT TO REMEMBER

My dad, Fredric Hamilton McCarthy, was born in 1897 in Chicago, Illinois and died in January 1977 at the age of eighty. In 1917, he married my mother, Genevieve McGrady, and they were married for sixty-two years.

My dad came home from work one Friday in the summer of 1931, and as he did every Friday night, he went to the local bank and deposited the check so he could write checks and pay his bills. The bank closed its doors that night. It took everyone's money that day and never opened its doors again.

My parents had no cash and their savings were gone. What were they going to do? My mother's sister, Mercedes, lived on the outskirts of Chicago, not far from our house in the town of Maywood. Aunt Dee Dee's husband, Dan Ryan, was a Chicago policeman.

We ended up moving in with the Ryans. I am not sure how long we stayed with them, and I don't recall where we slept in that little two bedroom flat. In fact, I don't have many memories of our stay there. I do remember my aunt saying, "Dan, I need some money."

There was no answer.

"Danny, I need money, *now*," my Aunt Mercedes would say, only a little louder.

"All right," he said.

My Uncle Danny went into the bedroom. When he came out, he was in full motorcycle cop uniform. He left the flat and returned a few hours later. He gave my aunt my aunt $40 or $50. That was more than most people made in a couple of months.

Uncle Danny had two bad habits: alcohol and gambling. In all the years Danny and Mercedes were married, the flat was the only home they ever had. They never owned anything: no car, no house, no vacations, no new furniture, nothing, just same old, same old.

One night, around 5:00 a.m., my mother woke me. Uncle Danny had just come home, and he was really drunk. We were being thrown out of the house. It was quite a mess. My dad loaded all our belongings into the old Model A Ford and drove us back to the house in Maywood, where we lived until our move to New Jersey.

I can understand how another family moving in with you in a small apartment could wear thin in a very short time. The sad part is that it took Uncle Danny a lot of booze to get up the nerve and ask us to leave.

My mother and Aunt Mercedes were very close all their lives, but now things were different. My dad and Uncle Danny never spoke to each other again. Mom and Aunt Dee Dee only saw each other a few times after that night, until Uncle Danny died.

Aunt Dee Dee moved from Chicago to my parents' house in Oaklyn, New Jersey. She lived with Mom and Dad a number of years until she passed away.

Aunt Dee Dee had two children, a boy and a girl. We lost track of them many years ago. I have no idea what happened to them. It must be in the genes. Some families stay together forever and other families go their separate ways.

Aunt Dee Dee loved to tell jokes. When she told a joke, she would laugh until she had tears running down her face. She could tell one joke after another. She never had much, but she was a happy soul.

Circa 1927

At age 7 (left), with my brother Bob, age 3

At age 14 (right), with my mother, age 40, and my brother Bob, age 10, on the Cape Charles Ferry from Norfolk, VA to Cape Charles, VA in the Delaware Bay

At age 9 (right), with my brother Bob, age 5

At age 13, in my Boy Scout uniform

At age 14 (left), with my brother Bob, age 10

THE FORGOTTEN SHOP TEACHER

During The Great Depression, the Works Progress Administration dammed the Newton Creek and dredged it to ten feet deep. The dam made the creek into a lake. The lake ranged from fifty to nine hundred feet wide and was two-and-a-half miles long. In the summer, you could hear the frogs croaking all night.

That fall, I entered the Oaklyn Junior High School. The school had twelve rooms for grades seven, eight and nine. The stage in the auditorium was also the gym. The staff was made up of a principal, an assistant principal, one secretary, twelve dedicated teachers and one janitor. How is that for a well-run school?

Our shop teacher was Mr. Chester Noise. Our first wood shop project was to build a corner shelf. Our second project was to make a bowl with a lid. The bowl was made of layers of black walnut and layers of maple. Several layers were glued together and turned on a wood lathe. The final step was to varnish it. I gave my bowl to my dad's aunt in Chicago.

By the end of December, I finished all the required projects for the year. My brother Bob and I needed new beds for our bedroom. Up until now, we slept on a steel frame with a spring and mattress—not much to look at. I asked Mr. Noise if I could make bunk beds that could come apart and be used as twin beds. As always, Mr. Noise said, "Sure."

Each headboard and footboard had two legs made from three-and-a-half inch solid maple turned on the lathe and tied together with fancy maple end boards and head boards. One bed sat on top of the other with three-quarter-inch steel pins to hold them together. When I first brought the beds home, we set them up as bunk beds with a ladder. After a short time, the novelty wore off, and then we changed the beds to twin beds. After sixty-nine years, the beds are still in use in our guest room.

Living on Newton Lake, I was dying for a motor boat. My dad finally said to me one day, "You build the boat and I will buy you the motor." I think my dad was playing a little game. This deal would get me off his back. If I did not build the boat, he would not have to buy the motor. Pretty slick.

At school the following day, I went to Mr. Noise's wood-working shop. I walked up to Mr. Noise's desk and said, "Mr. Noise can I build a boat here, in this shop?"

He thought for a minute or so, and said, "What kind of boat would you like to build, Fred?"

"About a 10-foot motor boat," I said. He thought for a few minutes and said, "If you can buy the materials, I will help you build the boat. Do you have any plans for the boat?" He asked.

"Yes, I have the plans for the boat, and I have saved enough money from my paper route to buy the materials," I said

"O.K., give me the material list and I will order the material from the lumber yard. But first, I will find out how much the materials will cost, to make sure you have enough money to pay the bill."

A few days passed before the lumber yard estimate arrived. The entire bill was $9.80, plus the paint. Remember, the year was 1940. A lot has happened in those 68 years. Today you cannot make a deal or commitment on a handshake.

The material arrived at the school one afternoon, and was put in the lumber racks. The first step was to build a jig. The jig would hold all the frames in place. The second step was to cut out the frame parts and assemble the frames using glue and bronze screws. After all the frames were assembled, they were mounted on the jig and clamped in place.

Next the keel and stem (bow piece) and transom (the back of the boat) are fastened into place. Once the frame is assembled on the jig and is fastened together, the frame is ready for fairing. The frame must be faired or shaped so that the planking will lie on the frame, and there will not be any sharp corners under the planking.

When the frame is completed, the boat is ready for planking. The planking is laid in a bedding compound and is screwed to the frame with bronze wood screws. The screws are covered with wooden plugs. The grain in the plugs should line up with the grain in the planking.

The hull is now ready to be lifted off the jig and turned right side up. Now that the boat is sitting right side up, the seats, rub rails, corner knees. and floorboards can be installed.

The next step is to prepare the boat for painting. Sanding, sealing, priming, and painting. What I just put down on paper took over three months to do in Mr. Noise's woodshop.

School let out for the day at 2:30 p.m. Mr. Noise stayed every day until 4:30. This would give the kids with big projects the needed time to finish their projects. I know now, if it were not for Mr. Noise, I would not be writing this story. He was a really dedicated man.

When World War II was over, I tried to locate this great man, but he just disappeared. The school had no record of his whereabouts, and I just kept running into blind alleys. I wish I had the chance to thank him for all he did for me.

NEW YORK SHIPYARD

1941 was a great summer. Skip Miller was my best friend. He lived on the other side of town. His house backed up to the Newton Creek in Oaklyn, NJ just like ours did. We both had 10' boats with outboard motors. Skip would motor down to our house or I would motor up to his house to play ping-pong. We didn't have a care in the world.

My paper route was my only commitment. Riding my bike on my paper route one day, I saw a run-down, 14' sailboat sitting alongside a garage. The hull was not in good shape, but I could burn the boat and salvage the screws and such.

I knocked on the front door, and when the man answered the door he saw my bike with newspapers in the basket. He said, "I already get the newspaper," and he started to close the door.

"No, sir, I would like to buy the boat next to your garage. Is it for sale?"

The man opened the door and walked out onto the porch. "How much will you give me for the boat?"

"Can I take a look at it, first?"

"Sure you can. I'll go with you."

We looked the boat over and I said, "It's in very bad shape, and I don't know if I can repair it."

He asked me some questions: Where did I live? How old was I? Did I have a girlfriend? Why, I don't know? After the questions, there was a long pause and the man said, "Would you give me five dollars it?"

I thought for a bit and said in a low voice, "I'll buy the boat for five dollars. I'll be back Saturday at ten o'clock to pick it up with my wagon."

On Saturday, I gave the man five dollars and said, "Thanks for selling me your boat." I went out to the garage and started to load the boat. It was bigger than I thought, and a lot heavier than it looked. I put three two-by-fours across my wagon and finally got the boat blocked up on some cinder blocks, and got the boat over the wagon.

To steer the wagon, I tied a rope to the wagon's tiller arm. After a lot of sweat, I got the boat on the two-by-fours on top of the wagon. That little wagon was lost under the 14' boat.

I was finally ready to start for home when the man came out of the house and said, "Don't you want the rest of the boat?"

"What else is there?" I asked.

The man opened the garage door and said, "Here's the mast, boom, tiller, and sails."

I couldn't believe my eyes. I thought I was just buying a sailboat hull, not a complete sailboat.

Finally, I got the boat six blocks back to my house. It took over four hours. The boat kept shifting on the two-by-fours. The wagon was destroyed, and so was I.

Skip and I talked about making the trip down the Newton Creek to the Delaware River. The trip one way was about ten miles, with one dam to go over.

We decided to use Skip's boat. Skip's boat was heavier than mine and had a bigger motor. We planned to leave on a Saturday morning. This would give us enough time to get back home before supper. No one would know what we were up to.

On the planned day, I motored my boat to Skip's house. We climbed into his 10' rowboat and started down the creek. About a mile from Skip's house was a dam under the Black Horse Pike. From the high side it was about three feet. The 3 foot drop was no problem. Our only problem was all the junk that was stuck on the top of the dam: logs, sticks, and any other thing you can think of. It was a nasty experience.

On the low side of the dam, Skip started the motor and off we went on our new adventure.

It turned out to be not much of an adventure, just a ride down the Newton Creek. We went under the low bridge, under South Broadway. In fact, all the bridges were very low, something like four to five feet. As we came out from under the bridge, we were in the New York Shipyard, in between all types of ships under construction: battle ships, aircraft carriers, landing craft, and many others.

After we passed through the shipyard, we were in the Delaware River. We made our goal. We motored around the Delaware River for a while, looking at all the ships. We guessed it was time to start for home; neither one of us had a watch, but the sun told us it was time to go.

Just before we entered the South Broadway Bridge, we were surrounded by a lot of men in uniforms: They all had guns and the guns were pointing at Skip and me.

One man jumped in the boat yelling, "PUT YOUR HANDS UP! PUT YOUR HANDS UP!"

I didn't know why he was so excited. We were out numbered five-to-one, and they had guns—even machine guns.

They took Skip's boat, and we were taken to the Coast Guard office in the shipyard and put in a room. We waited about thirty minutes before we were escorted into the captain of the port's office. He looked us up and down. After a minute or two, he asked us our names, where we lived and then told us how much trouble we were in for trespassing.

"What do you have to say for yourselves?" he asked.

"Captain, sir," I said, "We came by boat down the Newton Creek and under the South Broadway Bridge. There are no signs or fences under the bridge or on either side of the bridge."

The captain said, "Are you sure of that?"

"Yes, sir," we both answered.

Two Coast Guard men took us home. Both men had sidearms, and there were two machine guns in the station wagon. First stop was Skip's house. His father opened the front door. When he saw us with the armed Coast Guard men, his jaw dropped like a rock. If looks could kill, we'd both be dead.

Skip's dad was really mad. My house was next.

My dad thought it was the funniest thing he ever heard of.

The front page of the Camden paper, the *Courier-Post,* wrote in a big headline: "TWO YOUTHS INVADE IMPREGNABLE SHIPYARD."

Three days later, we were told we could come and get Skip's boat back. Skip's dad wanted no part of this. The boat could stay there forever, as far as he was concerned. My dad drove us to the shipyard.

We were met at the front gate. A guard took us to the place where we left Skip's boat...But there was no boat.

Forty-five minutes later, we found Skip's boat tied to the anchor chain of the aircraft carrier *Princeton.* The wind was blowing about twenty knots. Skip's boat was really bobbling up and down with the large waves generated by the strong winds.

Skip and I got in the bouncing boat. He started the three horsepower outboard motor. I untied the line holding us to the Princeton. By now, the docks were covered with workers watching us going out onto the Delaware River.

We had to go downriver to reach the Newton Creek, which emptied into the river. Out on the Delaware, Skip's boat was pitching up and down like a cork. It seemed as if it would take us forever to reach the Newton Creek.

As we went by each pier, more people were watching us. By now, there must have been a thousand or more people yelling something. We finally reached the Creek. Now there were several signs posted that read, "Keep out," and "No Trespassing."

There were several men waiting for us to go under the bridge. They were going to put steel wire under the bridge to close the openings. Just before we entered the bridge opening, I asked one of the guards, "What are all those people doing standing on the piers?"

"They were taking bets," he said.

"Betting on what?" I asked.

"If you kids would make it or not."

SUN SHIPYARD

Somehow, I found out that Sun Shipyard in Chester, Pennsylvania was looking for workers. The only requirement was that you had to be at least sixteen years old. This was the summer of 1942, and I was going to turn sixteen in a couple of days.

Without telling my parents, I walked to the bus stop and took the bus from Oaklyn to Philadelphia. I then took a train from Philadelphia to Chester. The shipyard was a short walk from the train station. Total time: two hours flat, from our house to the shipyard's gate. I filled out the yard's employment form, and was given an interview with the personnel director.

I didn't care where I worked. I just wanted to see how ships were built. Sun Shipyard, at that time, was building oil tankers. These oil tankers were over 400' long and 65' wide. They were known as "T2 Tankers." The yard had thirty ways. This meant they could build thirty ships at one time. A ship was launched every day, including Saturdays and Sundays, or thirty ships a month. Computers had not yet been invented. Everything was done by hand and drawn on paper.

When I got home that night, I was really excited. I announced that I had a new job at the Sun Shipyard. I think it was the only time my dad and I had harsh words. He said, "Do you know how many men get injured and killed in large shipyards? It is no place for a 16-year-old boy. You are not going to work in that shipyard!"

"Yes, I am. I'm going to learn how to build ships," I said, and went to my room.

I started on Monday on the 4:00 p.m. to 12:00 a.m. shift. I'd leave the house at 2:00 and get home at 2:00 a.m. I was very disappointed with my new job. They put me in the heavy pipe-bending shop. This shop bent steel pipe from 8" to 20" diameter. My boss was Polish and did not like the Irish.

The pipe came in 40 foot lengths. The first step was to put a wooden plug in one the end of the pipe, and drive it home with a big sledgehammer.

Then an overhead crane picked up the pipe by one end, and lowered it into a hole in the floor. The open end of the pipe was then even with the floor. Then the Polish guy would say, "O.K. kid, fill up." I took a big shovel and filled the pipe up with sand. Then I plugged the end. The crane lifted the pipe out of the hole and put it on the bending table.

The bending table was about 40' by 40' and 2' thick. The tabletop was a mass of 2" to 3" square holes. In some of the square holes were square pins to hold the pipe in place. After the pipe was pinned in the right position, blowtorches were used to heat the pipe until it was cherry red and then could be bent. Mr. Polish bent the pipe using hydraulic rams to get the desired shape. This took real skill. After the pipe was shaped, the crane picked the pipe up by one end and moved it over to the sand pile. The plug would be knocked out of the pipe and he'd say, "O.K. kid, beat pipe."

That meant it was time for me to beat the pipe with the sledgehammer to knock the sand out of the pipe.

For three days, I worked in the bending shop. All I heard was, "O.K. kid, fill up" or "O.K. kid, beat pipe." On the fourth day, I went over to the boss of the pipe department and told him I did not want to work in a shop. I wanted to work out on the ways.

"You're a funny kid," he said. "Everybody wants to work in the shops, not on the ways."

"Well, Mr. Boss, I want to learn how to build ships. I can't learn how to do that in a shop." "O.K. kid. Let's go," he said.

We walked into the yard and up the stairway of the nearest ship. Halfway up, the ship started to vibrate. The boss said, "What the hell was that?"

"I don't know," I said.

We finally reached the top of the stairs. I couldn't believe all the noise and confusion. People were everywhere: welders, chippers, and burners. The boss took me over to my new boss. His name was George Ledden. He was a farmer from New Jersey, he told me.

He got me aside and said, "Look kid, I work from four to eight. I can do more in four hours than most of these clowns can do in eight hours. So here's how it works. We give it hell for four hours, then I go my way and you go your way. Just don't get caught. If someone asks you what you're doing, just tell 'em you're lost, then ask for directions. You got it?"

George worked with 3" to 6" heavy pipe. We would go inside the ship, and he'd take all the measurements. I would write them down in his little book. Then we would go to the pipe shop and cut the pipe according to the drawing in George's little book.

The next step was to weld the pipe tack. If the pipe assembly matched George's little book, a certified welder would weld the assembly together. Some of them weighed over three tons.

The next trick was to get your assembly on board the ship. There were two cranes, and the ships had to share them. To lift a boiler or a main engine took both cranes and tied them up several hours.

The head rigger on our shift was called "Goosey Tony." He was short and on the fat side, but he was tough. You didn't mess with Goosey Tony. On this day, Tony was surrounded by a bunch of men who were trying to lift their work into the ship.

Tony kept saying, with his accent, "I'm-a lifting dis-a steam-a turbin. Go away, go away, come-a back when I'm-a done."

Tony had his back to me. I saw someone crawling on the ground. Suddenly, Tony jumped up in the air. Someone had goosed him. He swung around and looked me in the eye. I could see the fire in his eyes. Tony's fist came out of nowhere. He hit me square in the face with one of those huge, oversize hands. I went down on my back and laid there for a few minutes.

I took my spud wrench out of my belt holster and charged at Tony, yelling, "I didn't goose you, you dumb son-of-a-bitch!" A couple of guys grabbed me before I could hit Tony.

"Hey kid, I'ma sorry I'a hit you so hard," Tony said.

I thought he broke my nose, but I could see that he was really sorry he had hit me.

"Hey kid, whatta you doing here anyway?" he asked.

"I work with George Ledden and we need a lift."

"You got it, kid," Tony said.

"O.K. guys, put the turbine back on the ground and pick up the kid's stuff."

From that day on Tony gave me whatever I wanted. All the work had time limits. If you finished the job faster than the allotted time, you got paid primo or bonuses. George was so good we made lots of primo.

When George made up a big assembly, the crane would set it in place and every bolt-hole would match. I would see men making up an assembly of small pipes, and when the crane set it in place they would have to bang and pry to get the bolt-holes to line up. Not George.

P.S. The reason the ship was shaking when the boss took me on board to meet George Ledden was one of the burners did not shut off his gas line at the manifold when he left the ship. Another welder struck an arc, the gas exploded, and three welders were killed.

THE LIFEBOAT

Inside the Sun Shipyard fence were piles of lifeboats. Some piles had six or seven boats. They were mostly wooden and there were a few steel ones that were all rusted out. At the bottom of one pile was a boat that looked pretty good. I asked George Ledden if he knew anything about the lifeboats. He said he was not sure, but he thought they were free for the asking.

After nosing around and asking everybody I could, one name kept coming up: Captain Bill Smith. I wrote him a letter and dropped it off at his office in the shipyard.

A few days later the guard at the main gate said, "Captain Smith wants to see you right now."

I knocked on his office door and a voice from inside said, "Come in." Sitting behind the desk was a middle-aged man dressed in civilian clothes. He threw my letter across the desk and said, "Did you write this?"

"Yes, sir, I did."

"Well, young man, that letter of yours got me in a lot of trouble. In your letter it sounds like I'm trying to sell those old lifeboats."

"Captain Smith, I asked if I could buy one, hoping you'd say 'No, you can have one.' I felt funny just asking for one."

"I get it," he said. He thought for a while. "Next Saturday have your trailer here. I'll have a crane ready. Pick out the one you want."

"Thank you very, very much Captain Smith. What time should I be here?"

"Two o'clock sharp. Now get out of here," he said with a little smile on his face.

Somehow my dad found a wooden trailer with two sets of wheels and a bumper hitch. I was under age and didn't have a driver's license, so my dad drove to help me pick up the boat. We arrived at the Sun Shipyard at 1:30 and the crane was waiting for us. The head rigger said, "Which one do you want, and don't say the one on the bottom."

"I'm sorry, but that's the one I want."

The three riggers did not like this, but they knew I had my pick. It took almost two hours to get my boat loaded. The lifeboat was twice the size of my dad's 1939 Ford V-8. On the way home, two of the trailer's tires had gone flat. Now we knew why the trailer had three spare tires.

We unloaded the boat next to our one-car garage. I say we, I should say my dad, because he did all the work. In those days, this was a big undertaking, and my dad was the one that pulled it off, and no one got hurt.

The lifeboat turned out to have been built in Cardiff, Wales, where some of our ancestors were from.

At age 13, in the first boat I ever built, with a rebuilt WaterWitch motor bought by my Dad from Sears & Roebuck for $19 in 1939

The lifeboat, Oaklyn, NJ

THE LIFEBOAT ENGINE

World War II was going strong over in Europe. Germany was invading several countries, both large and small. Our president, Franklin Delano Roosevelt, said we were neutral and we would stay that way. Like all politicians, he twisted the truth.

Everyone wanted to protect our great country the best way they could. George Homan and I joined the New Jersey State Guard. We were both sixteen years old. The guards met every Wednesday night from 7:00 p.m. to 10:00 p.m.

George and I would take the bus from Oaklyn to Camden, where the armory was located. The first night we were issued hats, shirts, pants, and overcoats. They were left over from World War I and reeked of moth balls.

George and I felt like big shots. Every Wednesday, we would put on our WWI uniforms and get on the bus for the ride to the armory, on Haddon Avenue. Roll call came first, then some marching inside the building. Captain Sweeney was the officer in charge. After marching, he broke us up into small groups to learn about our guns. We were taught how to care for our weapons and how to take them apart and put them back together, blindfolded. My gun was a submachine gun, just like the ones you'd see Al Capone using on TV. Of course, TV had not yet been invented back then.

I needed an engine for the 26' double-end lifeboat I got from Sun Shipyard that summer. A private named Austin Hood in our company said he had a Model A Ford engine that he would sell cheap. "It's in a station wagon in the barn in a girl's camp in Medford, New Jersey, called Camp Ockanickon. The price is three dollars, but you'll have to take the engine out of the station wagon," he said.

"That's kind of cheap, Austin. What's wrong with the engine?" I asked.

"Nothing is wrong with it. The rest of the car is the problem. It's falling apart."

"Austin, you got a deal. When I get the engine, I'll give you three bucks."

That night, I told my dad about the engine I bought from Austin Hood. My dad said, "Three dollars for a Model A engine sounds awful cheap. Saturday we'll go take a look."

On Saturday morning, we got in my dad's 1939 maroon Ford V-8 and headed out to Camp Ockanickon. Back then, Medford was really out in the sticks. Medford Lakes was a summer place and very few people lived there year-round.

We found the Model A Woody station wagon in a rickety old barn.

"Looks like it's in pretty good shape to me. Are you sure you bought it?" Dad asked.

"Yeah, Dad. I bought it from Austin Hood. He is in my company at the State Guard," I said.

"O.K., if you're sure. Get the tools out of the car," In an hour we had the engine in the trunk of my dad's car. I finally had an engine for my 26' double-end lifeboat.

Austin Hood missed a few meetings of the State Guard. It was about a month before I saw him. "Hi Austin. Here's the three dollars I owe you for the engine," I said.

Austin pushed my hand back and said, "It's all a joke. That's not my station wagon. It belongs to the camp."

When I told my dad about the station wagon engine we stole from the girl's camp, he was shocked. In fact, I don't think he ever got over it. He felt bad about it for the rest of his life.

The following weekend, the Guard went on war maneuvers at Fort Dix. The Red Army verses the Blue Army. We all got poison ivy and we were covered with chiggers, tiny bugs that gets under your skin and itch like hell, and are hard to get rid of. After that trip, it was no more army for me.

MEETING THE CLOWERS

I served in the Navy from 1944 to 1946 in the Pacific. When the war was over, we left Japan and sailed to Norfolk, Virginia via Pearl Harbor and the Panama Canal. I sat on a cargo boom for the entire trip through the canal. It was really great.

We arrived in Norfolk, Virginia on December 7, 1945. The trip took about two months. The captain was Joe Finnegan. After laying around Norfolk for six weeks or so, the captain got itchy feet. Somehow, he talked somebody into letting the ship go to Bermuda to look over the place for the Navy Rescue Fleet.

Our first night in Bermuda, my friend Ken Zol and I went ashore. There was only one automobile in all Bermuda, an old wooden Ford Model A. Everyone used the narrow-gauge steam train that went all around the island instead. Ken Zol and I waited for the steam train, and we got off at the first stop. We were low on money and we did not want to get too far away from the crew boat landing. Down the road, a mile or so, we came across a very large hotel, the Belmont Manor.

With my friend George Homan (left), in our New Jersey State Guard uniforms, 1943

In my Navy uniform, 1944

Honorable discharge as a Private, Grade VII, from Company D, 10th Battalion, Infantry, of the New Jersey State Guard, August 8, 1944

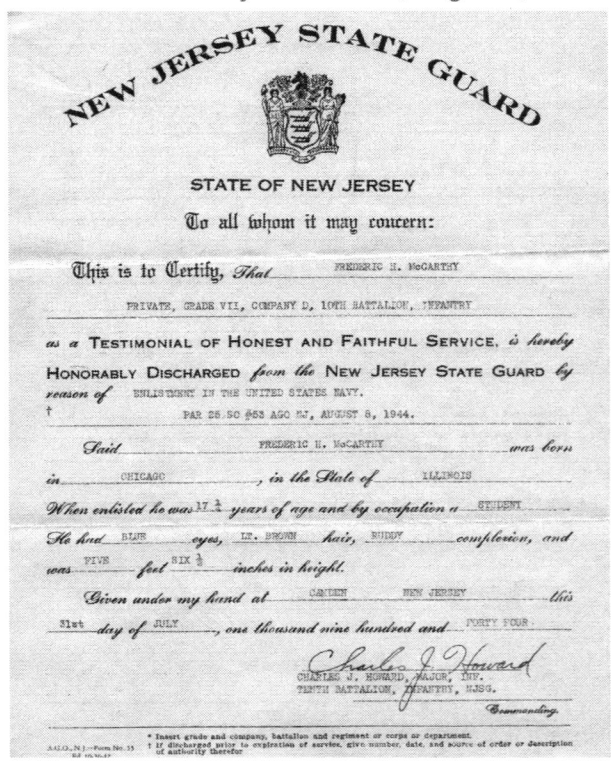

The doorman opened the door for us, but you could see in his face that he wasn't happy letting a couple of sailors into the hotel. We went to the bar and we both had a bottle of beer. Halfway through my beer, I said to Ken, "I've got to hit the head." The bartender pointed across the dining room to the men's room.

As I was crossing the dining room, a man sitting at a table accidentally pushed back his chair in front of me. Before I knew what had happened, I was almost sitting in his lap.

"Where are you going sailor?" he asked.

"I'm going to the head."

"Where you from?" "New Jersey."

"We're from New Jersey also." "What are you doing here?" I asked.

"We're here on vacation and celebrating my daughter's eighteenth birthday.

We flew in yesterday on the Pan Am Clipper. What's your name?"

"Fred McCarthy."

"I would like you to meet my wife, Mrs. Clower and my daughter, Bea Clower.

"Are you here alone?"

"No, my buddy Zol is at the bar waiting for me."

"Why don't you tell him to join us?" Mr. Clower asked.

"Okay, I'll go to the bar and ask him to join us."

I could see our ship's officers seated across the dining room. They kept looking our way, and it was very noticeable that they were unhappy about our presence on what they thought was their turf. Ken walked with me back to the Clower's table. About eight o'clock, Mrs. Clower asked me, "What time do you have to be back to your ship, Fred?"

"Nine o'clock, Mrs. Clower."

"Those Navy officers over there keep looking at us. Are they from your ship?" she asked.

"Yes they are."

"I thought so. Is that your Captain?"

"Yes."

"What is his name?"

"Joe Finnegan."

Mrs. Clower stood up from the table, cupped her mouth and yelled, "Hey Joe, come over here. I want to talk to you," and then sat back down.

There was a lt. commander at the captain's table who was second in command under Finnegan. He got up from the table and walked over to

Mrs. Clower and started to give her hell for calling the captain from across the dining room.

When Mr. Clower heard this, he got up from his chair, walked up to the commander and said to him, "How dare you speak to my wife like that," and pushed him back away from where he was standing in front of Mrs. Clower.

Zol grabbed me by the arm and said, "I think it's time to go." As we walked out the front door, we could hear the voices getting lower. When we got to the crew boat pier, there was no crew boat. We missed it by a half hour. The crew boat finally came and we went back to our ship.

For minor things, like fighting and drinking, you had to go to what was called "Captain Mask." The names were posted on a bulletin board. The next morning, I saw my name posted on the Captain Mask, along with fifteen others.

We lined up outside the captain's office. The first name called was "McCarthy."

"M" is in the middle of the alphabet. I wondered why I was being called first. What happened after we left the Belmont Manor?

I walked into Captain Finnegan's office, stood at attention and waited. In the Navy, you do not salute when you are inside a ship or building. You only salute when you are outside. The captain finally looked up from his desk and said, "Well, McCarthy, what do you have to say about last night?"

"Sir, we lost track of time and missed the crew boat by ten minutes."

"I'm not talking about missing the crew boat. I'm talking about the fight in the hotel. What do you have to say about that?"

"May I speak freely, sir?" I asked.

"Yes, you may speak freely, McCarthy."

"Well sir, I don't think you can blame me if your executive officer can't act like a gentleman and officer. How he acted was not Navy-like," I said.

It was true, but how was the old man going to take it? The captain looked me straight in the eye and said with a little twinkle in his eye, "McCarthy, we have two more days here in Bermuda. For the next two days you will have shore patrol duty from 0800 until 1600. Your area to patrol will be the Belmont Manor. You will also be the shore patrol on the last crew boat to return to the ship on these two days."

"Yes, sir," I said, and walked out the door.

Boy, our captain had a heart. It was as if he was saying to me, "you're right; the executive officer acted like a horse's ass."

A GREAT DAY

June 6, 1946 was a great day in my life. I said goodbye to this man's Navy. I got on a bus at Lido Beach, Long Island, NY, to Oaklyn, NJ—my hometown. Boy, what a day this would be!

At that time, you were discharged on the point system. That meant you were given points for what kind of work you did. When I was discharged in Lido Beach, I ran into a guy I knew from Oaklyn.

"What are you doing here?" he asked.

I grinned and said, "I'm getting discharged and going home."

"I've been in the Navy for a lot longer than you have. How come you are getting out the same time as I am?"

"What did you do and where?" I asked.

"I worked in DC in the supply department for three years, that's what. What did you do?" he said.

"I was running an ammunition ship all over the South Pacific, that's what I did."

I had my duffle bag over one shoulder and my rare, 30-caliber Japanese rifle over the other shoulder. The Japanese used 25-caliber rifles and a 30-caliber was rare. (I could have sold that Japanese rifle anywhere I went. I'm glad I didn't. It still looks great mounted on our fireplace.)

It took quite a while to get back to a normal life. When I finally got home from the Navy, I was only nineteen years old. At first, I thought I would like to be a high school shop teacher. I checked several colleges but with thousands of GIs coming home, most had a four-year waiting list. Who could wait that long?

The GI Bill gave veterans money to go to school. I could not get into a college, and I did not want to lose my GI Bill, so I signed up in a flying school at the Camden Airport. My class had eight students. All the instructors were ex-military pilots.

June 6, 1946 was a great day in my life. I said goodbye to this man's Navy.

Junior high school graduation

At age 16

With (standing, left to right) my father, Fredric H. McCarthy Sr., my brother Bob's best friend, Warren Zinn, and Bob, 1950. Warren was a Private First Class in the U.S. Marines, killed in action in Korea in 1951, at the age of 20.

Work After the War

MY FIRST JOB AFTER WWII

Western Electric Company ran an ad in the local paper for telephone installers. They manufactured and installed all the equipment for the Bell Telephone Company.

In those days, Bell Telephone was the only game in town. Keystone Telephone was briefly in competition with Bell Telephone, but somehow Keystone disappeared.

I applied for the job, along with five hundred other guys. I couldn't wait four years to get into college, so a job was the next best thing. We all took a test for the job and somehow I was hired, along with eleven other guys. We spent the next five weeks in the basement of the telephone building in Collingswood, NJ. One of the guys told me he'd been married for seven years. To me that sounded like forever.

In World War II, during the Battle of the Bulge, the Germans captured a hundred American GI's. They didn't know what to do with them, so they lined them up and machine-gunned them. One of the men in our class had been in that lineup but had been lucky not to get hit by a German bullet. As the men fell down around him, he fell with them, unharmed. He lay there for three days waiting for the Germans to leave the area. All his toes were frozen and had to be amputated.

Our subjects in the course covered everything the telephone company needed, except climbing telephone poles.

My first job was to install two switchboards in the Berlin, NJ telephone office. All the parts were shipped to the site. We were supposed to take drawings, erect wire and test the equipment before it was turned over to the telephone company.

The pay was not great, but every job was a challenge. We installed ten new switchboards in the Camden telephone office. The telephone operators were all women. The day shift had 600 women on duty. Whenever you picked up a telephone, an operator would say, "Number, please." You gave her the number you wanted, and she'd connect you.

After a couple of years, things started to change. I was sent to a new telephone building that was under construction. There was no turnpike then, just roads with traffic lights that took you through all the towns. We were on the road at 5:30 a.m. and returned home at 7:00 p.m. The car pool helped. The driver drove the car and the rest of us slept. We tried the boarding house route, but did not like the long nights with nothing to do.

This new telephone building showed me the future I would have with Western Electric. All the equipment came in completely finished. All we had to do was uncrate the equipment, bolt it to the floor, and hook up thousands of incoming wires to it.

The job was boring. Hooking up wires all day long did not have a future. I quit.

MY SECOND JOB AFTER WWII

I landed a job as a manufacturer's representative for J.M. Waldecker on Broad Street, north of City Hall in Philadelphia. My territory was anywhere I wanted to go.

I could draw up to $50 a week, and I had to pay all my own expenses. My commission was five percent of what I sold. I represented a spring company, a forging company, and a plastic molding company.

So I started to knock on all the doors I could. My dad said, "If you knock on enough doors, some will open; the main thing is not to get discouraged."

After a time, I started to get some sales, but not many. I called on RCA, DeLaval, and so many more companies that I can't remember their names. After several months, I started to get discouraged. I was working my butt off, traveling across four states, and getting nowhere.

One Saturday, I went into the office to write letters to the companies I'd been calling on. I found their mailing addresses in the files. The first file was "Delaval" of Trenton, NJ. They made huge steam turbines. In the file were several sale slips. What the hell was this? Delaval was buying things and I wasn't getting any commission on the sales. Now I started looking for other companies I had been calling on.

One place was in Oaklyn, NJ. On my third visit, the owner had asked me to quote on several forgings. He looked at the quote and said, "It seems a little high to me."

"These forgings must be made by a board drop hammer. That makes the price a little higher," I said.

"What is a board drop hammer?"

"I'm sorry, but I don't really know."

"When you find out, come back and tell me," he said.

Forgings are made by heating steel until it is red hot, and then placing the metal in a forge, which is nothing more than a large hammer. The metal is pounded into the desired shape. You probably have seen this in the movies. They put red-hot steel in a big machine, and the machine makes a big pounding noise and the sparks go in all directions.

You guessed it. The forgings were bought and paid for with no commission to me.

As I continued to look through the files, I found several more paid invoices, with no commission.

On Monday, I was in the office by 8:00 a.m., waiting for the great J.M. Waldecker. A little after nine, Waldecker came strolling through the door. "What are you doing here, Fred? You should be out selling."

When he sat behind his desk, I walked over, opened up my briefcase, and dumped the invoices under his nose.

"Mr. Waldecker, what do you have to say about these invoices?"

Waldecker sat there for a minute, then looked at me and said, "Fred, you were doing such a good job. I was afraid if I paid you all those commissions, at your young age, it might go to your head."

"Mr. Waldecker, at my young age, I've heard a lot of bullshit, but that's the poorest excuse for stealing I've ever heard. You're nothing but a lousy crook."

Lee Spring Company was Waldecker's biggest account. I knew that contract would be up for renewal soon. A man named Lutz, who'd retired from a large company, had recently bought it. I made an appointment, and we met in his private office. I told him I'd like to take over his contract for Pennsylvania, New Jersey, and Maryland. He thought I was too young for the job, but said we could talk more about it over lunch.

We went to the restaurant in Brooklyn's best hotel. I thought it would be just the two of us, but we were lead to a round table where six men were seated. I was introduced to each one and told what their job was: Mr. So-and-So, chief engineer; Mr. So-and-So, Accounting, and so on.

During lunch, Lutz browbeat each man, one at a time. They were so uptight they could hardly eat their lunches. Finally, he turned to me. "Well, Fred, what do you think of that?"

I got up from the table and said, "Mr. Lutz, I think you're nuts!"

I left the hotel and went back to the company's office to get my coat and hat. Lutz was coming in the door as I was walking out. "Where are you going?"

"After what I said to you at the restaurant, I figured I better go home."

"Why go home? I'm giving you the contract. I like someone who's not afraid to say what they think."

I couldn't believe that I was going home with the entire Lee Spring sales contract.

THE BIG ONE THAT GOT AWAY

The first few months selling Lee Springs went pretty good. RCA used springs as drive belts on all their 16mm movie projectors. That was a nice order every month. Now some of my legwork started to pay off. My dad worked for RCA Service Company. His office was in Gloucester, NJ.

The girl I was dating at the time lived in Pennington, NJ, just north of Trenton. Her father worked for a parachute manufacturing company. The ripcord that opens the parachute up is made of springs. Every parachute has a lot of springs in them.

The parachute company got an order from the government for several hundred parachutes. Her father told me if I would bid the job one-tenth of a percent lower than the competition, I would get the job.

The total spring order was over three million bucks. If my commission were only two percent of that, it would be great.

I jumped into my two-door Chevy and headed for Brooklyn. I thought how Lutz would drop dead when he saw this multi-million dollar order that I was going to drop on his desk. I couldn't wait to see his face!

After I took off my hat and topcoat, Lutz's secretary ushered me into his office. Lutz looked up from his desk and waited for me to say something. "Mr. Lutz, I think you'll like what I am going to tell you. I've got a three million dollar order here. All we have to do is beat the competition by one-tenth of one percent, and we can have the order."

I thought Lutz would be jumping up and down with such a deal. Instead, he kept looking at the drawings. Finally, after what seemed like hours, he said, "Tell the parachute people we will take 15 percent of the contract."

"But Mr. Lutz, this is a once-in-a-lifetime opportunity," I said.

"To take this contract, it would mean some new machinery, more help, and two shifts or maybe three shifts," Lutz replied.

I wanted to say: "If you can't take the heat, get out of the kitchen."

Lutz retired from a large company. I guess Lee Spring Company was just something to do: An office to go to and a way to get out of the house. Needless to say, I was really down. You work hard and when you get a really big one, the boss thinks it's too much trouble.

A couple of days later, I called my dad up at RCA, and asked him if he wanted to go to lunch. I picked him up at the front door of RCA in Gloucester. We had a nice lunch and I told him about the parachute deal. His answer was, "that's not the only thing out there."

We were on our way back to RCA. One block from dad's office, a guy goes through the red light and plows right into the driver's side of my late-model, two-door Chevy. My right arm is wrapped around the spoke of the steering wheel. From my elbow to my hand, it looked like the letter "L."

Dad took me to Cooper Hospital in Camden. We were in the waiting room three hours and still no doctor came to see me. Finally, when I was about to pass out, they set my arm in a cast, but it was never done correctly.

After that I couldn't drive. My contract with Lee Spring Company says that I must call on the customers once a month. No big deal; I can do it by telephone, I thought. Ah, but there's a fox in the hen house.

Lutz's daughter was getting married. His new son-in-law doesn't do a good job. I received a letter from Lutz saying, the contract reads "call on," not "telephone," the customers. So his son-in-law got a good job, and along with it, the possibility of a big order from Trenton, NJ.

THE PAPER TRAIL

Losing Lee Spring Company was a real letdown, but I feel things happen for the best. I answered an ad for a salesman to sell paper products for Camden Bag & Paper The company had a little storefront in Camden with the warehouse in the back. It was a father-and-son deal, with one man in the warehouse, and one man driving the truck. The routine was that every day of the week you had a route: Monday go out to this street, Tuesday go out to that street. Same routine every week, same stops, same customers.

The big profit was selling bags to farmers who had road stands. I made a list of everyone on my route: their location, name and phone number. The morning I picked for my farmers' run, I got a phone call from the Loveland Towing Company. They said the *Doris Loveland* was in Norfolk, Virginia and needed an engineer. Was I interested in the job? I told them I was in sales now and wasn't interested in any work around the water. I thanked them for thinking of me. That was that.

I got into my black, two-door Chevy and headed out to the farmland. At my first stop, I was told, "Your truck was here this morning, and we bought all the bags we need from the owner's son."

On my second stop and all the rest of them, the story was the same. That no good so-and-so. How rotten are these so-called business men? I thought.

That afternoon, I called the Loveland Towing Company. "Is the job on the tow boat still open?"

The next day, I was in Norfolk, VA on the *Doris Loveland*.

THE SAVANNAH TOW

The *Doris Loveland* was an ex-U.S. Army tugboat. The crew consisted of a captain, mate, two engineers, two deckhands, and the cook.

One afternoon in 1949, we left Norfolk for Savannah, GA, to pick up a large pipeline dredge and tow it to Port Newark, NJ. The captain was seventy-six years old and half blind, the cook was gay, the one engineer had spent fifteen years in prison; and one deck hand was a full-blooded Cherokee Indian. Some outfit!

We left Norfolk, VA, and headed out to sea. The *Doris Loveland* had a six-cylinder, direct-reversible, 400-horsepower, 350-rpm Atlas diesel engine for propulsion. Direct-reversible means when you go forward, the engine turns in one direction. To go backward, you stop the engine and start it up in the opposite direction. The engine is started with compressed air.

The man on the bridge signals the engine room what he wants the engine to do. He does this through a series of bells. The main bell was about fourteen inches in diameter, and the other bell looked and sounded like a cowbell. When the big bell rang, it was just called a bell. When the cowbell rang, it was called a jingle. One bell meant slow forward, two bells meant slow astern or backwards. To go full astern was two full bells and a jingle, and so on.

It took two men to run the *Doris Loveland,* one in the wheelhouse (bridge), and one in the engine room. There were two crews, one stood watch from 6:00 a.m. to 12:00 p.m. The second watch was 12:00 p.m. to 6:00 p.m. Each watch would relieve the other watch for meals. As you can see, you never got a good night's sleep.

The work was 20 days on the boat, and ten days off the boat. The big problem was they did not have a relief crew, so you never got your ten days off. It was summer. The weather was nice. The first couple of days, I had a hard time sleeping in new surroundings, hearing different sounds.

On the way out of Norfolk Harbor, I went up to the wheelhouse to talk with Captain Parker Noland. "When do you think we will get to Savannah?" I asked.

He replied, "2345 hours (11:45 p.m.), day after tomorrow."

I thought, What kind of fruit cake am I sailing with? This guy has only a compass and an old RCA radio that doesn't work half the time, and he is telling me the arrival time down to the minute.

At 2330 hours on the night we were to arrive in Georgia, I went up to the wheelhouse. The captain was not the talkative type. I sat down on the watch berth and didn't say a word. I was just waiting to see what was going to happen.

At 2345 hours, Captain Noland switched on the big searchlight. He turned the light left and right a couple of times, and off to our right was the Savannah River entrance. I couldn't believe my eyes! The old man really did it.

When we arrived in Savannah, there was the dredge waiting for us. It had an 8–10 man crew, with a cook who must have weighed 300 pounds.

On the third day, the *Doris Loveland* took the dredge in tow on our port side. When we reached the center of the river, the dredge was taken in tow on our stern. In congested areas, the tow is kept close to the towing boat. In open water, the tow is let out to six hundred feet or more. The towboats today have large winches with all the line (Hauser line) on drums. Push a button and you can take in or out the Hauser line. The *Doris Loveland* was not equipped with a towing winch. It took two to four men to take in the line.

The dredge was now about one hundred fifty feet behind us and we were off to Port Newark, New Jersey. It was a long slow ride up the Intra Coastal Waterway (ICW). When we reached Morehead City, NC, the dredge crew was out of food and the *Doris Loveland* was low on fuel. It took a lot of talking to get Parker Noland to stop for fuel.

In those days, marinas were few and far between. Parker Noland tied the *Doris Loveland* to the dock. A man came walking out, and I got off the tug to meet him.

"Do you sell diesel oil?" I asked.

"I don't have fuel here on the dock, but I can have a fuel truck come here," he said. "How much fuel do you need?"

"About 4,000 gallons," I said.

His face lit up and a big smile covered his face. "Four thousand gallons."

It was not long before the fuel trucks were on the dock.

After taking on fuel, we went to the city dock and picked up the dredge crew with all the provisions. I was on watch in the engine room and Parker Noland was in the wheelhouse. We left the city dock and headed back to the dredge. The *Doris Loveland* was going full speed. The old six-cylinder Atlas was doing her best.

I looked at my watch. We should have been near the dredge by now. At the throttle, I was waiting for the signal to slow down. The next thing I knew, I was on the engine room floor. We had just hit the dredge at full speed.

After stopping the engine, I ran up on the deck. The dredge crew was lying all over the place. Their big cook was carrying a large paper bag of booze. When the *Doris Loveland* hit the dredge, the cook went down on top of the paper bag. The bottles of booze broke and bourbon was running down all over the deck.

Fortunately, no one was hurt, but the dredge was. The *Doris Loveland* hit it so hard that one of the dredge's fuel tanks started leaking. What the dredge crew did to stop the leak, I do not know.

That afternoon, we started up the ICW again for Port Newark, NJ. The trip north took a lot more time than the trip going south. We had the dredge in tow, plus all the bridges to contend with.

One day I asked the mate, "Doesn't it make you nervous pulling that big dredge through all these bridges? What's the secret?"

"It's very simple," he answered, "You just steer the boat to the center of the bridge span, but don't look back. After a few minutes, if the boat doesn't slow down and you do not hear noise, you made it under the bridge."

When you left the C & D (Chesapeake and Delaware) Canal and entered the Delaware River, you would smell a horrible odor. The river stank so much you could not sleep.

Most tugboats do not have any inside passageways. When you left your cabin, you had to walk outside to the galley. After a shower, you walked outside to your cabin. This was in both summer and winter. Sometimes after a shower, you walked out to your cabin in a snowstorm.

EARLY YEARS

Aboard the tugboat *William J. Scott* (right), 1950

Most tugboats do not have any inside passageways. When you left your cabin, you had to walk outside to the galley. Sometimes after a shower, you walked out to your cabin in a snowstorm.

American Dredging Company

THE DREDGE *PENNSYLVANIA*

I left Loveland Towing Company in August 1949 because you worked 12 hours a day, seven days a week, and never got a day off. After a few months, this got pretty old.

I went to see the union agent, Vinnie Motsel, for the 825D Operating Engineers Union. I told him I was looking for a job on the Delaware River. Vinnie told me there were no openings, but I should keep in touch, and he started to walk away. He stopped, turned around and said, "You don't have any steam turbine experience, do you?"

"Yes. When I was in the Navy, I ran a 10,000-ton ammunition ship, the *USS Winston* (AKA 94). She was powered by a 6,000-horsepower G.E. steam turbine and three 600-kilowatt generators."

"That's great," Vinnie said, "You're now the first engineer on the dredge *Pennsylvania*. Go up the river where the dredge is working and tell the chief engineer you're his new first engineer."

On the dredge I met the chief, Harold Gregory, who was not happy to see me. After ten minutes, he told me I didn't have enough experience. I told Vinnie what had happened. He told me the chief wanted his son Harold to fill the job, and to go back and tell him that I was the new first hand and that was that.

I said, "Vinnie, if the chief doesn't want me, he'll be hell to work with. He might even hurt my reputation."

Vinnie said he didn't care. You're the new first, and that's that, he repeated. "It's this job or no job."

The chief was really upset when he saw me coming aboard the dredge.

The dredge was called the *Pennsylvania*; it was owned and operated by American Dredging Company in Camden, NJ. She had a 56-man crew, a 36' cutter head and suction pipe, two Babcock & Wilcox boilers, and one 3000-horsepower steam turbine. Dredging a 24-hour day, the boilers would eat 2,500 gallons of Bunker C fuel oil and was capable of digging one million cubic yards of mud a month.

I asked the chief, "Where's the library with the operating manuals?"

He said there was no such library and a good engineer knew all the equipment from memory.

EARLY YEARS

On my first watch, I met my fireman, a Greek named John Canavaris who was about sixty-five years old. He had been a fireman all his life.

"John," I said, "You know more about the boiler room than I do. It's all yours, and if you need help just call me."

The captain's name was Cocky Boyer and the chief mate was Harry Austin. Harry and I hit it off from the first day. He was neither a small man nor a really big man, but he was as strong as an ox.

Most everyone on the dredge had a nickname. "Bobby Pins" was always combing his hair, "The Preacher" was going to school to become a preacher, "Eye Bolts" had only one eye, and so on. I was just "Mac."

I never knew how old the dredge was. The *Pennsylvania* was just old and tired.

In the summer the living quarters were so hot that it was impossible to sleep. The galley and the eating area were one room shaped like an L. The stove and ovens were oil-fired and very hot, with all that cast iron. Frank, the cook, had one small fan that did not do much.

Needless to say, Chief Gregory had no time for me. Nothing would have pleased him more than if I quit the job. I guess that's why I stayed on the job so long. The pay was good, but the working conditions were pretty bad.

When I first went on the dredge, Chief Gregory did everything he could to get me to quit. The union knew that Chief Gregory wanted his son Harold to have my job, so he could not fire me. That would be too obvious.

My first run-in with Chief Gregory occurred when I was on watch one night and both boilers were down for repairs. It was my job to have both boilers on line by midnight.

At 10:00 p.m. Chief Gregory entered the boiler room. Both boilers were about 50 percent ready. Chief Gregory said, "What in the hell are you doing?"

"What do you mean, Chief?"

"It's almost ten o'clock and the boilers are not ready," he said.

"Chief," I said, "I was taught you should take eight hours to bring a boiler from cold iron to full pressure."

"Who told you that crap?"

"The United States Navy's Boiler School, that's who," I said.

"What the hell do they know? Light off all eight burners," he said.

I turned to John Canavaris, my fireman. "You heard the man, John. What does the U.S. Navy know about steam boilers? Light all eight burners and take the boilers up to steaming pressure."

John lit all of the eight burners, and in less than 20 minutes the boilers were on line. Boilers are made of steel, and the fireboxes are covered with firebricks. This mass of steel and bricks must be heated evenly. You start with one burner in each firebox, then every fifteen minutes you shut down one burner and light another burner. The idea is to heat the boiler evenly and slowly.

On the *Pennsylvania*, each firebox could hold a full-size automobile. The dredge had an oil barge that refueled it, as needed. The oil barge held one hundred thousand gallons of Bunker-C oil.

When the dredge was working around the clock, it would empty the oil scow every four days. When the job was finished, the dredge would go back to the company's yard. The crew was laid off until the next job came up. The engineers were kept on to make repairs. The repairs never ended; sometimes the dredge would be in the yard for months. After the chief and I had the boiler run-in, we had a lot of boiler work.

The boilers were water tube boilers, which meant that the water went through the tubes and the fire went around the tubes. On a steam locomotive, this is reversed: the fire goes through the tubes and the water goes around the tubes.

The boiler work consisted of cleaning these tubes, repairing the firebrick in the firebox, and so on. Cleaning out the tubes is not a nice job. On the very top of the boiler is the steam drum, which goes the width of the boiler and is less than four feet in diameter. On each end is a manhole cover. You can't be very fat to get through the manhole.

All the tubes enter into the steam drum and there are several hundred tubes. The water level in the boiler is measured in the steam drum where the water glasses are located.

To clean the tubes, you first remove the manhole covers, then pass through the hole, drop lights, air hose, turbine cleaners and a water hose. After that, you wiggle your way through the manhole (I think it should be called the "boy hole"), and crawl to the far end, hook up the hose to the tube cleaner or turbine, and start running the turbine down and up each tube.

After the first few tubes, you are now sitting in dirty water. Oh, I forgot, you should keep a bucket of ice water near by. You come out of the steam drum hands and arms first. If you have a man that's a little chunky, and he gets stuck coming out of the manhole and panics, two people must grab both his arms and start pulling. The third man douses him with the cold water. Eventually, he will come out.

It takes about five hours to do each boiler.

Boiler work is hard, dirty work.

THE CONDENSER

The dredge was between jobs in the Camden, NJ yard. It was a good time for repairs. The main condenser needed re-tubing very badly. She was a little run down.

Here's how a steam plant works: The boiler generates steam, the steam goes to the turbine, and the turbine turns the pump. After the steam does its job in the turbine, the steam is sucked into the condenser. The condenser has less than 28" of vacuum to carry out this job. Inside the condenser are a bunch of tubes, with seawater running through them. When the steam hits the cool tubes, the steam turns back into water. The water is then pumped back into the system, and around and around it goes. This is basically how it all works.

The chief gave me the job. On the bottom of the condenser was a 30" by 24" round collecting chamber, called the well. This was the chamber to pump out the condensed water. I thought the best way to do this job was drop the well, go up into the condenser, cut the tube in half, then drive the tubes out of each end of the condenser.

My helper and I started unbolting the well, so we could drop it down on the deck (it weighed about 300 pounds). The suction pipes were taken off, and the well was about 90 percent unbolted, when here comes the chief with his son Harold.

The first words out of the chief's mouth were, "What in the hell are you doing?"

"Well, Chief, I thought the best way of doing this job was to drop the well and get inside and see what we were in for. If things were O.K., we would cut the tubes in the center and drive them out of both ends."

The chief said, "That's the dumbest thing I've ever heard of. I've made a tool that fits the inside of the tubes. Just insert the tool and drive out the tube."

I was taken off the job and sent to do something else.

The next day I went to see how the chief and Harold were doing. They inserted the chief's tool into about 50 tubes and tried to drive the tubes out the other end. When a tube didn't come out, they would go to another tube.

It was time for the chief to eat crow. They dropped the well and found that the tubes they tried to drive out with the Chief's wonder tool had kinked the tubes in the middle. Instead of cutting the tubes once to drive them out, they now would have to cut the tubes twice, once on each side of the kink.

I happened to walk by the job when Harold looked up into the condenser for the first time. I heard him say, "Dad, I see things in here that aren't in the drawings." Drawings? What drawings? I thought.

Later on that day, I saw Harold and said, "Gee, Harold, do you have a drawing of the condenser?"

His comment was, "We have drawings of everything."

I asked, "How about drawings of the pumps? Do you have instruction manuals?"

"Sure, we have manuals on everything."

"Funny, I was told a good engineer didn't need instruction manuals. He should know everything from memory!"

GUS TATMAN

When I first went to work for The American Dredging Company, the engineer who I relieved was named Gus Tatman. Gus had been working on dredges all his life. He knew his job well and was willing to share his knowledge. Some people try to keep everything a secret. I guess they are afraid you will steal their job. But I learned a lot from Gus, who was a real nice guy.

The lever man on a dredge is the guy who really runs the dredge. What would be the pilot house or bridge on a ship is the lever room on a dredge. The lever man pulls the levers in the lever room, which is located up high on the forward end. Visibility is the name of the game.

The lever men are very competitive. Each one tries to dig more mud than the other guy. A vacuum gauge, with a recording chart, records how much vacuum is pulled. The more vacuum recorded per eight-hour watch, the more mud is pumped ashore.

One of our lever men was Oley Olson. Oley spoke with a very heavy Swedish accent and he was very proud of his Swedish background. When Oley was digging mud, a team of horses could not pull him away from those levers. If nature called, Oley would open the door, run out on the deck to the handrail, and relieve himself over the side. There was just one problem with this technique. The lower deck, twelve feet down, was about ten feet beyond the lever room deck. So instead of hitting the water, he was wetting the lower deck. Oley didn't care. He wouldn't dare take time from those levers to visit the head (toilet) on the first deck.

One night, Gus Tatman was walking forward to check something when down came Oley's water. You guessed it. It hit Gus right on the top of his head. Needless to say, Gus was really mad. When he told me the whole story, he ended with, "I'll get even with that Swedish S.O.B."

The following night when I came on board to relieve Gus, I couldn't find him. I walked around and finally saw him forward where the episode had happened the night before.

Gus was sitting on a five-gallon bucket right inside and under the lever room deck. He was holding some kind of long rod in his hands.

"What are you doing there," I asked him.

"Stick around kid and you'll find out," Gus said.

A few minutes passed and nothing happened.

"O.K., Gus, you are relieved. I've got the watch," I said.

The words were no sooner out of my mouth than down came Oley's stream of water. Gus stood up, walked a little forward and stuck the long rod into Oley's water. The next thing I heard was an ungodly scream. It sounded like someone was being killed.

Gus picked up his stuff and started to walk away.

"What in the heck, Gus, do you have there?" I asked.

Gus turned and showed me what he was carrying: an old spark coil out of an old Model T Ford, a small six-volt battery and the length of a small size pipe with a wooden handle.

"Gus, I can't believe it. You gave Oley the shock of his life," I said.

"Yeah kid, I told you I would fix that S.O.B. I don't think he'll pull that trick again. I'm keeping this stuff on board, just in case Oley goes back to his old tricks."

PAYDAY

The American Dredging Company's payday was every Thursday after twelve o'clock. It was a cash payroll—no checks, just cash. Several years later, the paymaster ended up as the company president.

The card games and crap games went on all night. In fact, some of the deck crew were professional gamblers. They worked on the dredge just for Thursday night.

One evening, Harry caught one of the pro deck hands cheating at poker. Harry didn't say a word; he just got up from the table. He took the fire ax down from the wall and walked back to the table, where the cheater was sitting with his pile of bills stacked in front of him. Harry drove the ax through the pile of money and halfway through the table.

"You're lucky it wasn't your head, you crook. Now just get up and get out of here, before I really get mad."

Another time the captain, Cocky Boyer, was really hot with the dice. At 5:00 a.m., the mess cooks came into the galley to start breakfast. Cocky was still rolling the dice. He was $3,200 to the good (in those days you could buy a pretty nice car for that amount of money). Cocky laid the $3,200 on the deck and said, "Shoot it."

Someone said, "I'll take a $100." Another said, "I'll take $200," and so on. Cocky said, "One person covers it all, or I don't shoot." The galley was dead quiet. No one said a word.

Finally, Cocky said, "Hey Chico, you want to take it?"

Chico laid down his paring knife, took off his apron, and walked over to the money lying on the floor. He laid his $3,200 on the deck and just looked at Cocky. Cocky really didn't want to bet his $3,200, but now he was trapped. He finally picked up the dice and shot a pair of snake eyes: two ones.

Chico picked up the money, put it in his pocket, and never said a word. He just walked back to his seat and continued pealing potatoes, just like nothing happened—just another day. Cocky picked up the dice, threw them overboard, went back to his cabin, and never said a word.

HARRY AUSTIN AND THE WHIRLY CRANE

The Whirly was an old steam crane that sat on a wooden barge, about 50 feet by 110 feet long. It was always with the *Pennsylvania*. The boom was about 60 feet long. The crane had an old upright fire tube boiler, fired by coal. Steam engines ran the winding gear that turned the drum holding the cables. The cables raised and lowered the boom. The boom had two hooks. A single whip had only one cable for picking up light loads, and the second hook had several cables for very heavy loads.

The Whirly was always doing something. On this day, Harry Austin and I were running it. Harry was the operator and I was the engineer fireman. Our job was to remove the runner from the main pump, which pumped the mud. The outer shell of the pump was about 14 inches diameter, and the impeller, better known as the runner, was about 8 inches diameter. The runner screwed onto the shaft from the main engine. Between the turbine and the pump was a large reduction gear that changed the high speed of the turbine to the low speed of the main pump.

To remove the runner, you needed to secure the single whip hook to a cleat on the far side of the dredge. This was a safety precaution. The second hook was wrapped around the runner. When pressure was applied to the second hook, it would unscrew the runner, if things went right. If a cable on the number two hook broke, the single whip fastened to the deck cleat would hold the boom from whipping back and smashing through the wooden crane house.

That day everything was rush-rush. The crew chief decided he didn't have time to set the single whip. Harry was in one of his happier moods. Every time he put a good stress on the cables, he would get out of the operator's seat and do a little dance on the inside deck. The deck crew wanted more strain. Harry would give them a little more; do his jig, and get back in the operator seat. By now, the crane and barge were starting to list.

I yelled to Harry, "That's it. She won't take anymore."

Harry continued to give a little more strain and do a little more dancing. I left the boiler and went up to Harry's area, and said, "This is it, Harry. She won't take any more and that's it."

I climbed down out of the crane, and when I stepped on the deck of the barge, the cable broke. The boom smashed right through the crane house. Harry was doing his dance and was able to jump out of the way. The boom smashed through the crane house, knocking the boiler out the back of the crane. This was the end of a good old steam crane called The Whirly.

HARRY AUSTIN AND THE STIFF LEG CRANE

The American Dredging Company sent us an old stiff leg crane to replace the whirly crane. A stiff leg crane looks just like what it is called. A large wooden beam about 20" by 20" by 30' stands straight up in the air and is supported by two smaller beams that keep the stiff leg from falling over. At the base of the stiff leg crane is a third beam that can swing from right to left and move up or down. This beam has hooks and cables that can be used to lift and swing objects around as needed.

At the top of the stiff leg crane is a large pulley called a shive. The cable from the winch or winding gear runs through this shive, down to the hook, and back up to the shive. There can be several shives in a block.

On this day, the 4:00 to 12:00 watch (on the water a shift is called a watch) had the job to replace the main cable on the stiff leg crane. This cable was three-quarters of an inch in diameter and was very heavy.

The deck captain sent one of the college boys that worked for the company during the summer months, up to the top of the stiff leg crane. The college boy was told, "Watch the cable as it goes through the shives. If the cable starts to climb out of the shive, kick the cable back into the shive with the heel of your shoe."

The 11:30 p.m. crew boat was along side the dredge with the 12:00 to 8:00 watch crew, plus anyone who lived on the dredge that went ashore. Harry was the deck captain on the 12:00 to 8:00 watch, and as he walked down the deck, he heard this loud scream.

When Harry looked up, he saw this man hanging by one arm at the top of the stiff leg crane. Everyone was looking up to see what happened, but not Harry. In a matter of seconds, Harry was on top of the crane. He found the college boy hanging by one arm with his hand under the cable and in the shive.

The shive is mounted in the pulley, called a block. The block on top of the stiff leg crane weighs about 300 pounds.

Quick-thinking Harry took a rope and tied the 160-pound, college boy to the stiff leg and with brute strength lifted the block high enough to get the boy's hand out from under the steel cable.

When the boy—I guess when you're 160 lbs. and working on a dredge you're not a boy—was free, Harry swung him over his shoulder and climbed down the stiff leg. I wish I could tell you the outcome of the man's hand. I can't because we never saw him again.

HARRY AUSTIN AND THE "A" BAR

Harry Austin was not a big man. He was about 5'10" and strong as an ox. Harry liked the girls, and he was always laughing and clowning around.

For a while Harry was dating a girl midget. She was less than four feet tall, and very attractive. Harry would take her with him to the "A" bar, in Marcus Hook, PA. Not a very nice neighborhood, to say the least.

His girlfriend could not see over the bar, so Harry would bend over, and placing both of his hands over her ears, pick her up by the head and sit her on the bar.

His girlfriend would stay on the bar until it was time to leave. When it was time to leave, Harry would pick up his friend by the ears and place her on the floor, and they would both walk out the door together.

HARRY AUSTIN AND THE STRAW

Harry Austin and I were dredging the Delaware River off of Marcus Hook, PA. I was the engineer and Harry Austin was the deck captain. Between the two of us, we ran all the watches. Watches changed every week, 12:00 to 8:00, 8:00 to 4:00 and 4:00 to 12:00, twice daily.

The crew boat ran back and forth from the dredge to a large pier. It was great. You could park your car on the pier and walk a few feet, and there was the crew boat.

On this day, Harry, who was quite a ladies man, and I had the 4:00 p.m. to 12:00 a.m. watch. John Canavaris was my fireman and Bill Smith was my oiler. Smith was new to the company. He was young and nice-looking. His wife was very good-looking, I was told, and she picked him up every night.

It was a beautiful summer night, not too hot, with a light breeze. About 11:00 p.m. Harry said, "Mac, I would like you to do me a favor."

"Yeah, Harry, what's the favor?"

"Give your oiler some overtime tonight."

"What for, Harry?" I asked.

"Don't ask questions. Just do it," Harry said.

"Harry, I can't do it. If we had a breakdown or for any other good reason, I could but, for no reason, I can't."

Harry was not very happy about my answer, but I had no choice. Harry told the crew boat captain to take him ashore. We were near the pier and it was a short run.

I didn't see Harry for a couple of days. When I did see him he was in the galley sucking a bowl of soup through a straw. His broken jaw was wired shut. I did not have to say, "Hey, Harry, what happened? How did you break your jaw?"

Oh, by the way, my oiler Bill Smith never missed a day's work.

THE GOLDEN GLOVES

One day, Harry Austin and Bobby Pins were on the ladder on the front end of the dredge. There was a big cutter head on the forward end, which turned when the ladder was digging on the bottom. The ladder was hinged on the aft end, so it could be raised up and down.

Inside the ladder was a three-foot pipe that sucked up material dug up by the cutter head. A suction pipe was connected to the pump, which was driven by a steam turbine. Mud and other materials dug up by the cutter head was pumped ashore.

I was up in the lever room looking down on Harry and Bobby Pins. Bobby was holding the big wedge while Harry hit it with a 12" maul, a big sledge-hammer. Clowning around, Bobby put his index finger on top of the wedge and said, "Hit her here, Harry."

Down came the maul, quicker than Bobby Pins realized. It hit him with a thump. He shouted, "Damn you Harry! You hit my finger."

"Gee, Bobby I didn't mean to hit your finger." Harry said.

When Bobby Pins took off his glove, his index finger was gone. Harry got him on a crew boat and off to the hospital.

I was still looking out the lever room window when I saw the Preacher, who was studying to be a minister, coming around the corner. He saw the gloves on the deck, and thought he would make them his own He looked around and when he didn't see anyone, including me in the lever room, he picked them up. When he put on the left-hand glove, he felt something inside. He took off the glove and shook it. When the smashed finger dropped out of the glove and onto the deck, the Preacher puked right down his chest.

THE C&D CANAL

One morning, the man on the elbow was not there. The dredge was searched and he wasn't found. A couple of small skiffs were put overboard to search and dredge the bottom for the lost man. The current was very strong. The crew figured that the man must have gone far down stream, so that's where they started the search, under Harry's supervision. After a few hours, an older man showed up on the canal bank. He watched the operation for a while. He called Harry over and asked him what was going on.

"We lost a man off the elbow last night, and we're dredging for him."

The elderly man said, "Did he fall off the platform?"

"Yes, we think so," Harry said.

"If he fell off the platform, you'll find him about thirty-five feet down stream."

Harry said, "We think the fast tide took him further down stream."

"Sonny, when a person drowns, he sinks to the bottom and remains there until the body starts generating gas. The amount of time this takes is controlled by the water temperature. The hotter the water, the faster the body will surface."

Harry didn't like what he heard, but to satisfy the old man, he made a pass with grappling hooks over the area. After the first pass, they found what they were looking for: the remains of the man we lost off the elbow.

COLLISION ON THE C&D

We were digging mud in the canal. It was about 8 p.m. I was on watch with John Canavaris in the fire room. The oiler and the throttle men were in the engine room. Everything was fine until, without warning, the dredge began to shake and list to starboard. I had no idea what had happened. Looking forward, I saw smoke coming from the fire room passage way. When I got into the fire room the smoke was so thick, I couldn't see.

I yelled at the top of my voice, "John! John! John! John!" After a few minutes, I couldn't breathe. There was an 18' escape ladder on the port side by the two boilers. When I reached the top, I saw that the side door was open and John was sitting on the discharge pipe that ran down the port side of the dredge. The first words out of John's mouth were, "I knew you would come up sooner or later out of the smoke."

I looked out the side door and saw the Japanese freighter that rammed us. The impact shut down the port boiler blower. The four burners in the port boiler room couldn't get any air: no air, no fire—just black smoke.

John pulled the four burners before he got out of the fire room. If he hadn't done that, God only knows what could have happened. Bunker-C oil is very thick, black oil, with the consistency of molasses. The oil has to be heated to a minimum of 180 degrees Fahrenheit to be sprayed into the boiler's firebox. The boilers burned about five hundred gallons per hour when the dredge was working. Can you imagine that much oil getting into the red-hot firebox with no fire?

EDDY BENNETT

God only made one Eddy Bennett. I don't think the world could stand more than one. He spoke with a lisp, and his lips were mangled and scarred. Here's why.

In the winter, Eddy would fish for snapping turtles using a six-foot steel rod with a hook on one end. He would go out in the marsh and look for bubbles coming up from the bottom. He'd probe the bottom with his rod;

hook the snapping turtle underneath its shell, and work it up to the surface. He would throw his catch into a burlap bag, then go find another one.

Some of the snapping turtles were quite large. He would sell them to the local restaurants, who would make turtle soup. But before Eddy sold his turtles, he would first go to a local bar.

He would place the largest snapping turtle on the bar and take bets for drinks. After the wagers were made, Eddy would turn the turtle on its back and rub its underside quite hard until it fell asleep. When Eddy thought the turtle was sleeping, he would flip it over and kiss it on its beak. One day, Eddy was doing his routine with his turtle when something went wrong. Eddy apparently had too many drinks and the turtle didn't get enough belly rubbing to fall asleep completely. When Eddy went to kiss the snapping turtle on its beak, the turtle clamped onto Eddy's lips and wouldn't let go.

I bought a war surplus Mark V hardhat and diving gear. My dad made a telephone system for the diving gear, and now the diver could talk to the tender. The tender is the person that dresses the diver and runs the show topside. The tender should check everything: the gear, air supply, the ladder the diver would go down on, and so on.

The tender should be a qualified diver, and be paid as such. The problem was that no one would pay for a qualified diver to do the job and the tender would wind up being anyone who was available at the time. One night, the *Pennsylvania's* oil barge sank. The corners of the barge had holes from hitting the docks. The wind was blowing and the waves splashed into the open corners of the barge, and the barge went down on the forward end. The forward end, which had the pump hose and valves, was on the bottom of the river.

I was on watch and couldn't get a replacement. At the time, Eddy was a deck hand. He and Harry Austin took my diving gear on our small barge and went to the sunken oil barge. I told Eddy which valves went to each tank compartment, and where the steam hose connection was.

Eddy was on the sunken barge when a tug came into the area with a big dipper dredge alongside. A dipper dredge is like an old steam shovel. Instead of crawler legs, it sat on a barge. They were getting too close to the sunken oil barge. Harry was waving his arms and jumping up and down and yelling for the tug to stop.

The tug and dipper finally stopped and the dipper dredge dropped its shovel right where Eddy Bennett was standing on the bottom of the river.

When diving in the Delaware River, once you go down three feet, it is, as they say, "like working in a tar barrel:" you're surrounded by total darkness.

The dipper dredge's shovel must have missed Eddy by a couple of feet, but Eddy could not see it. Eddy asked Harry on the diving telephone, "Harry, what was that big clunk I just heard?"

Harry, all sweaty, said, "It's nothing Eddy. Just keep working."

After several hours, Eddy got the steam hose from the dipper dredge hooked up to the sunken oil barge. The right oil valves opened and started pumping the sunken end of the oil barge. In a matter of a few hours, the oil barge was floating.

My diving gear was a real mess. Everything was covered with the black, sticky, tar-like Bunker-C oil. Everything you touched was dirty and sticky. I spent the night cleaning my beautiful new diving gear.

In those days, a diver got sixty-five dollars a day; not too bad when you could hire a full-time helper for fifty cents an hour. I sent American Dredging Company a bill of two hundred fifty dollars to raise the oil barge. If they had brought in a salvage company, it would have cost thousands. They sent me a check with a note: "We'll approve $65.00. Signed, American Dredging Company."

I was really steaming. What a cheap outfit I was working for. I just saved them thousands of dollars and now they want to stick me for $185.

I found out that the American Dredging Company's president was on the land fill, the place where we would dump the material we were pumping from the river. I got in my car and drove to the dump. I found Mr. President. I showed him the letter and the check and asked, "What is this?"

Mr. President said, "That's all the job was worth."

I explained the cleaning of the gear and so forth, but he didn't want to hear it. He just brushed me off. I said, "Mr. American Dredging Company President, you can go to hell and on your way, you can take your dredges, and my job, with you." Then I walked back to my car.

News travels fast. When I got back to the dredge to get my gear, Captain Cocky Boyer was waiting for me. He said, "Mr. President called me and told me what you said to him. But I talked him into keeping you on."

I said, "Captain, I wouldn't work for that snake for all the money in China. You tell Mr. President to kiss my you-know-what," and off I went.

The next day, I went to work for Merritt-Chapman & Scott, the construction outfit on the Walt Whitman Bridge. After leaving, I did a few diving jobs. Not having a good tender, I had too many close calls and decided to call it quits.

In my diving gear on a tug in the Delaware River with Eddy Bennett (in black watchcap), 1950.

My last job was in Dredge Harbor, New Jersey in 1953. A tugboat had sunk. Its bow was on the sandy beach, and her stern was sunk in twenty feet of water. Eddy Bennett was with me as my tender, along with the two guys who wanted the tug brought up.

I was to get a line under the tug between the rudder and the keel. On the first try, we used a gallon can on a light line, trying to put the can between the rudder and propeller, and have it float up with the line on the other side.

It was a good idea, but it didn't work. When I got down to the rudder, I saw that the pressure had crushed the can.

The day was shot, so we got our gear together and started home. We had just left the sight when Eddy said, "You know, Mac, we could slip on down home, get a little dynamite, come back and blow the wheel (propeller) off, and they would never know who did it. That wheel will bring a lot of money for scrap, and I know the man who would buy it."

That was how Eddy Bennett thought. Needless to say, we didn't blow off the wheel.

After raising the oil barge, Eddy said, "Mac, I've got one-hundred-eight dollars coming to me, and I would like to have it now."

I said, "Eddy, you know the deal. When I get paid, I'll pay you."

Eddy said, "Mac, you know Christmas is right around the corner and I have to get some presents for my wife, Sarah."

"Well," I said, " let me see if I can borrow the money from the crew."

I was able to borrow the money. When I paid Eddy, I said, "This is it. From now on, when I get paid, you get paid."

"That's for sure, Mac." Eddy got in the crew boat and left for shore.

About an hour later, the crew boat returned. I couldn't believe my eyes. The first man off was Eddy.

I asked the deck hand, "Why did Eddy come back to the dredge?"

"The only thing I know," he said, "is that I just won one-hundred-eighty dollars from him in a crap game he lost on the way in to the beach."

I was in Hack's Point, MD in Harry Austin's mother's house. We were sitting around the kitchen table and I asked Mrs. Austin, "All the stories I've heard about Eddy Bennett, I really can't believe."

"Mac," Mrs. Austin said, "Don't believe all the stories you hear about Eddy. He's 10 times worse than the stories you hear."

Eddy would come home after a job, with no money, full of booze. The first house on the street he came to, he'd go into and tell everybody to get out. Then Sarah would have to go to the neighbor's house and take Eddy home. You could hear her beating Eddy on the head with a frying pan, bong-bong-bong.

Mrs. Austin said to me, "One night Eddy was in my kitchen, sober. I had a pot on the stove boiling and I said, 'Eddy, do you see that pot of boiling water on my stove?"

"Yes, ma'am, I see it there, Mrs. Austin."

"Well, Eddy, if you ever come in my house drunk, I'll pour the pot of boiling water right over your head."

"I'll never do that Mrs. Austin," he said.

And he never did.

By the way, all the houses on Mrs. Austin's street looked exactly the same.

Before I met Eddy Bennett, he worked for Sun Oil Company cleaning big oil tanks on Sun Oil's tank farm. The Chesapeake City Bridge was damaged by a ship and put out of commission. A ferry was used to replace the bridge until the repairs were completed on the bridge.

One day on his way home from work, Eddy crossed the canal on the ferryboat, and while getting off of the ferry, he ran into another car. The driver in the other auto was injured. The ambulance came, and the injured man was placed in the ambulance. They were all waiting for the ferry. Eddy thought he would go into Ma Smith's General Store and get a coke. In the store, he looked in the mirror and when he saw his face, he thought he better get in the ambulance, too.

When Eddy was telling me this story, he said, "Mac, I got a bill from his lawyer, and in it was a bill for $250 worth of flowers. Now Mac, if I killed him, I wouldn't mind paying for flowers, but $250 for two broken legs isn't fair!"

Just before I left American Dredging Company, Eddy told me he was moving on.

I said, "Gee Eddy, we've got a good thing going. Why spoil it now?"

Eddy looked up and down the deck to see if anyone could hear him. "Mac, do you remember about four years ago, when that big meat truck was stolen in Chester, Pennsylvania?"

"No Eddy, I never heard of such a thing."

Eddy looked around again, and said, "Well Mac, I was in on that job. I was the only one never caught."

"So what, Eddy, does that have to do with our diving work?"

Eddy looked around again and said, "The guys are getting out of jail next week, that's why."

"Eddy, I don't see the connection."

"I was supposed to keep the money for them until they got out of jail, but I spent it."

That was our Eddy Bennett.

Eddy's wife was a nurse. She worked in a big hospital in Delaware. It was also a mental hospital. Eddy told Harry and me a hundred times, "If I'm ever sent to that place, you come in and kill me. If you don't, Sarah will kill me a little at a time."

Eddie later died there.

EDDY BENNETT AND FORT DELAWARE

In 1859, a few years before the Civil War broke out, Fort Delaware was completed. It was built on a marshy island out in the Delaware River called Pea Patch Island. The fort was shaped like an octagon and covered six acres.

After the war broke out, the fort was converted into a prison for the Confederate soldiers. The inmates knew the Commandant General Albino Schlep, as "General Terror." Approximately, 2,700 confederate soldiers died from lack of food and good water while being held captive at Fort Delaware. Scurvy, small pox, and severe malnutrition ran rampant, along with measles, diarrhea, and dysentery.

After the Battle of Gettysburg, the prison built to hold 4,000 inmates was holding 13,000 inmates. Out of the 32,000 prisoners held in Fort Delaware during the Civil War, 7 1/2 percent died while there.

For many, many years Fort Delaware just sat on Pea Patch Island, ignored by the world. During the summer months, a few people with boats would visit the fort. We would take our kids to the fort and let them play hide-and-seek. The fort was a great place to hide with all the rooms, tunnels, and cubbyholes.

The State of Delaware decided to restore the fort and make it a state park. The state found out that someone stripped the fort of all its brass and any other items that could be sold for scrap. Needless to say, the state had no way to find out who the culprits were and how they did it.

Here is how it was done, told to me by one of the two men that pulled it off. The two men had an old lifeboat. The boat was in Chester, PA. At high tide, the two men with their gear and food would leave Chester, PA, and let the tide carry them to Pea Patch Island. They would dock the boat and camp out in the fort. In about five days, the lifeboat would be loaded with the brass and other things taken from the fort. At high tide the two men and the lifeboat would let the tide carry them back to Chester, PA, where they would sell the scrap.

Now you know how it was done! Both men are not on this Earth now, so the State of Delaware is out of luck. Eddy did it again.

THE NEW DREDGE

Sun Ship Yard in Chester, PA, had built a new dredge for American Dredging Company. "Chief One Wing" was the chief engineer. He asked me to go along with him as first engineer. Half his shoulder had been blown off in an air compressor explosion. Somehow oil got into the cylinder head and could not take pressure when the heat from the compressor exploded the oil. For every pound of compression, the temperature goes up two degrees. For example, for 300 pounds of compression, the temperature would be 600 degrees Fahrenheit.

The dredge had a 20" pipeline. Driving the pump was a six-cylinder turbo charged diesel engine, built by the Worthington Company. The engine was handmade and nothing was interchangeable: No. 1 bolt, No. 1 nut, No. 200 bolt, No. 200 nut, and so on.

The dredge had several serious problems. The biggest was that the runner was too big for the engine. Turbo chargers were new and the engineer didn't know that the runner was too big.

When the engine was overloaded, the turbo just pumped more air into the engine. With more air, the engine could burn more fuel—the more fuel and air, the higher the cylinder temperature. The cylinder head temperature was above the specifications of what the engine could tolerate. As a result, we had to overhaul the engine three times in two months. Guess who got the job?

The engine was so big. To unbolt the connecting rods, you had to climb into the engine, in eight inches of oil, and unbolt the connecting rods. The bolts were 1 1/2" wide and 18" long: No. 4 rod, No. 4 bolt; No. 4 hole, No. 4 nut.

Things finally started to come together. Most dredges have two spuds on the back, which are controlled by the lever man, the guy who actually runs the thing. In front are two swing wires, port and starboard. The tug and crane barge take the swing wires that have a big anchor on each end and drop the anchor and wires in the water: one on the right side forward of the dredge, and one on the left side. The lever man can swing the dredge left or right. By raising and dropping the spuds, he can walk the dredge forward.

About 7:00 p.m., The American Dredging Company's president and the Sun Ship engineers went for a long dinner. I said to my oiler, "Mouse," who was so called because he looked just like a mouse, "Let's go take a look at the winding gear."

After thirty minutes, I said, "Look, Mouse, the right brake band is on the left side, and the left brake band is on the right side."

"Oh, yeah," said Mouse.

"Go get the tools. We're going to switch the brake bands."

The brake bands hold the spud up when swinging the dredge. We had just finished the job and put the tools away when the crew boat came along side with the president and the Sun Ship engineers. Mouse and I were having a cup of coffee. Mr. President said, "Is that all you people do? Drink coffee?"

"What would you like us to do, Mr. President?"

"Well," he said, "Why don't you help out on the winding gear problem?"

I said, "What's there to do?"

"You know, the damn thing doesn't work right."

"Oh, that," I said, "Mouse and I fixed it while you were out for supper."

"What do you mean you fixed it?"

I said, "Try it." It worked like a charm.

Mr. President said, "What in the hell did you do?"

I told him what the problem was. He said, "Meet me in the parking lot." Then he told The Sun Ship people how dumb they were. The company had lost lots of money and time with this problem. He was going to give me a big bonus or something. I waited in the parking lot for about twenty-minutes before he showed up. He told me what a good job I had done and handed me a sealed, white envelope. "Don't open it here," he said.

"Boy I'm going to be in Fat City!" I thought. I drove a few blocks and stopped the car under a streetlight. The time had come for the big news. I opened the envelope and took out...a gift certificate for a $15 Stetson hat.

BAD UNION REPRESENTATIVE

I left the American Dredging Company in 1953 and went to work at Warner Sand and Gravel, which had been started by Sap Warner. Whenever Bill McCullough, from Industrial Transmission Machinery, came down to the plant, he would go back to his office and tell everyone how wild and crazy we were. When "Big Bad Brown," who had worked with me at American Dredge, put three rounds through the office ceiling, that was the limit. "Those crazy people down at the sand plant even tried to kill me," he said. "I got out of that office just in time. Another minute and I would have been shot."

Well, the crew was a little crazy, but it was all in fun. Everyone worked very hard and was loyal to the company and each man respected his fellow workers. Bill McCullough was a little different. He was not a man's man, and that is why the crew did what they did.

At that time, I met Etta DelConte, who worked at ITM. After we got engaged, Etta would turn her engagement ring around so that McCullough wouldn't ask her who the lucky guy was. She did not want him to know the lucky guy was one of those crazy guys at the sand plant.

Etta and I were engaged on May 1, 1953 and the wedding was exactly one year later, on May 1, 1954. A lot happened that year. I finished the 26' boat, the sand plant closed down, Sap Warner ran off (to where I never did find out), and I got married.

When the sand plant closed down, I was out of a job again. I asked myself again, "Are there any honest people left in this world?"

I went to American Dredging Company's offices and was met by Vinnie the union guy outside the company's office. "I understand the *Caven* needs an engineer," I said.

I don't know if Greaser will give you the job, Mac, but I'll go in and ask him," Vinnie said.

When Vinnie returned, he said, "I'm sorry, Mac. Greaser said he would not touch you with a 10-foot pole."

"I left this company in good standing. Why would Greaser say such a thing? I'm going in there and find out why."

"You can't do that. I'm your union representative and you've got to go through me. That's how it works."

"Well Vinnie, if you can't get me the job, I guess I don't need you." With that, I started walking to the office door.

"You go in there, and I'll pull your union card," Vinnie shouted.

Turning my back on him, I walked into the office and up to the woman behind the desk. "My name is Fred McCarthy. The engineer's job on the *Caven* is open. Vinnie Motsel said Mr. Greaser would not give me the job, and I would just like to know why."

She picked up the phone. "I have a young man named Fred McCarthy out here who'd like to see you."

"Send him in," came out of the intercom.

As I walked into the office, Mr. Greaser stood up, reached out his hand and said, "Mac, it's good to see you. How is everything down at your sand plant?"

"To answer your question, Mr. Greaser, I'd like to know why you told Vinnie Motsel that you would not touch me with a 10-foot pole?"

"Mac, I haven't seen Vinnie in a couple of days. The job is yours. I am very glad to have you back. I hate to ask you this, but the *Caven* is in the R.T.C. shipyard with a broken propeller shaft, and the new propeller shaft isn't bolted to the engine. This is very short notice, I know, but would you go to R.T.C. and hook up the new shaft?" Greaser said.

"Sure, Mr. Greaser. I'll go home and change clothes. I'll be at the yard by 6:30 p.m. tonight."

"Mac, I can't thank you enough." He put out his hand and said, "Glad to have you back." We shook hands and I started to walk to the door.

"Mac," he said, "Vinnie has some relation who wants the job. I don't need more problems. If Vinnie tries to give you a hard time for going over his head, let me know. Sorry the sand plant didn't work out for you. My door is always open."

That night, I became one of the engineers on the tugboat *Caven*.

TUGBOAT SHAKER

The *Caven* was one of American Dredging Company's tugboats. It took loaded dump scows down the river to the landfill in Bridgeport, NJ, and dumped them by opening the bottom doors. From high to low tide was approximately seven hours. The tugboats had to make the trip in that seven-hour window. They didn't have the horsepower to pull the loaded dump scows against a flood tide. There were many times when the tugs got a late start. The captains knew they could not reach the landfill before the tide changed. They were told, "Don't come back with loaded scows." The only thing a captain could do was dump the scows, no matter where they were, before the tide changed and try not to get caught!

The shipyard that built the *Caven* made a super screw up. The *Caven* was powered by a six-cylinder Fairbanks Morris direct-reversible diesel engine. When the engine was set on the engine bed, and the propeller shaft was installed, something was wrong. The engine and the shaft coupling did not line up. The engine was a half-inch higher than the shaft coupling.

There were only two ways to fix the problem. One, you could take the engine out of the boat and rebuild the engine bed; or two, you could raise the propeller shaft a half inch. Both repairs would be very costly.

The buyers rejected the boat. Along came American Dredging Company. They bought the boat for a song.

When Mr. Greaser, the boss, sent me to R.T.C. shipyard to bolt up the propeller shaft on the *Caven,* I didn't know what to do. I called the port engineer and told him my problem. The port engineer told me where I would find the twenty-ton jack, to jack up the propeller shaft high enough to get the coupling bolts through the coupling. By using a twenty-ton hydraulic jack, the shaft was lifted up the half inch. Of course, the shaft couplings did not line up like they should, but it worked. The only problem was the boat vibrated so much that the plates on the galley table would jump up and down turning the *Caven* into a real shaker.

I could not believe what I was hearing. This was against all the rules, but you gotta do what you gotta do. The *Caven* was put overboard at 8:00 a.m. the following morning.

Planes

FLYING SCHOOL

I was only 19 years old when I returned home from the Navy. It took quite a while to get back to a normal life. At first, I thought I would like to be a high school shop teacher. I checked several colleges and with thousands of GI's coming home, they were all jammed. Most had four-year waiting lists. Who could wait four years? I got a job with Western Electric Company, which made and installed all the equipment for Bell Telephone.

I did not want to lose my GI Bill benefits, which gave veterans money to go to school. I could not get into a college, so I signed up at a flying school at the Camden Airport. My class had eight students. All the instructors were ex-military pilots. One had been an army transport pilot and the other a P-51 fighter pilot. We were flying Cessna 140s: a high-wing, two-seater with aluminum body, fabric wings, and tails with no wing flaps. It's a very basic airplane.

At flight school one of the things we had to do was a 720-degree turn. The idea was if you entered the turn heading north, you'd make two complete turns. You would be heading north at the end of the last turn, at the same altitude that you started with. This was a good hands-and-feet exercise.

My first instructor was an ex-cargo pilot. He said to me, "Give me a nice smooth 720." I checked my compass heading, made two complete shallow left turns and came on the same compass heading as when II had started the turns.

"Very nice. Very nice," he said.

A few days later I had a different instructor. "Give me a 720," he said.

I started my nice, smooth, standard-rate turn, just as before.

He grabbed the stick and yelled, "Who the hell taught you to fly? You're the boss of this airplane. When I say turn, turn this God damn airplane like you mean it, not like you're afraid of it."

He took over the controls and stood the plane up on one wing, then made two very tight turns in a matter of seconds, leveling out after the second turn. "That's how you make a 720," he said. Remember, you're the boss."

"What did you fly in the Air Force?" I asked.

"A P-51 fighter. Why?"

"I can see now why you fly like you do," I said.

For the next couple of weeks, I was a P-51 pilot. Then one day, the cargo pilot got in the Cessna with me and said, "Let me see how you're doing. Take me up to 4,000 feet over the practice area."

"O.K.," I said.

When we reached the area and 4,000 feet, the cargo pilot said, "Give me a 720." With that I stood the 140 up on its left wing and into the very steep turn.

My cargo pilot instructor grabbed the controls and put the 140 back into an upright position. "What the hell are you doing? Trying to kill us?"

I didn't say a word. I just let him ramble on. When he finally settled down, I said, "I wish you guys would get your acts together and have only one way to fly this airplane. Let's go home. I've had enough for one day."

I flew the little 140 back to the airport and after landing, I put the airplane back in the hangar and walked over to the flying school office and asked to see the director.

"I want one instructor," I said. "Not ten."

After that, I only had one instructor and things were better. In the 1940s, you came out of training as a real pilot. You were taught spins, lazy eights, real forced landings, full power stalls, and so on, and you flew by the iron beam (railroad tracks) and the concrete beam (roads) without radios. You were required to do things that are no longer allowed today.

I passed my oral test and my flight test in August 1946, the same month that I turned 20.

NAVY N2T, CLEMENTON AIRPORT

As soon as I finished flying school, I bought one-third interest in a war surplus Navy N2T, with my friend Bob Grissom. It was made by the Timm Company and it cost $200. It had two open cockpits and was made of plywood, and painted red. The engine was a 225 horsepower radial engine, made by the Continental Engine Company.

We were flying out of Blackwood, NJ. The runway was less than 1,800 feet long. The east approach was a real challenge. You had to fly next to a school and down through a hole in the trees. The runway began at the end of the trees. The N2T was very nose heavy, so you had to use very little brakes. The plane had flipped on its back once, when too much brake was used.

A new airport had opened on the White Horse Pike in Clementon, New Jersey. At the time, I didn't know that I would marry a girl from Clementon. I'll tell you about that later on. Across the street from the airport was a very nice restaurant called the Silver Lake Inn. The White Horse Pike separated the runway from the Silver Lake Inn, and was only a few feet from the road and the power lines were on the same side as the Inn.

The airport ran big ads in the local newspapers: "Big Fly In At The New Clementon Airport. Come See All The Airplanes."

At the bottom of the ad, it read, "Fly In Pilots, Join Us At The Silver Lake Inn For A Great Free Lunch."

Sounded like fun!

When the day arrived, I drove down to Blackwood and uncovered the two cockpits. The plane was outside. The only hangar housed the Warner Bird. After checking the oil lever and for water in the fuel tank, I was ready to start the engine. I climbed up on the wing, leaned over the cockpit and gave the engine a couple of shots of fuel and cracked the throttle. With no one in the cockpit, you had to make sure that when the engine started, it would not go too fast. You didn't want the plane to go running around the airport without a driver.

I put the crank in the hole and started cranking. I got the fly wheel winding. I took the crank out and pulled the clutch lever. The engine started on the first try.

The new airport in Clementon was only about 6 or 7 miles from Blackwood NJ. In those days, I never used a checklist. In fact, we didn't even have a checklist.

On takeoff, the plane handled sluggishly. It didn't want to climb. I couldn't find the reason. What the hell is wrong with the engine? I was only at tree level when I saw the problem. The carburetor heat lever was pulled out. How dumb could I get? I pushed the lever to the off position and the engine came to life. After that, they called me "Check List Kid" in all the local town airports.

Clementon, here we come!

I flew around the traffic pattern at 600 feet. On my approach, the runway looked awfully short, and those damn power lines were right on the end of the runway. I was always told, "Don't be ashamed to make a go-around," so I made one and then another. On my fifth try, I really wanted that free lunch. I put the plane in a very hard sideslip. To make a right turn, the pilot pushes the right rudder pedal and turns the yoke or stick to the right. The more you move these controls, the steeper and shorter the turn.

At age 9, building a model airplane

At age 10, at the Pine Valley School of Aviation in NJ

Starting the Navy N2T with Bob Grissom

In the Navy N2T, at Blackwood Airport in NJ, with my brother, Bob (left), 1946

A sideslip is a maneuver to lose altitude in a very short distance. You use the right rudder and left aileron or the left rudder and right aileron, depending on whether or not you are right or left handed. The more rudder and aileron you use, the faster you lose altitude. This is called crossing the controls.

I had the N2T dropping like a rock and finally got the plane on the ground. I got the free lunch and met Fred Tonyes, an airline pilot who would later get his ATC rating in my plane.

NAVY N2T, CAMDEN AIRPORT

One day, I thought I would fly the N2T to central airport in Camden, NJ, to show the N2T to some of the instructors I had in flying school. When I arrived at the airport, I forgot how long the runway was—5,000 feet next to Blackwood's 1,800 feet—it looked like it ran forever. I landed, parked the plane and walked over to the flying school.

I was talking to one of the instructors when a guy walked up and said, "I understand you just flew in from Blackwood."

"Yes, that's true."

"I'm trying to get a ride there. Would you take me with you?"

"Sure," I said, "I'll be leaving shortly."

The two of us left the flying school and started walking to the plane. When we had about 500 or 600 feet to go, the passenger saw the N2T and said, "Are you flying that N2T over there?

"Yes," I said, "How do you like her?"

"Would I hurt your feelings if I turned down your offer?" he said.

"Not really, but why don't you want a ride?"

"I was in the Navy, and was a flight instructor. I was instructing in the N2T basic training."

"Go on," I said.

"Well, one day, I had a student up for a check ride. We did all the maneuvers: spins, lazy eights, power on stalls, everything you could think of. We landed and taxied up to the parking ramp. As you know, the parking ramp has a gutter shaped indentation for the landing gear wheels to drop into. This lines the plane up into a perfect row."

"Well, we taxied up to the parking ramp and when the wheel dropped into the wheel indentation, I felt odd movements. When I saw what happened, I could have died."

"What happened?"

"When we taxied to the ramp and the wheels dropped into parking, the N2T broke in half, right behind the backseat. The plywood plane was full of dry rot. When I think of all the stress we put on the airframe, I still shudder. How lucky can you get?"

He walked off, and I flew the N2T back to Blackwood, thinking all the way back, "How can we check for dry rot?"

THE CLOWERS OF PENNINGTON

Having an airplane is one thing, but finding some place to go in your plane is another thing.

One Saturday, in the middle of summer, I was cleaning the Navy N2T at the Blackwood Airport. When I was finished, I stood back and thought: You're a nice airplane, but we have nowhere to go.

Then the light came on. That girl I met in Bermuda, she said she lived in Pennington, NJ, and was in the phone book. That would be a nice ride on a Saturday afternoon. Why not?

I'd call her when I got to Pennington Airport. If she is home, O.K. If not, I just had a nice Saturday afternoon outing.

The Navy N2T had a full tank of fuel with no water in the tank. Oil level was O.K. We were ready to go. I got the crank out of its holder and started the engine. I climbed into the front cockpit with my white helmet and yellow scarf blowing in the wind, and started out for the short 1,500-foot runway.

Taxiing the N2T was not easy. If you hit the brakes too hard, then the plane would nose over and land on her back. The short 1,500-foot runway kept you sharp. There was no room for errors.

I took her up to 2,000 feet while heading to the Delaware River. When I reached the river, I turned north and flew down the center of the river, until I reached Trenton, NJ, where the river turned west.

The Pennington Airport was just a few miles north of Trenton. It took me a little time to find the airport. It was nothing more than a small grass field with two lights at the end of the grass runway. Without the lights, you would never know it was an airport. A little windsock and a small office were helpful landmarks.

After landing, I taxied over to the little building and parked the N2T.

A man was standing in the doorway. I asked him if I could use his telephone to make a local call. He said O.K., and pointed to the telephone sitting on this little desk.

I picked up the phone and gave the operator the phone number. The phone rang a few times.

"Hello, Mrs. Clower. I know you won't remember me. We met in Bermuda a few years ago, when I was in the Navy."

Before I could say another word, she said, "Fred McCarthy?"

"I'm surprised you remember me after all this time."

"How can I forget that night in the hotel. We're still talking about it. Where are you calling from?"

"The Pennington Airport," I said.

"What are you doing there?"

"I thought about you people this morning, and decided to take a chance that you'd be home, being it's Saturday," I said.

"We'll be there in 15 minutes."

Fifteen minutes later, a black four-door Buick drove up to where I was standing. Mr. and Mrs. Clower and their daughter stepped out of the car. The daughter said, "Will you take me for a ride in your airplane? What kind is it?"

"It is a Navy N2T, and sure I'll take you for a ride, if it is O.K. with your mom and dad," I said.

Both parents nodded O.K.

Bea Clower had kinky red hair. I gave her a helmet with goggles, and had her sit in the backseat. I showed her how to fasten the seatbelt, and we were ready to go flying.

Now, all I had to do was get the plane cranked up. She was still hot from our flight up here. As I started to turn the crank, I said under my breath, "Come on old girl. Let's start on the first try. You can do it. You can do it."

She must have been listening to me. She came to life on the first try. We taxied over to the end of the grass runway, did our mag check, turned into the wind and the big seven-cylinder radial engine came to life, and we went flying down the grassy runway.

When we climbed to one thousand feet, we leveled off and flew around the area. Bea pointed to a large house with a very big pool, with lots of people in and around the pool.

"Can you buzz my friend's pool?" she yelled over the roar of the engine.

"Sure."

EARLY YEARS

Next to the swimming pool was a large cornfield. I went across it at about ten feet over the tops of the corn. Everyone started waving with towels and anything else they could find.

The second pass was even lower than the first pass. As we reached the airport, Bea said, "Buzz my daddy's car."

"Sure," I said.

After landing, we taxied over to her father's car.

Mrs. Clower said, "Freddy, would you come to dinner next Saturday? Say about 6:00 p.m.?"

"Sure, that would be nice."

They all climbed into the black Buick and drove off.

I guess the old girl was mad at me. It took me three times to get the engine started. I sat in the cockpit with my eyes closed and sweat running down my face, listening to the idling engine. The plane rocked a little, and when I opened my eyes, a man was standing on the wing. The next thing I knew, he reached into the cockpit and shut down the engine.

"Who do you think you are, climbing on my plane?" I asked.

"I'm with the CIB." (The CIB is now the FAA.)

He gave me a hand written notice that said: 1. Acrobatics over an airport. 2. Acrobatics with a passenger. 3. Acrobatics without parachutes. 4. Etc., etc.

After that, he climbed down from the N2T and walked off.

What a day!

The N2T was tied down in Blackwood before dark.

On Saturday I left Oaklyn around 5:30 a.m. I drove my 1948 Chevy business coupe, a two-door car that sat only two people with a very large trunk that was used to carry the salesman's samples.

The route was easy: North on the White Horse Pike to the airport circle, pick up Route 130 to Trenton, NJ, and Pennington was just a few miles north of Trenton.

Just a little before seven o'clock I arrived at the Clowers' house with a present for Mrs. Clower. Cocktails were at 7:00 p.m. and dinner was at 8:00 p.m. There was just the four of us: Mr. and Mrs. Clower, Bea and myself. Their son, Charley was still in the Army. I left for home around 10:00 p.m., and was home by 11:15 p.m.

At the time I was working for that crook, J.M. Waldecker, selling springs, castings, forgings and a couple of other items. Covering three states, kept me on the road a lot. Whenever I was in the Pennington area, I would stop in to see the Clowers.

Mr. Clower had a sister living in Lewes, DE. She was married to Roland Hasson. One weekend, the Clowers were going to Delaware for the weekend, and asked if I'd like to go with them. When I found out the Hassons owned a boatyard, the answer came out fast, "Sure."

The boat yard was located in the center of the town of Lewes. I met Roland's partners, Dick and Eva Thompson.

That meeting was the beginning of a 40-year friendship. Actually, it was more then a friendship. Dick and Eva became my second mother and father. When I think back, it must have been very hard on my mother and father, but at the time, I didn't see it. All I could think of was boats, any kind of boat. After that weekend, things were never the same.

Now that I am getting older, I can look back and see that things I thought were heartbreaking at the time were really blessings in disguise. Most things happen for the best, if you are lucky.

Example: Several months had passed since our weekend in Delaware. Bea's father said to me one afternoon, "Son, I'm going to build a house for you and my daughter."

"That's great, Mr. Clower. Bea and I will look for a building lot," I said.

"I already bought the building lot," he said.

"Where is it?" I asked.

"Just next door."

"Mr. Clower, thanks. It's very nice of you to build us a house, but I don't want to live next to my parents, and I don't want to live next to Bea's parents."

Before I could say another word, he turned and walked away.

That night, Mr. Clower invited a Dutch general for dinner. He worked for a company that made parachutes and was trying to get a big order. Both men had a little too much to drink, and when I walked into the kitchen, Mr. Clower said to the Dutch general, "General, here is the smartest boy in the world. You can't tell him a thing. He knows everything. For 25 cents, I would tell him to get out of my house."

That did it. I realized that I had never liked the man from the start. He was always trying to be the big shot. It was his way or no way. I reached into my pocket and put a $1 bill on the counter top and said, "Here is a dollar. You can keep the change."

After I said that, I turned around and walked out of the house, and drove home to Oaklyn.

I often think about that night. If I hadn't done what I did, I would have missed out on the great life I've had—and I would not have had fifty-five great years with my Etta.

Things do happen for the best!

NAVY N2T COMES TO AN END

The one-third share in the Navy N2T was still open. One day, a guy answered our ad in the paper, and we met at the airport. It was a beautiful Saturday afternoon. The wind was straight down the runway from the east, which meant you would fly away from the trees, not over them. I said to my partner, Bob Grissom, "You take him up for a check ride. You have a lot more flying hours than I do." Bob said, "You take him first and let me know what you think of him as a pilot."

I showed him the walk-around check. The walk-around meant checking the engine oil, checking for nicks in the propeller, checking for water in the fuel, etc. The pilot in command sat in the front seat and the co-pilot or instructor sat in the backseat. I said to our new buyer, "Sit up front. I'll get in the back and whatever you do, don't touch the brakes." We put on our helmets and goggles. Our buyer climbed into the front seat, and put on his safety belt.

To start the engine wasn't easy. You inserted the hand crank into a hole just behind the engine. Next to the hole was another handle that engaged the starter. So, it went like this: The pilot primed the engine in the cockpit, number two man inserted the crank and started turning it. The crank was very hard to turn at first, but as you turned the crank, the easier it got.

When you got the crank really turning fast, you took the crank out of the hole and said, "Contact" and pull out the little handle. The little handle would engage the spinning fly wheel, that in turn turned the engine over, and if you were lucky, the engine started. On a very hot day in May, it would take two to three times before the engine started.

That day we were lucky. It started the first time. After the engine started, I climbed in the back seat, and told our buyer, "Let's go." He taxied out to the runway. We went through the checklist, which wasn't much, and started to take off.

We flew the standard procedure: take off, make a climbing 180 degree turn to the left, level off at 600 feet, fly downwind parallel to the runway. When you reach the end of the runway, put the engine in the idle position and start your 180 degree left turn around the school, through the trees, and land on the runway.

Mr. Buyer was too high and too fast. I told him to make a go-around, and he said, "I can make it. I can make it." I shoved the throttle forward and said, "Go around."

We made three passes and three go-arounds. I landed the plane. I said to Bob, "You take him around. I don't like the way he flies." When Bob came back, he told the buyer that he wasn't ready for this airport, and the one-third ownership was not for sale!

Now this is hard to believe, but it's true. The buyer returned on Sunday with his girlfriend. The two got in the N2T and took off. Where they went, I don't know. They came back to the field and made the same mistakes on the approach: too high and too fast, but this time, there was no one to make him go around. The result was, he ran off the end of the runway, went through the fence and into a ditch. The plane was a total wreck. The only thing we salvaged was the engine (I still have the broken propeller). They both walked away without a scratch.

The following night, the three of us met in a diner in Haddon Heights for coffee. The first thing Bob said was, "Give me the 200 bucks you owe me."

Mr. Buyer said, "Why should I give you 200 bucks for one-third interest in an airplane you don't have?"

Bob wasn't very tall, but he was as strong as a bull. The next thing I knew, Bob pulled Mr. Buyer out of the diner booth, spun him around and hit him in the face. Mr. Buyer stumbled back the entire length of the diner.

"Fred, let's get out of here."

The diner was torn down several years ago!

THE BIRD

Now that the N2T was gone, I had nothing to fly. The airport owner had a two-wing airplane for sale. It was probably built in the early thirties. The plane was powered by a five-cylinder radial engine built by the Warner Company. The plane was called the "Warner Bird," and those powered by a Kinner engine were called "Kinner Birds."

The Warner Bird was for sale. The wings and tail were painted white and it had a bright red fuselage. The pilot sat in the backseat, and the front seat held two people—small people that is. The asking price was $700.

I went to the bank in Oaklyn, NJ, the town where I lived with my father and mother. The bank building was only about 50 feet by 50 feet. When I entered the little bank, the president was sitting at his desk. I walked up to him and said, "Good morning."

"Good morning, Fred. What can I do for you?"

"I'd like to borrow $700."

"All right, fill out these papers, and I'll submit them to the board. It meets on Wednesday. Come in on Thursday and I'll have an answer for you." Then Mr. President asked, "By the way, what is it for?"

My answer was, "I'm going to buy an airplane."

The week of waiting seemed like forever, but finally Thursday came and I was in the bank two minutes after it opened. "Good morning, Mr. President." (By the way, the president of the bank was the largest shareholder, and I dated his daughter in junior high school) "When can I get my $700?"

"I'm sorry, Fred. The bank turned your loan down."

I couldn't believe my ears. "I've been banking here since I was a kid." I was now 21 years old. "Close my savings account. I'm going to another bank." I didn't find out the real story until 30 years later.

Mr. President had called my mother and said, "Fred wants to borrow $700 to buy an airplane."

My mother's answer was short: "Hell no. Don't lend him any money to buy an airplane."

My mother didn't know I was flying, and getting the money seemed out of the question, so I made a deal with the airport owner. I could use the Bird any time I wanted, and just pay him a small rental fee. This would keep the plane running. There's nothing harder on an airplane then just sitting around collecting dust.

This was great. I could fly any time I wanted. I didn't have to worry about hangar rent, cleaning, and so on. It was a fun airplane to fly, sitting in the back cockpit with my yellow scarf flapping in the slip-stream, my white helmet leaning against the big head rest—hot stuff!

One day, my friend Jack Kern and I decided to fly up to Lancaster, PA. We rolled the Bird out of the hangar, checked the oil level and checked for water in the gas tank. We did a walk around to look the old Bird over.

Jack was a tail gunner on a B-17 in the 18th Air Force in Europe. He was shot down over Italy. He'd parachuted out of the B-17 and had been captured and sent to a prison camp.

I got in the backseat and Jack spun the propeller. Our procedure went like this: Jack said, "Off." In the cockpit I made sure the switch was off, and said, "Switch off." Jack turned the propeller three to five times to clear the engine cylinders and said, "Switch on." I turned it on and said, "Switch on." Then Jack spun the propeller and stepped back from the propeller. If everything went well, the engine would start.

This day, all went well. The engine started the first time. It was something to see. This old engine had most of the moving parts out in the open: valve stems, rocker arms, push rods, all going up and down.

We climbed into the plane, put on our helmets and goggles. In the front cockpit, you had to wear goggles, because there was no windshield. We were ready to go.

Down the runway we went and when we reached our approximate air speed of 40 miles per hour, we lifted off into the air. The reason I said "approximate" is that the old Bird didn't have an air speed gauge. We leveled off at approximately 1,500 feet (You now know what "approximate" means).

The shortest way from Blackwood to Lancaster, PA, was to cross South Philadelphia. We crossed the Delaware River with our scarves flapping in the wind. We were flying over the big cemetery in South Philadelphia when the engine started to sputter and lost its power.

Jack said, "What the hell are you doing?"

I said, "I'm not doing a damn thing! The engine is crapping out!"

"Oh, shit!" Jack said.

I looked down at the cemetery and couldn't see a clear piece of land. "Jack, I'm going to head for the river. If we're lucky, we'll find a boat we can ditch alongside of, and get fished out of the water." I headed toward the river in the distance. No boats. I turned south, just skirting the edge of the river. The Bird had about 15-to-1 glide ratio, which means for every foot of altitude lost, you could travel 15 feet forward.

I looked ahead and saw Muston Field, the Navy airport in South Philadelphia, next to the Philadelphia Navy Shipyard. I was stretching the glide as best I could. I knew I could not make the runway, so the next best thing was to land between the hangar and the Navy planes lined up on the parking ramp. I did a 90 degree turn around the control tower. The tower was giving me the red light, which means don't land (a green light means it's O.K. to land). When I went around the tower, I was looking up at the light, not looking down at the light. We landed as planned between the hangars and parked aircraft.

EARLY YEARS

The Bird was made for grass fields. When we landed on the concrete, we just kept rolling and rolling and rolling. When we finally stopped, I lay my head back on the head-rest and thought, How lucky can you get?

In a matter of minutes, fire engines, an ambulance, and about ten pieces of equipment led by a light-blue colored Jeep arrived. The Navy lt. commander in charge of the airport was clearly unhappy to see us.

"Are you out of gas?" he asked in a nasty tone of voice.

"I don't know Captain. I'll check."

The gas tank was just inches ahead of the front cockpit. Jack unscrewed the gas cap; reached into the cockpit; pulled out our short brush handle. He stuck it in the tank. When the brown handle hit the bottom of the tank, Jack pulled the handle.

"Nope, captain, we still have nine inches of gas."

"Are you the pilot?" the captain asked.

"Yes, I am."

"Put on your parking brakes and come with me to Operations."

"I don't have parking brakes."

"You don't have parking brakes? What the hell do you have in there?"

He stuck his head over the edge of the cockpit and looked at the instrument panel. It was painted red and didn't have a thing on it, except the compass. He said, "Don't you fly by the numbers?"

"What are the numbers, captain?"

"You know, air speed and altitude."

"No sir. I just go up and down with this stick, and steer with that pipe on the floor."

"I should go with you to Operations," he said

I said, "O.K., but first let me look at the engine." I climbed out of the cockpit, walked around the wing and looked the engine over. It didn't take long to see the problem: three rocker arms and three push rods were missing.

Being a Navy veteran, I thought the Navy would give me a little courtesy, but they didn't. The way they acted, you would think we were from Outer Space.

After filling out some papers for the Navy, I asked for some transportation to the Philadelphia Airport to buy parts to repair The Bird. The best the Navy would do was drive us to the main gate. Outside the gate, there were no taxis or any other transportation, so we started to hitchhike.

It took us an hour to make the four-mile trip. The Philadelphia Airport was very small in those days. You could park a car across the street from the terminal.

We found Kelsee's Shop and bought rocker arms and other parts. We finally got back to the Navy field. The Navy assigned an aviation machinist to help. I asked him where I could get some tools to fix the engine. The machinist took us to the tool room.

Out comes this good size toolbox, full of tools. The tool room guy asked me if I was ever in the service.

"Yes, I was in the Navy."

"OK," he said, "Here's pencil and paper. Put your Navy serial number at the top of the page, and list all the tools in the box."

I started to do what he asked but realized it would take me all day to write down all the tools in the box.

"Just give me a screw driver, a pair of pliers, a hammer and a long-nose pliers."

I took the tools out to the Jeep. Jack, the machine mate and I drove to the Bird and replaced the push rods and rocker arms. It didn't take very long to finish the job. Now that the parts were in, we needed to set the push rod clearance. But we didn't know the clearance, and even if we did, we had no way to measure it.

I took the rocker arm and moved it up and down a little. I heard a clicking sounds—click-click-click. I said to Jack, "What does that sound like to you?"

"Make it a little tighter."

I made the clearance a little smaller. When I moved the rocker arm up and down, the click-click-click was softer.

"What do you think, Jack?"

"Sounds good."

I tightened everything up and I climbed in the cockpit. Jack spun the propeller. The engine came to life. I let it run about five minutes and then shut it down.

The aviation machine mate said, "That engine sounds like it's about to fall apart."

"That engine never sounded so good," I said

By now it was late, and the weather wasn't good. It was starting to rain. The aviation machine mate drove us back to Operations and Mr. Lt. Commander walked over and said, "I want you out of here, now. After you take off, don't make a turn until you are at least a mile away from the end of the runway."

"Mr. Lt. Commander, this airplane was not built to fly in this kind of weather. It's too dangerous," I said.

His next remark was, "I said NOW!"

We went to the plane, started the engine and taxied to the end of the runway. By now, it was really raining. The tower gave me the green light. I shoved the throttle forward and off we went. At about 200 feet or so, we were in the clouds. We dropped down a little and flew just under the clouds.

I was still over the runway. I thought, "The hell with you, Mr. Lt. Commander," and made a sharp right turn and crossed the Delaware River. Jack had his head down in the cockpit to stay out of the driving rain. He was just looking over the rim of the cockpit, looking down.

We flew to the area where I thought the Blackwood Airport should be. But I couldn't find it. I kept turning and looking, turning and looking. I was getting nervous. It was starting to get dark. What will I do if I can't find the airport?"

I was still really low, which made it even harder to find the airport. I was starting to panic. Time was running out. Suddenly I was right over the airport. What a relief!

A few minutes later, we were on the ground. We taxied to the hangar. I sat in the seat for a few minutes, and when I got out of the plane, the first words out of Jack's mouth were, "What was that joy ride for?"

"I couldn't find the airport, Jack."

"Hell, you flew over it about 10 times!"

THE BIRD, NEW YORK TRIP

It was summertime. The weather was hot. Some friends invited me to spend a weekend on their farm just over the New Jersey border in New York State. I told them the Bird carried enough fuel to get there, but not enough fuel for the return trip.

"No problem," they said. On the farm they would mow the grass for a landing strip and have enough fuel (in five-gallon cans) for my return flight. Sounded like a fun weekend.

I rolled the Bird out of the hangar, checked the gas, closed the hangar door and stowed my bag in the front seat. Starting the Bird was really a two-man job. When you don't have a second man, it goes something like this: Stick your head into the cockpit and make sure the mags are in the off position (Remember, the mags are magnetos that gives the spark to the spark plugs). Put the throttle in the off position. Now just look around to make sure everything's in order in the cockpit.

The next step is to make sure the chocks are in front of the wheels. You don't want to get run over when the engine starts. Now you grab the propeller with both hands, and pull it down to make it turn and spin. As the propeller moves or spins, you step back. The engine should not start, but you never know. You always consider the worst thing that could happen.

After you pull the propeller through three or four times, it's time to get the old girl's engine going. Now back to the cockpit to turn both mags to the on position, and crank the throttle to the idle position. Then, back to the propeller, but this time the engine is ready to start. Grab the propeller with both hands, and pull it down with all you've got, and then step back. With any luck, the engine should be running. Years ago, this is how you started most small aircraft.

My friend gave me all kinds of directions, along with roads and landmarks. The flight was very pleasant. The farms and small towns were a beautiful sight. Back then most towns had their names painted on a roof somewhere in the town. This was a left over from the first airmail service planes. I crossed into New York State and some small mountains started showing up ahead.

After 30 minutes, I knew I should be at my destination. I made some left and right turns looking for the farm. This must have been my lucky day. Ahead of me was the farm, people, cars, and a mowed runway. I made a pass over the runway. It was too short. If I had to make an emergency landing, I could do it, but there wasn't enough room for take off.

The trip was for nothing. I made a really low pass over the runway waving to the waiting people. If I started the trip home, I had a big problem. The folks on the farm had gas for my return trip home, but I couldn't land. No landing, no fuel. A quick estimate said I would run out of fuel halfway home.

On the flight up to the farm, I didn't remember seeing any airports. A problem like this I didn't need. If I crashed the Bird, I would have to pay the airport seven hundred dollars, which I didn't have. Up ahead I saw a large baseball field. Next to it was a highway with a gas station. There was a baseball game in progress and bleachers full of people. This was going to be a piece of cake. All I had to do was make a pass over the baseball field and wave to the players to move over so I could land.

I made a low pass and frantically waved to the players to move out of the way so I could land the Bird. As I waved, the players just waved back. Couldn't they understand that I want to land on their field? I made three more passes, and the same thing happened every time. If I landed during the game, the guy I might hit was the center fielder. Well, it's him or me, I thought. I hope he can run fast.

I came around into the wind and started the approach. About halfway to touchdown, the center fielder got the message and moved out of my way. The next thing I knew, I was on the ground with the engine idling. I said to myself, How do I get into these situations? My heart started to get back to normal and I taxied up to the gas station.

As soon as I reached the pump, I shut down the engine. When the gas attendant walked out of the office, I expected him to go starry eyed and say something like, Oh my God, is that a real honest to God airplane? or something like that. Instead, he just walked up to the cockpit where I was still sitting.

In a very unimpressed voice, he said, "High test or regular?" as if this happened every day.

"Regular," I said.

A few minutes later, a New York police car drove up with two troopers. I got out of the Bird to meet them. One trooper asked me what happened and I told him the whole story. He thought for a few minutes.

"If my partner and I blocked off the road, would you have enough room to take off your airplane?" he asked.

"Yes sir, plenty of room."

I paid the gas bill and got the Bird fired up. The trooper dropped off his partner with a big flashlight, then drove the police car about a quarter of a mile down the road and flashed his headlights, which meant, "Go."

I gave the Bird full throttle and down the road we went. About halfway down to the police car, I was airborne. I made a right turn and headed home to Blackwood, NJ.

THE BIRD, FINAL TRIP

One day, my friend Jack said, "Let's go night flying." "Why not," I said. "I've never flown at night."

The Bird had no leading lights, no running lights and no instrument lights. Of course, the instrument light was no problem, because we had no instruments. It was starting to get dark, so we decided to make one go-around. The weather was calm and quite warm. We took the Bird out of the hangar and did the checks. Jack spun the propeller and off we went.

We flew through the trees, and it was pretty dark. Jack turned around and kept pointing at the gas cap. I couldn't believe my eyes. The short exhaust stack was throwing blue fire all around the gas tank cap. In the daylight, you couldn't see this blue fire. What a shock that was.

We put the Warner Bird back in the hangar and I never flew her again.

THE PORTERFIELD

In 1947, I bought half interest in a war surplus 1943 Porterfield plane which had been used for observations and short trips between small airports. It had two seats, one forward and one aft. The pilot in command sat up front. Around the cockpit was lots of Plexiglas for observation flights. The power plant was a small, 4-cylinder engine that put out 65 horsepower. The last time I flew the Porterfield was a trip to Atlantic City. This was many years before the casinos. The person sitting in the backseat was quite heavy.

The active runway for our return flight took us right over downtown Atlantic City. At the end of the runway was a small body of water. Back then Atlantic City didn't have a control tower. It was a hot summer day, and we taxied out to the active runway then checked the mags.

Airplanes have two spark plugs in every cylinder. Each set has its own magneto, called mags for short. They provide the electric power to make the spark. When you check the mags you turn off number one mag, and if the engine rpm (revolutions per minute) only drops a little, you know it's working. Then you make sure No. 2 is O.K. Then you're ready to go.

We taxied into position at the end of the runway. I pushed the throttle forward as far as it would go. The little 65 horsepower engine was doing the best it could; this airplane could have used another 25 horsepower. We slowly gained speed and finally lifted off about 300 feet from the end of the runway. Looking out of the front windshield, all I could see were very tall hotels. As our climb continued, I didn't think we would clear the tops of the buildings in front of us.

I figured that the best salvation would be to line up with the streets between the buildings. If we didn't clear the buildings, we could fly down the middle of the street. When we reached the first buildings we were below the rooftops; I could look in the windows. I was in a sweat and it wasn't caused by the heat. By the end of the block, we were on top of the hotels and out over the ocean. I can't understand why anyone would design and build such an underpowered airplane. The next owner wasn't so lucky. He ended up in the treetops. He was unhurt, but the Porterfield was totaled.

EARLY YEARS

Love and The Sand Plant

THE SAND PLANT

In 1949, when I went to work for the American Dredging Company, Sap Warner was president. Not long after that, he was replaced by Mr. Greaser. In 1953, Sap and Harry Austin were starting a new business, and Harry asked me if I was interested in joining them.

"Sap has some ground in Bridgeport, NJ. That area has very good sand, and a mile or two south of there the sand is pure white. We have to build a sand plant to wash the sand. There was a sand plant on the site a few years ago. The pound and a small dredge were left by the previous owners," he said.

"What equipment will we need to build a sand wash tower?"

"Nothing," Harry said.

"How can you build a sand wash tower without a crane?" I asked.

"The tower has six legs. We can get someone to set the six legs in place, and we can lift the cross members with a chain hoist. Then Blacky will weld them in place," he said.

"How tall are the six legs?" was my next question.

"About 40 feet," Harry said.

"When we get off watch at four o'clock I'd like to take a look at what the place looks like," I told Harry.

By the time I got off the dredge and drove to Bridgeport, it was 6:00. Sap Warner was still in his little office. I introduced myself and we shook hands. He was rather short and on the plump side. I guessed he was in his mid-fifties—and he was a talker.

We got in his two-door Willys Jeep and drove out to where the sand wash tower was going to be built.

Warner told me about his connections with the state inspectors and contractors, and how much money could be made here, and anyone that invested in his operation was going to make a lot of money.

I was 26 years old. It all sounded great. I thought anyone who had stockholders in a real company was really going somewhere. This seemed like a great opportunity.

We drove back to the little office, and I said I would buy $1,000 worth of stock: 10 shares.

Building the sand tower at Warner Sand & Gravel, in Bridgeton, NJ, 1953

The dredge and conveyor

Over the years, I had saved $2,500, thanks to my mom and dad, who did not charge me room and board. Today, $2,500 does not sound like a lot of money, but in 1953 you could buy a pretty nice house for $3,000.

The next day, I gave Chief Gregory notice that I was leaving American Dredge. His eyes lit up and for the first time he acted like I was a person. Now his son Harold could be promoted to an engineer. When the dredge was not working, everyone was laid off except the engineers. The engineers were very hard to replace. Now that Gregory's son was an engineer, the chief did not have to lay him off when they went to the yard. Needless to say, Chief Gregory was the happiest man in town. He didn't care if I gave notice. The faster I left the job, the quicker his son got my job.

The night after I met Sap Warner, I drove home and told my mom and dad about my new job. My dad thought it was great, but my mother thought I was very foolish to invest $1,000 without more information and background on Mr. Warner.

"Mom, he was president of American Dredging Company. He can't be that bad."

It ended up taking us quite a while to build the 40-foot sand-washing tower. The sand was pumped from the pond, up into a hopper, located in the tower, by the small dredge. The water would go to the top of the hopper as the sand settled to the bottom. When the hopper was full, the man on duty would open the ball valve, and the sand would drop into the waiting truck. The truck would then go to the office to be weighed. The going price was 35 cents a ton.

The ball valve at the bottom of the hopper was made with a 16-pound bowling ball. When it lost its shape from the abrasive sand, someone would go down to the bowling alley and buy another used bowling ball.

Believe it or not, we were doing O.K. Even at 35 cents a ton. The operation ran 10 hours a day, five days a week. Warner got Harry and me in the office one morning. He said he had a great plan worked out. Arundale, a company in Baltimore just completed building a large stone processing plant; they'd sell the old equipment for next to nothing. "Here is my plan."

"We buy what we need from Arundale's old plant, ship the equipment to New Jersey, and build a stone processing plant with a large stone crusher. We could make any size stone we wanted."

"That sounds great," I said. "But where do we get the stones to crush?"

"I can get a deal with American Dredge to dig material from their Bridgeport landfill. That fill is loaded with stone, and it is only three miles away," Warner said.

Harry said, "It sounds good to me, Sap. Let's do it."

We drove to Baltimore in Harry's two-door Dodge Ram. We met the Arundale group in their very plush men's club. I guess we looked pretty tacky. Even the guy who cleaned the men's room was not very pleasant.

Warner did all the talking. He put on a good show and we bought what we wanted for peanuts.

DONUTS AND CONVEYERS

To build a stone plant, we would need more than a chain hoist. Warner gave me the job to buy a truck crane, a dragline, and a conveyer.

I went to Thorofare, NJ, to a company that sold used equipment, everything from railroad engines to whatever. First was the unit truck crane. The crane was mounted on a Mack truck and had 50 feet of boom. Second was a Northwest crawler crane. The crane was old, but it was in good shape, and the price was right.

The first two items were easy, but a conveyer, that was another story. What did I know about conveyers? Answer: nothing. I let my fingers do the walking and found in the Philadelphia phone book Industrial Transmission Machinery located at 209 North Third St., Philadelphia, PA.

On Monday, I cranked up my new 1953 Victory Ford and drove to Philadelphia. Finding a place to park a car in Philadelphia is not easy. It took me 20 minutes to find a parking place. ITM was located in a storefront and was owned by three men: Bill McCullough, Jim Burns, and Paul Austin.

I was met at the door by a 21-year-old girl named Etta DelConte.

"Good morning, I would like to get some information on a conveyor. My name is Fred McCarthy. I'm with Warner Sand & Gravel."

"Mr. McCullough will be with you in a few minutes. Would you like a cup of coffee?" she said.

"Yes, with cream and sugar," "How about a donut with your coffee?"

"No, thanks."

"Oh, you think you're sweet enough?" she said.

Some girl!

Miss Donut ran the office. She did the bookkeeping, answered the phone, did the typing, and bought the donuts on her way to work. Her 20-year-old sister Marie assisted her. The two sisters ran the whole show. The three owners did the selling.

After about five minutes, I met with Mr. McCullough.

"Mr. McCullough, we have to move material from the ground up to about 30 feet. The material consists of sand, stone, and other things you would find on the bottom of the Delaware River," was my opening statement.

McCullough called over Mr. Austin and told him about my problem. Austin said, "The best way to move material like that is by a conveyer belt, but conveyer belts are very costly."

"What is the cheapest way to do it?" I asked.

Austin said, "Well, the cheapest way is not always the right way. Bucket type conveyers are the cheapest to buy, but they are the slowest and they are costly to maintain."

I asked the two men all the questions I could think of and said I would go back to the company and talk the matter over with my partners.

On the way out of the building, I thanked the girl up front for the coffee and told her that I would be back for donuts.

It was mid-afternoon, and by the time I got back to the office, everyone would be gone, so I just drove home. On the way home, I thought about the coffee and the donut conversation with Etta in ITM's front office.

OUR FIRST DATE

I arrived at Mom and Dad's house around 3:00. On my way home, I decided to call Miss Donuts, and ask her for a date. I took ITM's business card out of my wallet and picked up the telephone. The operator said, "Number, please," and I gave the telephone operator ITM's telephone number. In a matter of seconds, the phone rang.

On the other end of the phone, I heard, "Hello ITM." I recognized the voice. It was the Donut Girl.

"Hi, this is Fred McCarthy. I was in there today asking about a conveyer system, and you offered me a donut with my coffee."

"Yes, what can I do for you?" the Donut Girl said.

"Well, if you're not married, I'd like to take you out tonight for dinner and maybe a movie."

"I think you want to speak to my sister, the blond girl," Miss Donuts replied.

"No," I said, "I want to talk to you, the dark-haired girl that gives out the donuts."

"Where do you go on a Monday night?" she said.

"The same place you go on a Saturday night."

"Are you sure you don't want to talk to my sister?"

"No, I would like to take you out tonight. Where do you live?" I said.

"I don't know. You're a perfect stranger. I don't even know you," was her answer.

"Well, I live with my parents on Oaklawn Avenue, in Oaklyn, NJ. Is seven o'clock too early for you to get ready?" I asked.

A long pause.

"If you live with your parents," I said. "I'll come in the house and meet them. If they don't like me, I'll turn around and walk out. Fair enough?"

"I don't know," was Miss Donuts answer.

"By the way, I don't know your name." I said.

"Etta DelConte," she said.

"And what's your sister's name?"

"Marie Piazza," she answered.

"I guess your sister is married," I said.

"Yes, Marie is married, and her husband's name is Hank."

"O.K., Etta, I'll pick you up at seven o'clock. What's your address?"

"I'm in the telephone book," she said, and hung up the telephone.

Now, I said to myself, was that a brush-off or does she want me to pick her up?

Sure enough, there was a DelConte in Clementon, NJ.

Oh hell, what do I have to lose? I'll put on a suit and tie and drive to Clementon. If it's a brush-off, I'll just turn around and go home.

Now, this part of the story is what I was told later on. Etta and her sister Marie left work and got on the bus and went to Etta's house. She told her mother the whole story. Her sister Marie said, "Mom, he is an old man. He is too old for Etta. If he comes, you should not let Etta go out with him."

Etta changed her clothes and waited for the old man to come to the house. She'd never given him her address. That could mean, don't bother me, I'm not interested. What a mess. At 7:00 sharp, a brand-new Victory Ford drove up to the Clementon house.

Marie said, "That's not the same guy. This guy is a lot younger and better-looking."

Marie met me at the front door and invited me in. "Please sit down. Etta will be out shortly."

I sat down on the sofa. I thought my parents' house was small, but this house was really small. The whole house was the size of a two-car garage.

EARLY YEARS

In a few minutes, Etta entered the living room, where I was sitting with her mother. My old Greek biology teacher in high school always said, "When you boys start dating girls, look at their mothers. What you see is what the girl will look like in 25 years." Good advice. Etta's mother was a beautiful woman.

We sat around for a short time just talking. I guess Etta's mother was checking me out.

When we got in my car, Etta said, "That's funny, my mother always tells me to be home by eleven o'clock. Tonight she never said a word."

We had dinner and decided to skip the movie show. The next day was a workday and it was getting late. I said, "I'm building a boat in my parent's yard. Would you like to see it?"

"It's alright with me, but I'm not getting out of the car," Etta said.

"You don't have to get out of the car, Etta. I'll just turn on the car's spotlight.

We drove to Oaklyn, which was on our way to Etta's house in Clementon. The 26' boat I was building was near the curb. I stopped the car, turned on the spotlight, and there the boat was. Out of the water, a boat looks bigger than it does when it is in the water.

"That's a very big boat," Etta said.

"I hope to have it done by next spring," I said.

From there, we drove back to Etta's house in Clementon. We sat in the car for a short time, then Etta went into the house and I drove home. Did we kiss good night? I do not remember.

THE CONVEYOR

The items we purchased from the Arundle Company finally arrived. Warner talked me into buying another $1,000 worth of the company stock. Now my $2,500 savings was down to $500. At the time I thought it was a good investment.

The first 10 years after getting out of the Navy taught me a lot of dos and don'ts. This should have been a don't.

We started to build the stone plant. At the base of the tower, we built a ramp and a cinder block pit. The trucks loaded with the material from the landfill would back up to the ramp and dump the material into the pit.

We bought the parts needed to build a bucket-type conveyor from Miss Donut's boss, Bill McCullough. The conveyor would pick up the material in the pit and take it up to the screen wash. The screen wash was a large revolving drum that was set on an angle. Water was sprayed onto the material. The water would clean the material as it rolled down the revolving screen drum. After leaving the screen wash, the material went to the shaker. By this time, the material was just rock and stones. The mud and sand were washed away by the screen wash.

As the stone traveled down the tilted shaker, they dropped through according to size: little stones first and big stones last. Any stones over two inches would drop off the end. The idea was to set the crusher at whatever size you want the stones to come out, and get the big stones through it. From the shaker, the stones would roll down the pipe into piles according to size.

One day, I was talking with Warner, Harry, and Blacky about 200 feet from the tower. Eddy Brounky was on top doing something. As we were looking at the tower, Eddy slipped and fell off the 40-foot tower. On his way down, he hit every cross beam and landed on a pile of big rocks.

We were all stunned. No one rushed over to Eddy because we all knew he was dead. As we slowly walked over to Eddy's body, with our hearts pounding, he stood up and brushed himself off.

"Eddy, don't move until the ambulance comes," someone cried out.

Eddy looked over and said, "I'm O.K., I'm O.K."

"You're going to the hospital," someone else said.

"No, I'm not," Eddy answered.

Harry finally got Eddy in his car and drove him to the hospital. When they returned, we all thought that Eddy would look like a basket case. End result—no broken bones or cuts, just a few bruises.

One morning, "Big Bad Brown from Brown Town," who had been a deckhand on the dredge and was now working at the sand plant, came into the office. I was talking to Etta's boss, Bill McCullough. Brown had fire in his eyes.

"Mac, where did you buy that goddamn conveyor? That thing belted me with rocks all damn night. Look at me, I'm all black and blue."

I said, "I bought it from him," and pointed to McCullough.

With that, Big Bad Brown (he was about 5'8" tall) whipped out the little 32-caliber revolver he always carried, and put three rounds through the office ceiling. McCullough ran to the door. He almost pulled the door off the hinges. He got in his car and drove down the dirt road, leaving a huge cloud of dust. When he got back to his office, he told everybody, "Those people at the sand plant are crazy. They tried to kill me!"

THE BLACK DRESS

Etta DelConte and I started seeing each other more and more often. One of Etta's sisters, Gloria, was married to Clifford Weedeman. Cliff was from Minot, North Dakota and was in the U.S. Air Force stationed at McGuire Air Force Base, next to Wrightstown, New Jersey.

In 1953, McGuire had only one aircraft, one small hangar and a few airmen. Cliff was the crew chief on the aircraft, a twin-engine Beachcraft. The Beachcraft carried eight passengers and cruised around 165 miles per hour.

Gloria and Cliff had a three month-old baby boy named Henry. I would leave the sand plant around five o'clock; drive to Oaklyn; take a shower and get dressed; get in my 1953 Ford Victoria and drive to Wrightstown, where Gloria and Cliff had a small apartment.

When Gloria knew I was coming, she would get Cliff to take her to the N.C.O. club and leave Etta to baby-sit young Henry. This is how it would work. I would get to the apartment around 7 o'clock. Eight o'clock was the baby's bedtime. Trouble was, when you put Henry in his crib, he would just cry and cry.

The only way to get Henry to fall asleep was to take him for a car ride and settle him down. Etta would wrap Henry up in his nightie, then the three of us would drive around for thirty minutes to an hour and thirty minutes. By the time little Henry was in his crib and sound asleep, it was time for me to go home. It was not a great, fun date, but we had a long time to talk.

A few months passed. The sand plant was doing well, and Etta and I were seeing a lot of each other. One night Etta and I were just sitting around talking. Out of the clear blue sky, Etta said, "Are you ever going to get married?"

I thought for a few minutes and said, "Someday, I guess."

"How about May 1?" she asked.

"Etta," I said, "Don't be offended, but I would never marry an Italian girl."

"What is wrong with Italian girls?" she asked.

"Nothing is wrong with Italian girls. They are great."

"I don't understand," Etta said. "You said you would never marry an Italian girl, and then you said Italian girls are great. That doesn't make sense to me."

"Etta, what happens to an Italian girl when she gets old?" I asked.

"I don't know. I guess they just get old," she answered.

"Wrong," I said. "They get old, fat and wear long black dresses. That's the reason I would never marry an Italian girl."

We were married May 1 the following year.

Let's see how many of my predictions came true: We have been married fifty-five years. Etta is 78 years old and is two pounds lighter than she was the day we were married. She is a sharp dresser and a good golfer. I am 83 years old and thirty pounds heavier than the day we were married.

THE BIG WEDDING

Etta and I were married on May 1, 1954. Etta wanted a church wedding, so we arranged an interview with the priest of the St. Lawrence, Father O'Neil. The first thing Father asked me was, "Are you a Catholic?"

"No, Father, I'm not a Catholic."

"Would you become a Catholic to be married in our church?" the old priest asked.

"If that's what it takes, Father, I guess I would," I replied.

"Well, son, if you knew a little more about the Catholic religion, you might have a different outlook," was his answer.

"My mother and father are Catholic. And my mother's family has a lot of well-known priests," I said.

"Well, son, tell me the names of these well-known priests," the old priest said in a sarcastic tone.

"One is the dean of Marquette University, another is the Pope's representative."

"Stop right there. Give me their names," the priest said, as he was getting a large book off the bookshelf.

"Father Magee is the dean of Marquette University, and Father McGrady is the Pope's representative."

The old priest thumbed through the large book and after finding the names, he turned to me.

"You are a traitor to the Catholic Church. I will never marry you in my church." He turned and walked out of the room.

Etta's Uncle Al Caruzzi lived in Roslyn, PA, which is near Willow Grove Park. Etta found out that some of the churches in Pennsylvania would marry a mixed couple. A mixed couple meant that one person was not Catholic.

The wedding was set for May 1, 1954 at St. William's Church, in

Roslyn, PA. Etta's Uncle Al would give her away, and my brother Bob would be my best man.

The big day came, and the wedding went off very well. Skip Miller took 16mm moving pictures, and Russ Homan took all the still shots. There was no color film in those days; everything was black-and-white. Unfortunately, the photo lab messed up the moving pictures, but the still shots were O.K..

Later I found out that my mother was really upset with the priest who married us and his church. I didn't notice it at the time, but all the lights and candles were out on my side of the altar, which made my side of the altar very dark.

After the wedding, everyone had to drive about thirty minutes to get to the reception. Are you ready for this? The reception was in Cliff's and Gloria's house in Clementon, NJ. The house was very small. The bar was set up in the basement and was stocked with a quarter keg of beer My dad and brother lost half the beer when they tapped the keg), one fifth of Seagram's Seven, ginger ale and some root beer. Upstairs, there was tea, sandwiches and coffee. Total cost of our reception: $72. Can you see the young people today having their wedding reception in an unpainted, cinder block basement?

The reception lasted until 5:00 p.m. Etta and I went to our 1953 Victory Ford and away on to our honeymoon. Yes, the car was whitewashed with, "Just Married," in big letters, and several cans were tied to the back bumper. We had not planned our honeymoon trip. We just got in our Victory Ford and took off. We got as far as New Castle, DE. We found a motel, washed up, changed our clothes, and went out to dinner. Back then, about the only restaurant was a diner. After dinner we went back to the motel.

In our time, you did not play house for a few years and then get married. With us, everything was new. I guess that has something to do with how we've been together for 55 years. It has always been teamwork

THE HONEYMOON

The second day, we drove from New Castle, DE to the Sky Line Drive, in the Blue Ridge Mountains. We found a state-owned lodge on top of the mountain. Our room was really great. The wood-burning fireplace made the room feel very cozy and romantic. The fire took the chill off this very lovely place.

Walking down the aisle with Etta, at St. William's Church, in Roslyn, PA, on our wedding day, May 1st, 1954

At our wedding reception in Clementon, NJ

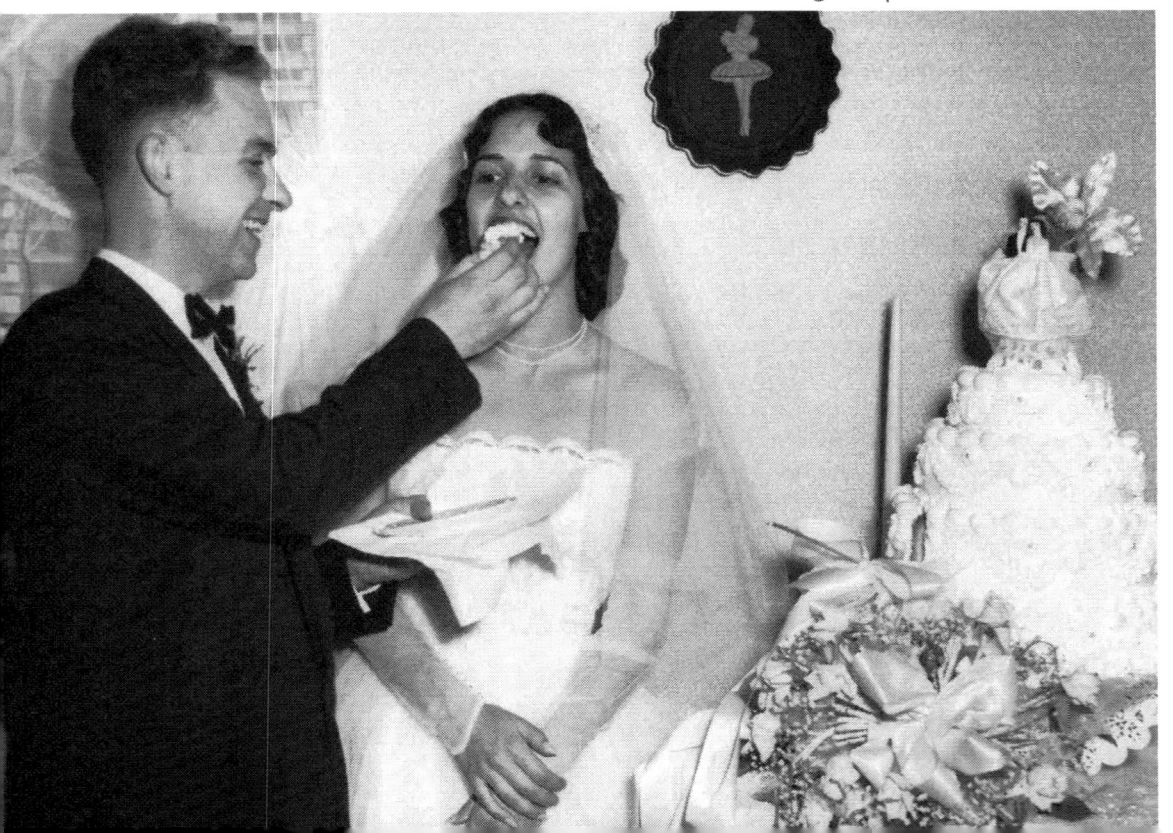

Etta throwing her wedding bouquet

Leaving for our honeymoon in my 1953 Victory Ford

We showered, changed our clothes, and went down to the dining room. When we walked in, we were shocked. There was a buffet that was unbelievable. The table seemed to be endless with roast turkey, roasted pig with an apple in its mouth (which we'd never seen before), beef, and everything else you could think of. It was the biggest spread I'd ever seen.

After dinner, Etta was very uncomfortable. The place was so quiet and dark. When we turned off the lights, the fireplace lit up the ceiling and you could hear a pin drop.

The next day, after breakfast, we headed down the southern end of the Skyline Drive. That afternoon, we ended up in Tennessee on a Cherokee Indian Reservation. That stop was uneventful, with a typical motel and souvenir stores. Etta bought cream and sugar bowls to remember our honeymoon and they are still in our kitchen today.

I said, "Etta, I have an aunt and uncle living in Chicago. I haven't seen them in a long time. Would you like to see Chicago, and meet them?"

"Sure. Sounds great," she said, and off we headed to the Windy City.

I was only ten years old when we moved from Illinois, so I didn't know the area. Near my aunt's and uncle's house, I saw two cops standing on the corner. "I'm looking for Kedvale Avenue. Can you help me?" I asked.

"Didn't you see the sign?" the biggest cop said.

I scanned the intersection. "I don't see any sign saying Kedvale Avenue!"

His reply was, "What are you, some kind of smart-ass. Can't you see the sign, 'No Left Turn'?"

"No officer, I really didn't see the sign."

The big cop turned and said to the other cop, "I think we ought to run this wise guy in, don't you?"

"Yeah, I think you're right," the second cop said.

"I'm looking for Kedvale Avenue because my uncle lives there. He's a cop, too."

"What's his name?" the big cop asked.

"Ryan," I said.

"Danny Ryan?"

"Yeah, that's my uncle," I said.

"Get in your car, kid. We'll give you a police escort to your uncle's flat. Follow us."

I didn't know my Uncle Danny was so well known in the police force.

"Lead on," I said.

EARLY YEARS

I hadn't been in my aunt's flat since I was six years old. My Uncle Dan was drinking and I already told you about how he and my dad had a big run-in. They never spoke to one another again. That's Irish for you!

My dad never drank. His father was an alcoholic, who died when my dad was only seventeen. I guess that's what kept my dad from drinking.

My dad's father and uncle were big-time painters in Chicago. I mean big time. I remember my dad telling me about the time they had the contract to paint all the bridges on the Chicago North Western railroad. After the painters put the first coat of paint on the bridge, the inspector would come along with chalk and put a big "X" on the newly painted bridge. When the second coat of paint was applied, it would cover up the "X." That's how the railroad knew the bridge had two coats of paint. My dad started out as the water boy. He'd bring drinking water to the working painters. His second job was to wash off the chalk "X." Dad was 16 years old.

Everyone thought the McCarthy painters were heavy drinkers. Every painter had a whiskey flask in his hip pocket. Before they started painting, he'd mix the contents—turpentine—from the flask into the paint. Turpentine thins the paint to go on faster and easier.

Frank Lloyd Wright, the well-known architect, owed the company money. Bills were sent, but not paid. My grandfather went to Wright's office and asked for the money. Wright said he could not pay the bill at the time. My grandfather reached down and picked up a very old piece of Chinese artwork and said, "When you pay me, I'll give you back this trinket." He put the artwork in his pocket and walked out the door. That piece of Chinese artwork was in my father's bureau drawer till the day he died. I never found out what happened to it.

Etta and I rang the bell on my aunt's and uncle's flat. When my Aunt Mercedes answered the door, she didn't recognize me until I said, "Hi Aunt Dee Dee. How are you?"

She sure was surprised; she had not seen me in 16 or 17 years, since I was nine or 10 years old. Uncle Danny was in the living room. After all the questions, Aunt Dee Dee made coffee and snacks. As we talked, I could not stop looking around their flat. After all those years of working on the police force, they never owned a car, a house, or anything of value. Their rented flat had all worn-out furniture and rugs.

Etta and I spent a nice afternoon with my Aunt Dee Dee and my Uncle Danny. There was no room to put us up for the night, so we said goodbye and left. We drove the Ford Victory out of Chicago and found a motel. The next morning we headed back to New Jersey.

We stayed with Etta's sister and brother-in-law, Gloria and Cliff, until our apartment was ready. It seemed like forever until we could move into our apartment. We slept in a single bed. Little Henry was still a baby, and of course Gloria put him in our room. The bed was so small, that if you didn't hold on, you would fall out of bed. For board, Etta and I paid for all the food.

THE *ETTA*

When Etta and I were married in 1954, I was working for Meritt-Chapman & Scott. The job was building the foundation for the Walt Whitman Bridge that ran between Camden, NJ, and Philadelphia, PA.

In August it was very hot, and I was captain on the crew boat, which carried the workers back and forth when changing shifts: 8:00 a.m. to 4:00 p.m. and 4:00 p.m. to 12:00 a.m. In between shift changes, the boat did some light towing. Most of the time, I worked the 4:00 p.m. to 12:00 a.m. shift. There were always some people working overtime, and I would stay until two or 3 a.m.

At the time, Meritt-Chapman & Scott was working on the Camden-Philadelphia Bridge and the Turnpike Bridge, a few miles up the river. One afternoon, the vice-president of Meritt-Chapman & Scott came on our boat. He was looking for a boat from 26' to 30' to run between two jobs. He asked me if I knew of any boats that would do the job.

A month before, I had just finished building the *Etta* in my parent's side yard, under a big oak tree. Etta and I, along with my brother Bob and Dad, launched the boat at the Farragut Boat Club in north Camden, where my dad was commodore. I told the club members that we would launch the boat and then leave in a couple of days. They thought this was funny, figuring that we would be like all new boatbuilders: launch the boat, then take several weeks to finish the job. We launched the boat on Saturday, and left for Lewes, Delaware the following Friday, then returned Sunday night. It was a 200 nautical mile cruise. All went well.

I showed the VP the boat, talked about price, and he finally said, "Bring in the boat papers and I'll give you a check for it."

Boy, how lucky can we get, I thought. Married 90 days and now selling the boat that I'd worked on for two years. The price we sold the boat for was one-third the price of a small house.

Before I went back to work the following day, I got a phone call from our union rep. "Hey Mac, I hear you are selling your boat to Meritt-Chapman & Scott."

I said, "Yeah, I think so."

"You know you have an unlimited union book. They are very hard to get."

I said, "What's this all about?"

"You know it's customary for us to get 10 percent."

"In other words, you want 10 percent of my boat or you'll pull my union book?"

"Well, I really didn't say that."

"Then what did you say?"

"Well, Mac, you figure it out."

My next statement was, "You can take your job and your union book and shove it!"

Well, there we were, no money, no job, nowhere to turn to. Etta's mother said, "I think you married a gigolo."

Etta told me, "You like to build boats, so let's go into the boatbuilding business."

"Go into the boatbuilding business, with no money? It's impossible," I said.

"Well, we have the $800 we got from wedding presents," she said.

Working on the *Etta*, 1953

The *Etta*, my first 26' boat, 1954

Etta told me, "You like to build boats, so let's go into the boatbuilding business."

"Go into the boatbuilding business, with no money? It's impossible," I said.

"Well, we have the $800 we got from wedding presents," she said.

Partnerships

Life Begins with Etta

OUR FIRST APARTMENT

In 1954, Etta and I moved into our first apartment, just off the White Horse Pike, Route 30, in Oaklyn, NJ. The apartment was small and had only one bedroom. The building was two stories high. We were on the first floor. Our rent was $58 a month.

Across the street was the Ritz Movie Theater. The actor, Michael Landon's father was the projectionist. Michael Landon went to Collingswood High School. The English teacher, Mrs. Melinger, was the person who got him into acting. She was a tough old bird. Mrs. Melinger told me that I would grow up to be an ignoramus. "How can you get along in this world without a good background in English?" she asked me one day.

"It is easy, Mrs. Melinger. I'll just get a good secretary." This was not a good answer, but what the heck? The best grades I ever got from Mrs. Melinger were "Ds" and I did not get many of them.

One day after work, I was taking a shower when I

heard a very faint knock on the bathroom door. I wrapped a towel around me and opened the door.

Etta pushed her way into the bathroom. She looked like she had seen a ghost.

"Etta—Etta, what's the matter? You look like you're scared to death!"

"There was a knock at the back door. When I opened the door, there was a man standing there," she said.

"So, what's wrong with that?" I asked

"I'll tell you what's wrong with that," she said. "He's over six feet tall, doesn't have one strand of hair on his head, and only one eye. He looks like a monster!"

I started to laugh, but Etta was too nervous to see what was so funny.

"Etta, that's 'Eye Bolts.' Where's Eye Bolts now?"

"I don't know. I closed the back door on him," Etta said.

"Go see if he's still there. If he is, let him in, and give him a beer. Eye Bolt's elevator does not go all the way to the top floor, but he's harmless," I said.

I guess Eye Bolts would put you on guard the first time you saw him.

We lived in that apartment for over seven years. The reason we moved out of the Oaklyn Apartments is a long, long story.

THE ORDEAL

For some unknown reason, Etta could not get pregnant. We both went through several exams. The doctor could not come up with an answer to our problem. No matter how hard we tried, nothing happened.

After trying for several years, we decided to adopt a child. In 1960, Etta went to the Catholic Charities and filled out all the adoption papers. When the Catholic Charities found out I was not a Catholic, all the doors closed.

The next step was to go to the Children's Home Society, a state-controlled organization. Again, Etta filled out all the paperwork. The Children's Home Society told us that we would have to get permission from the Catholic Church before the state would consider us for an adoption.

At the time, we were living in the Oaklyn apartment. So we went to see Monsignor Bazzelli, the pastor of St. Aloysius in Oaklyn. He told us that he would need to get permission from the diocese. As soon as he got the approval from the bishop, he would call us.

Every other Wednesday, I would stop by the rectory and ask Monsignor Bazzelli if he had heard anything from the bishop. The answer was always the same: "No, I haven't heard anything from him. He's a very busy man."

Weeks turned into months and I was getting tired of hearing "He's a very busy man."

One morning, I said, "Etta, I'm going to Camden to see this bishop guy. We are not getting anywhere the way we are going."

"Good luck," she said.

Etta could not go with me because she had to go to work. Etta had always worked in a one- or two-girl office.

"I think I would like to work for a big company," she said one day.

"Sounds okay to me, " I said. "Why don't you give it a shot? The only thing is, I think you might lose some of the freedom you have now."

"I know, but I want to see what it's like."

"You'll never know until you try it," I said.

The next day, Etta called in sick. She took the bus to Camden and walked to the main office of the Campbell Soup Company. She filled out the employment form and was interviewed by Mr. McGrady.

I think Etta interviewed the interviewer. She wanted to know how many breaks they got, how long was the lunchtime, and so on. When they told her there were no breaks and what the pay would be, she got up and told Mr. McGrady she was not interested in the job. The pay was half of what she was already making.

That night, Etta told me the whole story. The next day, Etta received a telegram from the Campbell Soup Company. After reading the job offer, Etta called them.

Would you please tell Mr. McGrady that I'm not interested in his job offer? Thank you very much."

When Etta got home from work the next day, there was another telegram from the soup company. It read, "We will meet your present salary."

Etta was still not happy with the offer.

On her lunch break the next day, she called the soup company and repeated what she had said before. Later that afternoon, another telegram arrived, which read: "A fifteen minute break morning and fifteen minute break afternoon."

Etta and I talked about the offer that night.

"Etta, the soup company's best offer is what you have now. What are you gaining?"

"Yes, I understand what you're saying. I want to work in a big company, but what if I don't like it? What will I do then?"

On Etta's lunch break the next day, she called again and said she didn't want the job.

That evening, the fourth telegram arrived. This time the message was quite lengthy. It read something like this: "The Campbell Soup Company has purchased Swanson Food. We are offering you the position of head auditor."

The pay was fifty percent higher than their last offer and it included the two coffee breaks. Not only was Etta going to work in a big company, but she would be a boss. Not bad for a 28 year-old woman.

THE BISHOP

I got into the 1953 Ford Victory and drove to Camden to see the bishop. The rectory was right around the corner from the Stanley Movie Theater.

When I was fifteen years old, Skip Miller's father worked for the Warner Brothers Movie Company, which owned the Stanley movie theater. Every Saturday and Sunday, the Stanley Theater had two great stage shows with a twelve- to sixteen-piece orchestra and some of Hollywood's top stars.

Mr. Miller got me a job as an usher on the weekends. I had to wear a uniform: red pants, short red jacket, stiff dickey shirt front and a bow tie. I worked the balcony. The steps seemed to go straight up and down. As the people entered my station, I would usher them to a seat, lighting my way with my flashlight. All day and into the night, it was up and down the stairs.

I walked up the steps to the front door of the rectory, rang the bell and waited. A few minutes passed. An elderly woman opened the door.

"Can I help you, young man?"

"I would like to see the bishop," I said.

"I'm sorry young man. The bishop is not in."

"Is the bishop not in to see me or just not in?" I asked.

"The bishop is at the Vatican in Rome. Is there something I can do for you?"

"My wife and I would like to adopt a baby. Monsignor Bazzelli said we had to have the bishop's blessing before we could adopt a baby. We've been waiting for the bishop's consent for several months now. I would like to know the bishop's answer," I said.

"Oh, I can help you there. Please come in. Have a seat in the waiting room and I will be right back."

I sat down in one of the big stuffed chairs and waited. Ten minutes later, the door opened and the woman walked into the waiting room with a folder under her arm. She sat down at a very large desk and opened up the folder.

"Is your name Fredric H. McCarthy, Jr.?" she asked.

"Yes."

"Is your wife's name Henrietta McCarthy?"

"Yes."

"Do you live in Oaklyn, New Jersey?"

"Yes."

"Mr. McCarthy, I'm very sorry to tell you this, but the bishop turned your request down several months ago."

"Turned us down? For what reason?"

"Because Monsignor Bazzelli did not give you his approval."

"Why didn't Monsignor Bazzelli tell us this?"

"I'm sorry, I have no idea why the Monsignor didn't tell you."

I thanked her for her time and walked out the door. As I got in my car, I was so mad I couldn't think straight. That S.O.B., he was the one who shot us down, and he didn't have the common decency to tell us the truth. He just strung us along all those months. The closer I got to Oaklyn, the angrier I got. The last six months kept running through my mind, including the shock of being told by Children's Home Society that we must live in a house, not an apartment, and how the baby must have a private bedroom.

Etta and I had spent weeks looking for a house. The first was in Cinnaminson, NJ. The location was good, because our shop was in Riverside, NJ, three miles down the road. The house was quite large, well constructed, and had four bedrooms. The only problem was the price: a whopping $27,000. No way would we be able to pay $131.50 a month.

We kept looking and looking. Everything was either poorly constructed, in bad location or not worth the money. The longer we looked, the better the Cinnaminson house seemed. Etta and I finally decided it was Cinnaminson or nothing.

We made five basic changes. One, we removed the three windows from the living room and replaced them with one big picture window. Two, we put the fireplace in the family room, not in the living room. Three, we took the powder room out of the family room, and moved it downstairs with a door opening into the family room. Fourth, we omitted the hallway wall next to the living room. And finally, we changed the heating system from gas to oil. These changes brought the price up to thirty thousand dollars.

Our development was called Wellington Park. When they started Wellington Park East, the builder would ask, "Can we show your house?" The new homes were an exact copy of our house with all of the changes we made.

All this was going through my mind as I drove home. We were in hock for thirty thousand dollars to adopt a baby. Now we couldn't get approval?

By the time I got to Monsignor Bazzelli's rectory, I was like a bomb ready to explode. I parked the car and went up to the locked front door. I rang the bell and waited. No answer.

After ringing the bell several times, I started to knock on the door with my fists. I was just about ready to go when the door opened. It was Monsignor Bazzelli.

"You S.O.B.! You turned Etta and me down for the adoption, not the bishop. Then you strung us along for months because you didn't have the guts to stand by your decision to turn us down. You think you're so holy. You are a hypocrite!"

I turned and walked to my car and drove back to our one bedroom apartment.

THE CINNAMINSON HOUSE

The Cinnaminson house was a really great house. The construction was outstanding. The bottom half was brick on all four sides. The upper part was white shingles. The five levels kept us in shape. With five levels, you were either going up the stairs or down the stairs.

The first level was a large basement. Off it was a two-car garage and the family room. Next came the kitchen, dining room, and living room. The next level had three bedrooms and two baths. The top level was large enough to make a small apartment. We used it as a large bedroom.

The house was to be completed by December 30, 1960. But, like happens with all builders, the completion, or should I say, the move-in date was February 1, 1961.

Etta had a baby shower for her sister Marie on February 10. I didn't know half the people there. In the family room were my record-winning, 14' blue marlin and a sailfish. Etta had her tournament-winning bull dolphin hanging on the wall. I walked by two young girls looking at the fish on the wall. One said to the other: "Who in the world would buy anything like that?" If she only knew.

There was a time when I thought the house was jinxed. Everything was going wrong.

We were buying plywood from a company in Baltimore, MD called Harbor Sales. The logs were shipped from Africa to Holland. The Dutch would peel the logs and make plywood, and sell it to Harbor Sales. Every year, the Dutch representative would take Etta and me out to dinner.

Not long after we moved into the Cinnaminson house, Joops came for his yearly visit. We left the shop about five minutes before closing time. Halfway home, I had to turn around and go back to the shop. I'd left my paperwork in the office. We were on the other side of the railroad tracks, across from our building, when Joops said, "Fred, what are all those people in front of your factory?"

I stopped the car, rolled down the window, and looked across the railroad tracks to watch what was going on. "Joops, that could only be one thing. Union. Some union is trying to unionize our shop," I said.

"Oh," Joops said.

"I hope my men are not dumb enough to sign the union cards. The union will promise them everything and give them nothing."

At dinner that night I said, "Joops, how many languages do you speak?" "Seven."

"Do you speak the other languages as good as you speak English?"

"Yeah, about the same."

"Joops, I can't believe how well you speak English, no accent at all, and you speak English better than we do. What's your secret?"

"Well, Fred, when I am talking to you, I do not take your English and translate it into Dutch. I think English and put Dutch out of my mind. That is the secret."

The next Monday, before lunch, I received a phone call from Blacky Cordillo of the Seafarers Union.

AN AFTERNOON ON THE FRONT PORCH IN CINNAMINSON

Etta and I were sitting on the front porch of our big, empty house one afternoon. A paper boy rode up our driveway on his bicycle. He walked up our front walk and gave Etta a newspaper. Here's a free copy of the *Courier Post*."

"Well, we don't have time to read the newspaper," Etta said, "but thanks anyway."

The boy looked a little disappointed. "I hope you change your mind."

When I was his age, I had a paper route, too. It was a six-days-a-week job. I knew how hard it was to get new customers. Saturday was collection day. Some people would pay me in pennies, and no one gave me a tip. After I paid the newspaper from my collection, I had 56 cents left over.

Etta started reading the free paper. A few minutes went by and she said, "Let me read you this article."

"What's it about?"

"It's written by a priest, Father O'Neil of the Camden Diocese. Listen to this. If you own your own home, and you have a spare bedroom and you do not have any children, you are being selfish not to adopt a homeless child. Can you believe this?" Etta said.

By the time Etta finished reading the whole article, I was ready to throw up. "Etta, go in the house and get a pen and pad. We're going to write this priest and tell him how it is in the real world."

Etta and I composed a letter to Father O'Neil. The letter was not nasty or belligerent. It just told Father O'Neil what a couple goes through when they try to adopt a child and are turned down.

A couple of days later, we received a letter from Father O'Neil asking us to come to his office. Etta made an appointment for the following day. We drove to Camden in our 1958 Ford Thunderbird. Our meeting lasted about 45 minutes. We told Father O'Neil the whole story, from day one, up to my last visit with Monsignor Bazzelli. Father O'Neil was a good listener; he did not butt in, he just listened.

When we finished our story, no one said a word. Finally, Father O'Neil said, "Now I know why you two sent me the letter. I wish I could help you, but I can't."

"I don't understand, Father O'Neil," said Etta. "Why can't you help us? We played by the rules. We've done everything we were asked to."

"I'm sorry, Mrs. McCarthy," he said.

"Father, it seems to me that the church made up its mind years ago," I said. "If someone is not Catholic, they can't adopt a child. I think selling religion is more important to the Catholic Church than the welfare of a small child. If you don't join our team, you can't play the game. Etta, I think it's time to leave."

I stood up, took Etta's hand and walked toward the door. Father O'Neil stood up and said, "Thank you both for coming. I really wish I could help you, but I can't. Monsignor Bazzelli is a very powerful man in the church. I cannot afford to fight him,"

"Let's go Etta. I can see now, it's a one-man show. I've heard enough." We walked out and went to our car.

On the way home, I said to Etta, "Boy, he is some dude, shiny patent leather shoes, expensive clothes—and did you see his rings?"

"Yes, he was quite a dresser," Etta said.

"For some reason, I feel I know him from some place," I said.

We drove home with the wind gone out of our sails.

About six weeks later, our neighbor Tony Corredetti, invited us to a big dinner outing. There were over 150 people in the room. When the dinner was over, the guest speaker walked up to the podium; lo and behold, it was Father O'Neil.

I can't remember what his subject was. All I knew was that his face looked very familiar. "I know that guy," I said to Etta.

"Well, why don't you go up and ask him," she said.

"Ask him what?"

"Ask him if you look familiar to him."

Father O'Neil finished his speech. He was walking away from the podium when I stopped him. "Father O'Neil, wait a minute, you look very, very familiar to me, but I can't remember from where."

"Collingswood High School," he said.

"You're not that kid that chased all the girls and drank beer underneath the football bleachers, are you?"

"That was me," he answered.

Now I remembered why Father O'Neil looked so familiar to me.

ETTA'S FIRST FLIGHT

Etta and I had not been married very long when one Sunday night we drove down the White Horse Pike to the Clementon Airport, across from the Silver Lake Inn. I pulled into the parking lot and stopped in front of an ugly dark-blue Ryan Navion. I said to Etta, "That airplane is called a Navion and it's owned by a very good friend of mine."

The Navion is an all-metal, low-wing plane powered by a 225 horsepower Continental engine and has retractable landing gear. The original Navions were built by North American, the company that built a great fighter airplane, the P-51. Some are still flying today. American took the wing and tail design and put a wide cabin between the wings that held four people. Ryan took over from American and after 1949 built the Ryan Navion.

Etta and I sat in the car about five to 10 minutes, and then I said, "Come on Etta. I'll show you the Navion."

"Are you sure your friend won't mind?" she said.

"I've known him for years, he won't mind," I said.

We walked through the gate to the parked airplane. I removed the tie ropes, climbed up on the left wing, and slid back the canopy. I said to Etta, "Climb on the wing like I did, and take a look at the cockpit." On the Navion, you climbed up on the forward side of the wing (most other airplanes you climb up on the back side of the wing). "Etta put your foot over and step into the cockpit and sit in the right seat. You will really like it."

"O.K., but I hope it is O.K. with the owner."

"Don't worry, it's O.K.,"

After Etta was in the right seat, I climbed in the cockpit and into the left seat.

Etta was amazed with all the details, switches, and knobs. "Looks very complicated to me," she said.

"I'll show you how to start the engine, and when you hear the engine running you'll really get the feeling of an airplane," I said.

Etta had never seen a real airplane before. "Don't start the engine. We are going to get into trouble," she said.

I primed the engine, stuck my head out of the cockpit, and said, "Clear". With that I pushed the starter button and 225 horsepower came to life. "Isn't this great, Etta?"

No answer.

We taxied to the end of the runway, did the pre-flight check, closed the canopy, shoved the throttle forward, and the next we knew, we were flying. It was late in the afternoon. The air was calm. I made a big flight pattern, came around and landed. I taxied back to tie down and shut the engine down. "Well, Etta, what do you think after your first airplane ride?"

"We went up and down so fast," she said. "I don't know what to think. Are you sure your friend doesn't mind? He must be a good friend."

"Well, Etta, the truth of the matter is, I am the friend."

"I don't understand what you're saying."

"It is a roundabout way of saying I bought the plane,"

There was a long pause, then Etta said," How in the world are we going to pay for it?"

"It's very simple. In our marriage, I do the buying and you do the worrying."

I thought Etta would be really bent out of shape, but she just took it in stride. This is why our marriage has been so great over the last 55 years.

The following Wednesday, Etta and I went to the airport and flew the Navion for about one hour. Three days later, we left for a seven-day vacation to Florida and the Bahamas with the Flying Farmers.

NAVION FLIGHTS TO LEWES, DELAWARE

Etta and I had very dear friends in Lewes, DE: Dick and Eva Thompson. Dick and his partner Roland Hasson owned and ran the Lewes Boat Yard.

The boatyard had two marine railways. The large railway could pull boats up to 70 feet in length. The workshop was in a large Quonset hut left over from WWII. Another railway ran into the Quonset hut. This railway could pull boats up to 42 feet long. The good times we had in Lewes are a story in itself.

Etta and I would climb into the Navion on a Friday night or Saturday morning and take off for Lewes. Going by car to Lewes was a 2 1/2 to 3 1/2 hour drive. It was only a 45-minute flight in the Navion. We really looked forward to our Lewes outings.

After take-off, we'd fly south over the Pine Barrens, which are a million acres of pine trees and sand. Under the sand is a massive watershed. They say this is the purest water in the entire world. The people who live in the woods are called Pineys. It's the same idea as calling people who lived in the hills Hill-Billies.

After we left the Pine Barrens, we'd fly over Delaware Bay. The course we took was the wildest part of the bay. When we flew over the water, the engine went on automatic rough. The farther out on the water we flew, away from the land, the worse the engine sounded. When we reached the other side of the bay, the engine sounded better. When the east end lighthouse came into view, it was time to begin a very shallow descent. The idea was to be 500 feet above the light.

On the other side of the channel was Lewes Boat Yard. As we passed over it, I would rev the engine to let Dick and Eva know that we had arrived. Lewes didn't have an airport, but Rehoboth, which was only six miles away, had two grass runways.

With Dick and Eva Thompson (left), and Alec (right), at the Lewes Boatyard, in Lewes, DE, 1955

With Etta, and our friends, Marie and Russ Homan, in the Navion before the Easter Parade in Atlantic City, 1955

Alec, who lived with Dick and Eva for many years, would get in his car when he heard the Navion overhead. He'd pick us up at the airport. By the time he got there, we had the plane tied down and were ready to go back with him to the boatyard.

Back in those days, Lewes was a very large menhaden fishing town. Menhaden are small fish, about 14" long and too oily to be edible. There were two processing plants in Lewes and seven or eight boats working out of each fish house. Each boat carried a captain, mate, engineer, and oiler. These four men were white and the 25 members of the crew were of color.

This is how it worked: the lookout in the crow's nest would scan the sea looking for a school of menhadens, better known as bunker fish (as they were called by the locals). The bunkers would swim in a large circle that looked like a big black donut in the water.

The purse boats were put overboard, and when they got to the school of fish, one boat would go right and the other would go left, pulling out the net as they circled the school of fish. As the boats came full circle, the net surrounded the whole school of bunkers. The Striker boat held up the backside of the net to keep it from sinking.

Picture this: the purse boats would be at 12:00 and the Striker boat would be at 6:00. When the net was full, the boats would start to make the circle smaller and smaller.

When the net was about 40 feet in diameter, the mother ship would come alongside and start bailing out the net. The engineer's job was to run the joist that emptied the net into the ship's fish hole. The mother ship would leave early in the morning and return that afternoon or night. The distance the mother ship had to travel to find fish determined how long of a day they would be at sea.

Later they used spotter airplanes—small single-engine planes that left early in the morning to spot fish. When they found them, they'd radio the location to the mother ship. This saved a lot of time. Spotter plane pilots had to be pretty brave to fly so many miles out in the ocean, day after day, in a single-engine airplane. It would be a long swim, if you had to ditch the plane that far out in the ocean

When the mother ship got back to the processing plant (called the fish house), the fish would be lowered on a long conveyor belt that traveled up the long pier to be processed.

By the way, menhaden oil is used in all types of products, such as paint and fertilizer.

As the bunker fish traveled on the conveyor belt, they were counted. The crew was paid by the number of fish they brought in and not by how much they weighed. The captain was paid seven cents per thousand; the mate, five cents per thousand, and down the line it went. On a good day, a ship brought in several million fish a day (multiply seven cents per thousand times 12 million—if you were captain, that's not a bad day's pay in the 1940s).

In those days, the Rehoboth Airport did great when the bunker boats were working. When the boats came in on Friday afternoon, most of the officers would charter a plane to fly home for the weekend, returning on Sunday afternoon.

The bunkers are all gone now. The fish houses are gone, too. The smell of fish that traveled for miles is gone and the airport is now a shopping center.

One Sunday afternoon, Etta and I were getting the Navion ready to fly home. The airport manager walked over to us and said, "Mr. McCarthy, as you know, Rehoboth and the area depend on the summer tourist trade."

"I know that, but what does that have to do with us?"

"Look around you, and tell me what you see."

"Nothing, why?"

"Well, every time you come to our airport, and you do come quite often, it rains. As you can see, it is starting to rain while we are talking."

"Are you saying we're like a black cloud?"

"No, not exactly that, but if you would come until June, and skip July and August, it would be a big help."

I still don't know if he was kidding or if he meant this.

We cranked up the Navion and took off for home. As we crossed the Delaware Bay, the weather really got stinky. I said to Etta, "I don't think we can make it home, the weather is getting worse. Etta, where can we go?"

"Bridgeton, NJ, isn't far. We can go there and get a motel for the night."

"O.K.," I said.

Bridgeton Airport was a grassy strip, without landing lights and it was almost dark by now. We came around and lined up with the runway. We got ready to flare out for a landing, a little too high and a little too fast. Etta had her own names when we were flying. The landing gear was the 'feet,' etc. The high grass was wet and slippery. We were three feet off the ground, eating up the runway. Etta said, "Put on the brakes, Fred."

I said, "I can't put on the brakes; the feet aren't on the ground."

We finally touched down. The wet grass was like being on ice. We slid off the end of the runway into a field of high corn. Making a 180-degree turn in the middle of a cornfield, we made a lot of cornmeal. We found a motel, spent the night, and flew home the next morning.

This story was told to me by one of the old-timers who lived in Lewes back in the Depression days:

The fish house would send a truck to Baltimore with a couple of men of color, with a pocket full of money. The men would go to a bar and buy drinks for takers. When they got drunk, the two men would load them on the truck and head back to Lewes. When the poor guys woke up in the morning, they were out on the ocean. Somehow, they kept the poor souls on board the boat for 30 days. They were given a list of what they had used, such as food and boots. When all the deductions were subtracted from their pay, there was only $5 left.

They would take the $5, head to the police station and tell them how they were shanghaied on the fish boat for 30 days. The cops would ask them how much money they had on them. When they said $5, the police would lock them up for vagrancy. If the story is true or not, I don't know, but I heard this story more than once.

With the Navion, at the Burlington County Airport, 1955

Flying Farmers

FLYING TO FLORIDA

In 1955, we met a peach farmer named Sharpless Richey at the Moorestown Airport. He owned a three-tail Blanco airplane that was designed by Giuseppe Blanco and built in the late 1940s. The wings were made of wood and covered with fabric. The fuselage was welded steel tubing covered with fabric. The landing gear was retractable. The company advertised speeds of 150 mph with a 150 horsepower engine.

The Flying Farmers were going on a fly-in in Florida. Sharpless asked, "Would you like to go as an associated member?"

Etta and I talked it over, and said, "Why not?"

They anticipated more than 100 airplanes from all over the country. We'd meet in a little town called Orlando, FL. At the time, no one thought of a guy called "Walt Disney". We met Sharpless and his farmer friend, John Traino and his 15-year-old son Gregory at the Moorestown airport early one Saturday morning.

Both men were on the big side. When all three got into the small Blanco, there wasn't room for their luggage. So Etta and I ended up with all of their luggage in our backseat.

Once airborne, we found out the head winds were very strong. The Navion and the Blanco flew side-by-side for the first hour or so. But as the Blanco burned off fuel, the little plane picked up speed. Within three hours, Sharpless was out of sight. Our first fuel stop was in southern Virginia. When Etta and I landed, there was Sharpless fueled up and waiting for us.

The wind was blowing about 20 knots. Unicom was our only radio communication. You flew the iron beam, a railroad track ,or the concrete beam, the roads. There was no autopilot, radar, or GPS, just a compass, an air map, and a road map.

Our next stop was Savannah, GA. I always fueled my own airplane, but in Savannah the airport did the oil check and fueling. Everyone was hungry and in a big hurry to get to Orlando. We ate a quick sandwich, climbed back into the airplane and took off. A short time later, Etta said, "I thought you were going to get gas back there."

I said, "I did get gas. Why do you ask?"

Etta's reply was, "How come the gas gauge says empty?"

PARTNERSHIPS

I looked at the gas gauge with its needle just over the empty mark. My first word was "Shit!"

At this moment we were over the Okeechobee swamp. Looking down the jungle looked like a Disney movie. I made a 180-degree turn. I thought I remembered flying over a farm that had a crop duster by the barn. Every minute seemed like an hour. I saw the barn and the crop duster and what looked like a landing strip. After I landed, we taxied to the farmer, a middle-aged man who asked, "Can I help you two?" I told him the whole story. He was kind enough to give us enough fuel to get to Orlando. We thanked him and off we went again. When we arrived in Orlando, we were amazed by how many planes were flown by farmers.

The next day we all got on buses. The first stop was Cape Canaveral. First, we went into a large auditorium. After a few minutes an Air Force general walked up to the podium. "Apparently, you farmers have a lot of clout in Washington. And I see you have your wives with you. My wife isn't allowed on the Cape, and if my wife can't go on the Cape, your wives aren't going on the Cape," he said. "Put your wives back on the buses." Then he walked off the stage.

After leaving our wives (they made a tour of the Tupperware factory), we spent an hour watching movies, one crash at a time. This rocket blowing up on a pad, this one falling over on the pad, this one reached 50 feet in the air and blew up, on and on and on.

After watching billions of dollars blowing up, we were taken out on the pad. They showed us a rocket that was going to take a monkey up for a ride, then we returned to the bus. We were driven to a big orange grove and then to the processing plant, followed by a nice lunch at the Ranch House, where hot dogs, soda, orange juice, and a hundred one-pound bags of pecans were served.

We returned to Orlando for a nice dinner and a lot of hangar flying (hangar flying is sitting around and talking about flying). The Flying Farmers were a great bunch of people: friendly, soft-spoken, and polite.

FLYING TO THE BAHAMAS

The day after the Orlando outing, we all flew to Fort Lauderdale. The only airport in Fort Lauderdale was one the Navy left behind after WWII. It had the typical three, 5,000-foot runways, heading in different directions.

By the time the last plane landed, the count was around a hundred airplanes. Two brothers flew a new Cessna 180: a high-wing, four-passenger plane. It was quite fast and big. The older said, "My kid brother does most of the flying, because I'm 82." I asked him how old was his kid brother. He said, "Only 80."

I asked the 82-year-old, "How do you like a high-wing plane over a low-wing plane?"

"Well," he said, "You know we're from Oklahoma, and Oklahoma doesn't have too many airports."

"Yes," I said, "But what does a high-wing plane have to do with how many airports you have?"

"Without airports we have to land on the roads, and we need a high-wing to clear the mailboxes," he said.

Now, the big surprise was that the town of Fort Lauderdale had arranged a parade with school bands, Miss Ft. Lauderdale, and other marchers. They also had open cars for the Flying Farmers to ride in as the parade drove through town. We all felt like big shots.

The only ocean-front hotel back then was the Ocean Gulf Hotel. The room cost $38 a night, but as Flying Farmers, we paid $8.

The next day, we were going to fly over to West End, Bahamas, which was about 70 miles east over water. After dinner that night, we were going to see a movie. The movie was *How to Ditch a Plane in the Ocean*. Of the hundred or so planes, there was only one Navion—only one—and we had it. The lights went down and the movie started. The heading in large letters was, "WHAT TO DO IF YOU HAVE TO DITCH IN THE OCEAN."

I said to Etta, "Can you believe this? They're using a Navion to show how to ditch in the ocean. Is this telling us something?"

The Navion had a sliding canopy that would just pop off when you pulled the release lever. There were no doors to open or wings over your head. You just popped the canopy and stepped out.

The next morning we all went to the airport. The Navy or Coast Guard would fly two planes back and forth, one on each side of the column of airplanes. Sharpless was the first to take off, and Etta and I, with their luggage, would be number two. After Sharpless cleared the runway, we hit the power and started our roll. At 2,000 feet, we leveled off. Sharpless was in the lead about a half-mile ahead of us.

Out in the distance, the weather didn't look too good. The farther we went, the worse the dark clouds got.

I tried to call Sharpless on the Unicom, but for some reason he didn't respond. I guess he'd switched to another channel. I said to Etta, "I don't know what to do. If Sharpless flies into that storm, I don't want to follow him; but I don't want to leave him."

The Blanco was getting smaller and smaller. Etta started peeling a tangerine. She turned to me and said, "Have a piece of a tangerine."

"Don't bother me," I said. By now the Blanco was the size of a golf ball. I can't help him. I can't leave him. What should I do?

"Have a piece of tangerine."

"Don't bother me, Etta."

Suddenly, I was in a panic. I was in the middle of the storm. It was as if someone had turned down the lights. This was real IFR (Instrument Flight Rule) stuff. At that time, I couldn't even spell the word "instrument," let alone fly IFR. I was afraid to make a 180-degree turn (in the turn I could lose control). Then I started to think, if you're in IFR weather and you are not a qualified IFR pilot, you can help the situation by slowing the airplane down—that way things don't happen as fast.

First, I lowered the landing gear. Ah, that made a difference. Next came the flaps. I lowered the flaps to the first notch. This is about 10 percent of their travel.

Next came the trim settings. You can set the trim to make the airplane climb or descend. If you set the trim in the middle, the airplane would hold its altitude and wouldn't climb or descend. I played with the trim a little while, and finally, the Navion was flying almost by itself.

"Boy, I got it made," I thought. All the instruments were looking good. "All I have to do is sit back and wait until we break out of this weather."

"Have a piece of tangerine. I'm taking the seeds out."

"Don't bother me, Etta."

I wished I were as calm as Etta. I was in a cold sweat and Etta was slowly eating a tangerine.

When I thought we'd made it, the "artificial horizon instrument" started indicating our left wing was down and our right wing was up. (This instrument today is called the altitude indicator. Don't ask me why they changed the name.)

I turned the wheel (or yoke) to the right to level the wings. Partway into the correction, I turned the yoke back to where it was. My gut feeling told me that this wasn't right. Then I thought back, "The instruments are always right. Pilots get killed because they don't believe the instruments."

I turned the yoke again to the right. My mind told me that the correction was not right.

A few seconds later, the artificial horizon started to move again. This time the nose started to rise, but didn't stop. It indicated that we were doing loops—over and over it goes. I was lucky. This time the instrument was wrong (we were in the Bermuda Triangle).

Now I had to fly compass, altitude, air speed, needle and ball, the very basic flight instruments. We were doing quite well. Etta finished her tangerine, and we were still flying. The good Lord was sitting on our shoulders the whole time.

We finally broke out of the storm. The sun was shining bright and the world looked beautiful: the blue sky and the deep blue ocean. We made it!

A few minutes later, we saw West End on the Grand Bahama Island. The runway was straight ahead of us and I could see the red Blanco on the final approach.

We climbed out of the plane, kissed the ground, and walked over to the waiting people. Everyone shook our hands, and thanked us for coming to their island. Food was set out on a big table along with a bowl of punch. After the fourth glass of punch, we realized it was half rum.

We later found out that after Sharpless Richey and Etta and I took off, that the rest of the airplanes were held back due to the big storm between Ft. Lauderdale and West End, Bahamas.

The storm passed and the other ninety-some planes took off and headed toward West End. The two Navy or Coast Guard planes went home due to the storm. Old Mother Nature can be very nasty when she wants to be.

After all the planes were in the air another storm entered the picture. By the time the planes reached the Bahamas, the storm was sitting right over the airport. Can you picture ninety-some planes looking for an airport in the middle of a storm? It was a miracle that no one was killed. One plane landed on a road, thinking it was the airport. Two more planes landed on the same road. It was a mess. Planes were scattered all over the island. The storm moved on and eventually, all the planes landed on the West End's 5,000-foot concrete runway. What a miracle happened on this day!

BAHAMAS' WEST END

Our luggage was unloaded from the Navion and we were led to our room, which was small but nice. The place had been built before WWII. During four or five years of neglect, the jungle had taken over. There were several of these buildings, but only a few were refurbished. The rest of the buildings looked like ancient ruins in South America.

As soon as we got in our room I said to Etta, "Before we unpack, let's go for a swim."

"Sure," she said.

We put on our bathing suits and headed for the beach. The water was warm and clear blue like crystal. We swam and walked on the beach until it was time to dress for dinner. When we returned to our room, we were amazed to see our bags were empty and everything was hung up or placed in drawers. Pretty nice! We changed into street clothes and walked to the dining room.

We were seated at a table for two. We ordered the soup, main course, and dessert. When the soup arrived, it was cold. I called the waiter over and said, "This soup is ice-cold. Please take it back to the kitchen and put some heat under it."

The waiter looked a little confused. He turned around and walked off. A couple of minutes later, a very big man in a white jacket and large hat came to our table. He was the head chef. "Is something not to your liking, sir?"

"Yeah," I said, "Our soup is ice-cold."

"But sir, that's vichyssoise," the chef said.

I replied: "I don't care what it's called, it's ice-cold."

Then our head chef said, "But sir, vichyssoise is served cold, never hot."

As our faces turned red, I said, "Oh."

Well, we got through the meal. It turned out great, but Etta and I still don't eat ice-cold soup, vichyssoise or whatever it's called.

After dinner, a lot of us went to a club to hear steel drum music. We'd never heard of steel drums and didn't know what to expect. The club was the size of a four- to six-car garage. The floor was just plain dirt and the walls looked like the inside of a garage. "Spider" and his band, which consisted of five more steel drummers were setting up. There were no amplifiers or speakers. The first number was a tropical island song. The singing and the steel drums were very loud. We'd never heard anything like it before. Spider was quite a guy. He sang and played the steel drums like a master. Give Spider a word and he would turn it into a song in about five minutes.

We found out later that Arthur Godfrey had heard Spider sing and play the steel drums and was so impressed that he took him to New York and put him on his daily radio show. Back in those days, Godfrey was really big-time. Spider didn't like New York, and it wasn't long before he packed up and went back to the islands.

Someone in the group said, "Give us a song about the Flying Farmers."

Spider asked a few questions and within a couple of minutes there was a great song about the Flying Farmers. What a wonderful time we had that night. To this day, I've never heard a steel drum band as good as old Spider.

The next morning it was time to leave. The drill was something like this: clear the Bahamas' customs, fly to Palm Beach, FL, and clear U.S. customs, then start the trip back to NJ.

Before we cleared the local customs, the manager of the hotel walked over to Etta and I and said, "I've got a big problem."

"What's your problem?" I asked.

"Two entertainers who were playing in the hotel last night have no way of getting back to Florida, and no one will take them."

I looked at Etta and said, "What do you think?"

"I don't know." she replied.

I said to the hotel manager, "I'm not too crazy about the idea."

"Well, we're really in a jam. You're our only hope," he replied.

"We'll take them with us on two conditions," I said. "One, if we can make room for them. We already have three other people's luggage. And, number two, you do all the paperwork to clear them off the island and any other papers for U.S. Customs."

"I can't thank you enough," he said." You've saved the day. I'll get them right away." Off he went, full-speed.

We checked the Navion over, rearranged the baggage, and waited for our two passengers.

"Here they come," Etta said.

I couldn't believe my eyes. Two stocky—no, not stocky, fat is a better word—women both carrying suitcases and instruments came walking down the ramp. When they got to the plane, we shook hands and introduced ourselves. We stowed the luggage and the two women got up on the wing and kind of flopped into the backseat with their instrument cases in hand. Etta helped with the seat belts and I untied the down ropes.

The women in the backseat started moving around and without warning, the Navion's tail went down and its nose went up. The nose wheel was now dangling in mid-air. We were all shocked.

It was said that whatever you could put in a Navion, it would lift. I thought that with Etta and me sitting in the front seats that would bring the nose down. You steer the Navion with the nose wheel when you're on the ground. I turned around and told our two passengers that when I started the engine and the nose came down, we would try to take off. We'd use half the runway, and if we couldn't lift off, then we would come back to the

PARTNERSHIPS

ramp and they would have to get out. O.K.? The ladies didn't look too happy, but nodded their heads in approval.

I started the engine and the Navion came to life. The nose wheel came down and we were ready to roll. We taxied to the runway. We did our magnetos check and carburetor heat check. "Is everybody ready?" I said. Everyone said, "Ready." The throttle went forward to full power and we started to roll…500 feet…700 feet…1,000 feet, and at 1,500 feet, I put some back pressure on the yoke. 1,800 feet, the nose wheel left the ground. At 2,200 feet, we were off the ground. We made a very slow climb out over the dark-blue ocean. We leveled off at 3,000 feet. I settled back in the seat with a sigh of relief. The next thing I heard was violin music from the backseat.

One of the ladies leaned forward and with a heavy alcohol breath, said, "What is the Flying Farmer theme song?" Etta said, "I don't know."

For an hour, all we heard was laughing and violins. We landed in Palm Beach and parked the plane. The ladies said, "Can we take you to lunch, dinner, or something? We are so grateful to you both for getting us back from the island."

We said, "Thanks, but we have another 1,000 miles to get home, and we want to get started as soon as possible. Thanks, anyway."

We cleared U.S. Customs. Etta went for coffee and I fueled the Navion. As I finished fueling, a Customs man in uniform told me to return to Customs with him. When I got to the counter, a Customs agent, Mr. Fatso, threw some Customs forms on the counter and said, "Your passengers didn't sign these forms."

"I don't know those people. As a favor to the hotel, I just brought them with us. I don't know anything about them, I said.

"They sign, or you go back to the West End," he said.

"Look, friend," I said. "I brought these people in here to you. If they didn't sign some form, that's your fault and problem, not mine. You find them. I'm going back to New Jersey."

When I got back to the Navion, there were four armed guards standing around the plane. I said to the nearest guard, "Someone in your office made a big screw-up and I'm not going to be the fall guy. When my wife comes back, don't get in my way because I'm leaving."

The guard said nothing.

Etta walked up to me and said, "What are all these men doing here with guns?"

"I'll tell you later," I said.

"No, I want to know now," said Etta.

"You know those two women we brought back with us? They weren't told to sign a certain form. Now Customs wants us to bring them back or we go back to the West End. How the hell are we going to find them?"

"Easy," said Etta.

"What do you mean, easy?" I asked.

"Because they are in the restaurant having lunch."

"Etta, go quick and bring them here."

Etta got the ladies. We took them into Customs. They signed the papers, and we all left. The Customs people never said sorry or that it was their fault, nothing. The Navion and the Blanco took off and headed home to New Jersey

FLYING FARMERS GOING HOME

The Blanco and the Navion took off with the Blanco leading. At 5,000 feet we leveled off and started up the coast of Florida. The coast from Fort Lauderdale to Palm Beach was almost unpopulated and Palm Beach was like a small city. Most of the houses had large blue-painted swimming pools. It was the winter haven for the very rich. From Palm Beach to Jacksonville there wasn't a heck of a lot to see.

We were just north of Jacksonville when Sharpless comes on the radio. "I'm losing rpm! I'm losing rpm!"

"What's the trouble?" I asked.

"I don't know, Fred. I think it's one of the mags. I see a pretty good-looking field up ahead. I'm going to land in it."

"O.K., Sharpless, I'm right behind you."

"Why are you landing?" Sharpless asked.

"I can't leave you out there all alone."

So down we went. I was about a hundred yards behind him and I could see that the field had short grass: flat and dry. I watched the Blanco touch down and roll to a stop. The door opened and out came the two men and the boy.

I said to Etta, "This is your first airplane trip and your second emergency landing. I think that's a record, Etta."

Etta was very calm; you would think that she did this every day.

We were on the ground without a problem. I taxied over to the Blanco and shut down our engine. We climbed out and walked over to Sharpless. I said, "You guys O.K.?"

John Traino said, "Boy, that was an experience."

A couple of minutes later four men came walking out of the woods carrying sidearms and rifles. They were dressed in overalls and hats. One said, "Are you in trouble? Can we do anything for you?"

Sharpless said, "I lost a magneto. I can't fly without it."

The man said, "My truck is just over there in the woods. I can go get the mechanic over at the tractor shop. They work with mags all the time."

"That would be great!" replied Sharpless. "How long do you think it will take?"

"About 30 minutes," he said.

The three men stayed while the fourth headed for the woods. I asked the men, "What are you doing with all that artillery?"

"We're hunting wild boars."

"Any luck?" I asked.

"We just started when we heard your airplanes."

Traino said, "I can see what the rifles are for, but why the sidearm?"

"Snakes," replied one of the men.

"What kind of snakes?" asked Traino.

"Rattlesnakes. We wear leather boots and carry pistols for protection."

Traino asked, "Are there many snakes around here?"

"More snakes than people," he answered.

The conversation continued about the area, wild boars, the weather, and so on. Before long, a truck came out of the woods with two men in the cab. They parked near the Blanco. Sharpless had the hood already open, and by now the plane engines had cooled down. The mechanic stuck his head under the cowling and did some magic tricks with the magneto. About 15 minutes later, he called, "Let's try it." Sharpless climbed in the cockpit and yelled, "Clear!"

The engine came to life. A minute or so later, Sharpless revved the engine up to full power. "Turn off mag one—O.K.... Back on. Now turn off mag two—O.K. Great, we are ready to go on our way."

Sharpless said, "I can't thank you enough. You really saved the day for us. What do I owe you?"

"Glad we could help. You don't owe us anything, and that goes for the mechanic, too," the man said.

Flying has changed over the years. Way back when, we practiced forced landings. When you were flying, you always had a field in sight where you could land in an emergency. Also, your instructor would pull the throttle back to the idle position as if you had lost your engine and had to make an emergency landing. In the back of your mind, you had a field in your head, good or bad, and you knew you could make that field.

You would head into the wind, line up on the field you had picked, and make an approach. You knew in real life you couldn't make a go-around. You only had one shot, and it had to be good. If you were right and could make the field, the instructor would let you go down below the trees, about 10 feet off the ground, before he'd let you put on the power and go.

When we went out to practice, we would look for a farmer working in his field. When he was heading into the wind, we would drop down and come across the field behind the tractor, about five feet off the ground, then pull up at the last minute. Needless to say, the poor farmer wanted to kill us. A forced landing was no big deal, if you had a good field to land in. Today, instructor pilots are not allowed to teach this maneuver, like so many other maneuvers.

Our next plan was to fly to Pinehurst and spend the night. It was a long trip to New Jersey. We thanked the men again for their help. We took off and headed north. The Navion carried 39 gallons of fuel. And the Blanco carried a little more.

About 15 miles south of Pinehurst, I called and told them we were coming in for the night. A voice came back, "Man, you can't land here. We got 17 inches of snow on the runway. You can't land here!"

Sharpless and I talked on the radio and decided to change our heading for Fayetteville, NC. I said to Sharpless, "I don't know if I can make it to Fayetteville. Looking at the map I see an army camp with a runway between here and Fayetteville. If I can't make it there, I'm going to land on the army camp." Sharpless said, "O.K., I'm with you. You lead the way."

The fuel problem was looking better as we approached the army camp. I called Sharpless. "It's a little tight, but I can make it to Fayetteville."

"Great!" he said.

Thirty minutes later, I said, "Fayetteville Tower, this is Navion 4375KELO."

"4375KELO, this is Fayetteville Tower"

"I'm about 15 miles west of you, low on fuel, and would like a straight-in approach."

"4375KELO we are plowing the runways. DO NOT, I say, DO NOT approach the field."

"Fayetteville Tower, 4375KELO. I can't wait for you to plow the runway. We were going to land in Pinehurst, but they have 17 inches of snow on their runway. I'm really stretching it to get here."

"4375KELO, O.K. approach the field and tell me if you can find a clear spot to land."

"Roger."

I could see the fueling area. There was a clearer runway leading up to that area. On the final approach, if you looked straight out the windshield, not up or down, that's where your wheels would touch down. Keeping the same altitude, if you were short of the runway, you'd add a little power; if you were a little high, you'd cut back on the power. The Navion was such a great airplane, just a little slow in the speed department.

We taxied over to the fueling area and just as we pulled up to the pump, the engine died from lack of fuel. After that, with a half a tank of fuel, I always began to think about landing. One-third of a tank was considered empty.

Sharpless landed, we took on fuel and tied both planes down. We got a taxi and went to the closest motel. Fayetteville wasn't much in those days. We found a little restaurant within walking distance, then had dinner and hit the sack. When we got up, everything was covered with more than a half-inch of ice, and I mean everything. We almost broke our necks walking to the restaurant. The day went very slowly. There was nothing to do but sit around. There wasn't even a television in the hotel.

We called the airport several times and got the same answer, "Still closed." On the second morning, things started looking a little better. The airport was open. We checked out of the motel and took a taxi to the airport. The driver dropped us off next to the two planes. We couldn't believe our eyes. Both planes were covered with thick ice. Breaking the ice off with our gloved fists took almost three hours. It seemed like forever.

After the ice was finally removed, it was time to go. About 75 miles south of the Chesapeake Bay, the ceiling got pretty low. We were flying on the Iron Beam and had no idea how long we would have this cloud cover. Sharpless saw a couple of sucker holes in the clouds and said, "I'm going up on top. What are you going to do?"

"I'm staying with the railroad tracks. I don't trust those sucker holes," I said. They are called sucker holes because many times after you fly through them, the holes close in and you don't know where you can descend. What's the bottom altitude? What's under the clouds? By flying the railroad tracks, you can make turns and see what's out there.

Thirty minutes later, the clouds opened up and there was the Blanco out in front of us. Home we went. They say, "When you get your pilot's license, it's only a license to learn." How true it is.

Sea Mac

BOTTOM DESIGN

Our company started out in a rented two-car garage in Merchantville, NJ, in 1954. The boats were named "McCarthy Prams." Senator McCarthy was going wild at that time and he was so disliked that we needed a new company name. My dad came up with the name "Sea Mac." If you want to buy a boat, see Mac.

Before Etta and I were married, I'd built a 26' plywood cabin cruiser, designed for me by Bill Deed. It was powered by a single Chrysler Crown engine and had two bunks, a small galley, a private head (wash stand and toilet). The steering station was out in the cockpit, with just a windshield for protection.

I contracted Bill Deed to design the boat. Bill was well known at the time. He had letters from Franklin D. Roosevelt, who had been Secretary of the Navy, about Bill's design of a 110' sub chaser, as well as about other designs.

The reason I'm telling you all this is because Etta and I went to Perth Amboy, NJ, to talk to Bill about designing a 14' runabout for us. The address Bill gave us was a rundown hotel. We found him living in one room in the hotel. He had a small drawing board over an old-fashion steam radiator. Here was a man who had done great things for the marine industry, living in a hotel room—one step above a flophouse.

We told Bill we wanted to build a 14' plywood runabout. Bill said he'd have something in about two weeks. We paid Bill a moderate fee and drove back to our Oaklyn apartment. Two weeks later, the drawings arrived. The 14' runabout that Bill designed was not a difficult boat to build.

I was building six prams a week. The prams were 8' rowboats, with a square front and back. In between building the prams, I built the first 14' runabout. The project took me about a month to finish. We took the boat to our dealer, Bill Guist, in Brigantine, NJ. Bill lent us a hand-steered, 20-horsepower outboard motor.

The boat was designed like most boats those days: A keel down the centerline with several cross ribs. The method has been used for hundreds of years. The sides and bottoms were planked with $1/4$" plywood; Douglas fir was the easiest marine plywood to find.

PARTNERSHIPS

Etta and a Sea Mac

Piloting a Sea Mac

We ran the boat in the roughest water we could find, hour after hour, for the entire weekend. At one point, the Coast Guard stopped us. The first words out of their mouths were, "Hey, what are you trying to do, sink that boat?"

"We're trying to see if we can break the boat up," we said.

That kind of ruffled their feathers. So we told them the truth, "This boat is a prototype, and we're trying to see how good it is."

By the time Sunday rolled around, the little boat started to show it couldn't take what we needed it to. The boat had to take whatever came along.

Another trip to Perth Amboy was necessary. Etta and I met with Bill in his hotel room. I told him the whole story. The thin bottom, the cross frames, and ribs acted like a series of knives that just sheared the bottom planking. Bill said, "I guess we need a thicker bottom plywood. Let's use half-inch instead of quarter-inch. That should do the trick."

"Bill, I could never bend half-inch plywood."

"Could you bend 3/8" plywood on the bottom?" he asked.

"I guess I could, but it won't be easy."

"Let's give it a try," he said.

"O.K., I'll give it a shot."

And back to Oaklyn we went. We found we could bend the 3/8" plywood on the bottom, but the plywood had to be soaked in wet sawdust overnight.

The second prototype was built using the 3/8" plywood, and we used the same testing method. After the first weekend, the boat looked good. Maybe the 3/8" plywood was the answer. The testing continued. After a couple of more weekends, the boat started to show fatigue. The same problem was starting to show up. The ribs were starting to shear the bottom plywood.

There's got to be a better design, I thought. If the frames or ribs are shearing the bottom, let's do away with ribs and frames; it's just common sense. We'll increase the keelson size (a keel on the inside), because we don't want to increase the drag. A larger keelson would be created, and we could run stringers from the transom forward, until they ran out of bottom surface.

Our 14' runabout would have a transom frame and three frames forward of the transom. The main reason for these frames was to hold the boat's sides apart and to keep their shape.

By this time, we had moved out of Merchantville and had rented the old ice house, next to the Prevonie Railroad Yards, in Camden, NJ.

The ice house was insulated with fine, powdered cork—truckloads of cork. Jim Briody, a friend of my Dad, was kind enough to lend me one of his three-yard dump trucks. I never kept a record of how many loads of cork I took to the Camden City Dump. The truck body did not have covers like they do today. As I drove down the street, I left a fine layer of cork dust. By the end of the week, North Camden looked like Cork City.

These were great times. Today, you need a permit for everything, plus lawyers and engineers to spend your hard-earned money. Back then you just had building codes. If you followed the different codes, no one bothered you. You did not have to pay a landscape engineer to tell you what kind of tree you could plant.

I tested the new bottom design in a hurry. I decided to plank the bottom with 1/8" fir plywood. If the 3/8" plywood started to fail after many hours of pounding, the 1/8" inch plywood should fail very quickly if the design was not good.

Let's give it a shot, I thought. We built the boat and brought it down to the boat yard in Brigantine, NJ, along with Bill Guist's outboard motor. The boat was really lightweight with the 1/8" bottom planking. Faster, too. The bottom was so thin that it seemed like you could put your fist through it, but it was almost indestructible.

No matter what we did to the boat, except running it on a rock pile, it just kept going and going and going.

The fore and aft stringer design was born.

While still building the 8' prams, we introduced the Sea Mac, our 14' deluxe runabout. The bottom was 3/8" utility plywood, the sides and deck were 1/4" mahogany plywood, with Philippine lumber cover boards and stringers. Retail price: $395.

The Sea Mac 14' was a big hit. We now had ten employees and we could not keep up with orders. Our biggest problem was bending the 3/8" plywood bottom. We tried several different ways to clamp the plywood to the boat's frame, but nothing worked.

One night after all the workers left, I said to Etta, "Go home, Etta. I'm going to stay here until I solve this bottom problem."

"What's the problem?" she asked.

"You'd never understand," I said.

"Well, tell me anyway," she said.

"O.K. But it's a waste of time. After we build the frame and shape, it's ready to accept the plywood sides and bottom. The sides go on first and are shaped to accept the bottom plywood. The problem is, once the sides are fastened to the frame, there is no way to clamp the bottom to the frame. The bottom plywood must be clamped to the frame before it can be fastened to the frame. Do you understand my problem, Etta?" I said.

"I don't see any problem," she said.

"I didn't think you would understand the problem," I repeated.

"I see your problem," she said. "But it's not a problem to me."

"Oh, it's not?"

"No, it's not a problem to me," she said. The side plywood bends very easily, because it's only $1/4$ of an inch thick. The bottom plywood is $3/4$ of an inch, and it is very difficult to bend, because it is thicker and the bottom has a lot more bend than the sides do."

"You now see my problem," I said.

"It's not a problem," Etta answered.

"O.K., smarty, what's the answer to my problem?" I said.

"Simple, put the bottom on first," Etta said.

"That's not the way it's done. All boats have the sides on first," I said.

Starting the very next day, every boat built in our shop had the bottom put on first.

THE ICE HOUSE

The first thing we did after moving from Merchantville to the ice house in Camden was to build a spray booth. My dad suggested we make a wooden frame and cover it with asbestos board, and secure the board with brass screws. This would make the structure spark-proof.

Everything was going along pretty well. Thompson Mahogany was supplying our lumber. We were framing the boats with a wood called Philippine mahogany, which was actually cedar. Fessenden Hall was supplying our fir plywood. Most people thought this plywood company was owned by two people: Mr. Fessenden and Mr. Hall. Actually, Mr. Fessenden Hall was a strict Quaker, no drinking, no smoking, no foul language, and so on. He always wore a jacket and tie. Soon after we moved into the ice house, he showed us a new, state-of-the-art plastic-covered plywood. This plywood would solve all our problems. Paint would stick better, the fiberglass tape we covered the seams with would hold better, and the plastic would not crack chip or crack like plywood fir does.

Piloting a Sea Mac, 1956

Sea Mac with the new bottom design, 1956

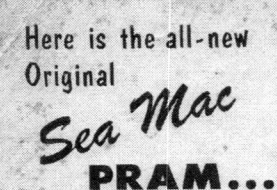

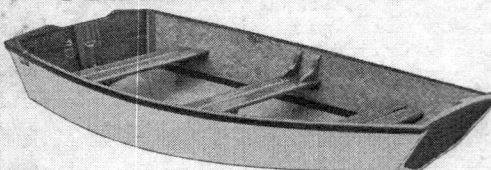

Sea Mac ads
Fine Hardwood Association award

We built 25 14' runabouts, using the new plastic-covered plywood called "Harbor Right." The boatbuilder's dream come true.

Soon, we started to get complaints from our owners. The fiberglass tape covering the bottom seams on the Sea Mac boats was coming off. How could this happen? It never happened before we started using Harbor Right. We found out the hard way that Harbor Right would not stick or bond with fiberglass.

We brought in an attorney to look at our problem. His final answer was, "You can go broke in one of two ways. The first way is to sue Fessenden Hall. The second way is to replace the defective boats with new boats."

Boy, that was some choice.

Etta and I finally decided to save our good name. We would replace the boats, all 25 of them. As the old boats came back to our yard, we would pile them up in the area next to the freight yard.

Our dealer from Woodbury, NJ, came to our office one day to place an order for some more 14' runabouts. Now we were buying plywood from Harbor Sale. Their office and warehouse was located in Baltimore, MD. The plywood was manufactured in Holland using beautiful African woods: African cherry, utile, and gaboon. Using these different woods really took our boat to the top.

The following year, we came in first place with one of our 14' runabouts from the Fine Hardwood Association. Our boat was on display in Chicago, IL, in the Museum of Science & Industry. We are the only boat company to ever receive this award, and that was over 50 years ago.

The Woodbury boat dealer saw the pile of Harbor Right boats and said, "What are you going to do with all of those?"

"I have no idea," I replied. He looked them over and said, "Give me a good price and I'll buy them, as is."

I said, "I don't want them back on the water. I want them destroyed." Mr. Woodbury Dealer came back with, "I'll take them to my yard and make any repairs they need. After the repairs I'll slap some paint on them and put them in the rental fleet down at the bay."

"I'll think about it and let you know what we're going to do with the boats."

On Friday afternoon, just before quitting time, a little old lady named Mrs. Baker came into the shop. I introduced myself and asked what I could do for her. She started off with, "We bought one of your 14' runabouts several weeks ago. We noticed last weekend something is coming off the bottom in long strips."

"Mrs. Baker, I know the problem you're having," I said. "Bring the boat back to us, and we'll replace it with a year-later model at no charge."

"I can't believe my ears," she said. "My husband is out in the car. I'm going out to tell him, right now."

When Mrs. Baker returned, she asked, "How can we get our boat here and take the new boat back to Long Beach Island, NJ?"

"Very simple," I said. "The boat company will lend you a boat trailer to make the swap."

She went back to the car to tell her husband the latest development. When she returned, she was all smiles. "Why can't we take the new boat to Long Beach Island now, and drop off our boat and your trailer Sunday night?"

"Sounds like a good idea," I said.

Mr. Baker drove his car to our loading area. We hooked one of our boat trailers to his car, loaded and tied down the new boat on the trailer and off they went. Before they left for Long Beach Island, they told us what a great company Sea Mac was. They still couldn't believe they were getting a brand-new boat that cost more than the one they were returning. They were two happy people.

On the returned boats there were items we could salvage: steering wheels, deck hardware, running lights.

After they drove off with the new boat in tow, I said to myself, "Was I just swindled out of a boat and trailer? If I was, it was a slick trick."

On Monday, the returned boat was in the yard sitting on our trailer, as promised, but the returned boat was not a whole boat. Our Mrs. Baker, that sweet grandmother-type, had stripped the boat down to bare bones. The only things left were not removable, such as the paint. Anything we could salvage was gone.

The Woodbury boat dealer kept calling every other day, "Just sell me five boats." Well, like a fool, I finally gave in and sold him five boats off the pile. When you're young, you do some foolish things, and this was one of my best stupid moves.

Several days later, a man and his wife drove up to the shop pulling a trailer. Sitting on the trailer was a 14' Sea Mac runabout.

Yes, you guessed it. The boat was one we had already replaced. Our loyal Woodbury dealer sold the boat saying it was a trade-in. The next day we were in Woodbury picking up the other four boats. Needless to say, we never sold another boat to Mr. Swindler.

We learned the hard way.

THE CHERUBINI FAMILY

We only spent one winter in the ice house. The building was too small and needed a heating system. Our sales were growing, and we needed more space to meet the demand for our 14' runabouts.

Tom Cherubini was one of our workers. Tom came from a talented family. I'd never met people like them. They just reeked with talent, but they lacked common sense. Tom said to me one day, "My father and brothers have no work, and you can't build enough boats."

Tom's father, and brothers Joe and Frit, built 14' and 16' runabouts. The name was "Sea Scamp." Their boats were good-running, well-made boats. Their shop was just 20 miles north of us.

"Tom, why don't you ask your dad and brothers to come see me. Maybe we can work something out. I don't know what, but it's worth talking about."

Tom said, "I'll ask them."

Our spray booth and drying room were not warm enough to dry the paint and varnish. The brothers that owned the ice house did not want to talk about the problem. We needed a quick fix, that did not cost a lot of money. Tom said, "Why not use salamanders? You know the things they put out in the orange groves, when it gets too cold?"

"How does a salamander work?" I asked.

A salamander is nothing more than a steel pot with a five-foot smoke stack on top of the pot. You put kerosene in the pot and light it. When the kerosene boils, the fumes burn and go up the stack. You can control the heat by how much air goes into the pot.

A burning pot in a spray booth sounds like a disaster ready to happen, but it's worth a try. A salamander only cost $17 back then.

We found that if the salamander was burning when you sprayed, the spray booth exhaust fans would pull out the overspray, which sometimes burned in the salamander flame like a sparkler on the fourth of July. It sounds pretty hairy, but it worked.

One day, I was in the spray booth painting a boat, when the fire marshal came in the booth. When he saw the little sparkler in the salamander's flame, he almost tore off the door trying to get out of the spray booth.

Mr. Cherubini and his two sons showed up, agreed that they would make the decks and seats for the 14' runabouts. These parts would be varnished and ready to be installed on the boats. We would pay for the parts when delivered to our shop. Also, we agreed, to give each other 30 days' notice if we decided to stop the work.

The parts started coming. The workmanship was very good, nice woodwork and good varnished finishes. Our production was now going great.

The two brothers who owned the ice house finally decided to fix the heating system. It would take a few weeks to complete the work. We were shut down for heating repairs, and I forgot our time agreement with the Cherubini's. The parts kept on coming. We had to borrow money to pay for the parts that were being delivered. Our two landlord brothers happened to own the local bank. That helped solve the problem.

We had decks and seats all over the place.

Finally, the heater was fixed, and we were back building boats. It didn't take long to use up all the decks and seats. When our next shipment did not show up, I called Mr. Cherubini and asked him about our deck and seat delivery. He said he was a little behind, but they would be along shortly.

The next day, I drove up to see what was going on. We had people that needed these parts to keep working and dealers waiting for boats. When I entered the Cherubini's boat shop, I didn't see any parts ready for shipment.

"Mr. Cherubini, where are my decks and seats?" I asked.

No answer.

Next to where I was standing was the new 14' runabout I had lent to Mr. Cherubini for a reference boat. If any questions came up, they could go to this reference boat and see how it was made.

"Mr. Cherubini, I'll be back to pick up my boat."

He replied, "When you pay me for these parts, you can have your boat."

"When you finish the decks and seats, and deliver them to us, I will pay you for them, not before," I said.

I looked up a lawyer I knew in town and told him the story.

"I'm talking to you as a friend now, not an attorney. To get your boat back would take a lot of time and money, more money than the value of the boat," he said.

"As a friend, not an attorney, what should I do?" I asked.

Mr. Lawyer Friend said, "Get six of the biggest guys you have in the shop. Go up there and physically take the damn boat. Don't say anything, just get in and out of the place as quick as you can."

"Sounds good," I said.

The next day, I hooked a trailer up to a station wagon. I walked into our shop and picked out six of the meanest-looking men I had. We went out to the station wagon and I told them the whole story.

"If anyone does not want to go, there's no hard feelings," I told them.

The biggest guy said, "Sounds like fun, let's go."

We all got in the station wagon and headed for Burlington, NJ, to retrieve our boat. When we got there, we all walked in the front door and the six guys picked up the boat and walked out the door before anyone could say a word.

In less than five minutes, we had come and gone, with the boat in tow.

Tom Cherubini came to me one day, and said, "My family has been building boats for years, and never made any money Doctors make all the money, I'm going to be a doctor."

"When is this going to happen?" I asked Tom.

"This is my last day," he answered.

The Cherubini family did not believe in giving an employer any notice when they quit a job.

Joe Cherubini worked for me over 16 years. When I returned from lunch one day, I asked Dick LaCates, the shop boss, "I do not see Joe, where did he go?"

Dick answered, "At eleven o'clock, Joe walked up to me and said, "I quit," and walked out the door.

I found out later that Joe rented our old shop and he and his two sons started to build sailboats. A short time later, his two sons walked out the door, on Joe.

"Tom, are you about 27 years old?" I asked.

"That's correct," he said.

"How much college do you have, Tom?" I asked.

"Never finished high school," Tom said.

"And you're leaving us today to become a doctor?" I said, "I wish you all the luck in the world, Tom."

Tom walked out the door to become a doctor

Tom ended up being one of the top eye surgeons in the world. He had a practice in New York City with big-time patients.

MIKE CHACCIO THE CROOK

By 1957, the ice house was really getting too small for us. We had to find a new building. In Riverside, NJ, there was an automobile dealership building owned by Mike Chaccio. I met with him and looked over the place. The shop part of the place was large; in the front of the building was the auto showroom, plus an office with desks and chairs, and a large safe. In the shop area were shelves, a time clock, welding machine, benches, and a lot of odds and ends. The rent was $1,250.00 a month. We would have to build a lot of boats to pay that kind of money. Chaccio said to me, in his Italian accent, "What would you give me for all this stuff?"

"You know what you want for all this stuff. Tell me what you want, and if it's a good price, I'll buy it."

"Give me five hundred dollars, and it's all yours," Chaccio said.

"I'll let you know in a couple of days about the building and the contents."

At the time, I didn't know I was dealing with a sly, lying crook. Etta and I talked about the move. It was a lot of money but the ice house was at its limit. We had to give it a shot. I called Chaccio and told him we would rent his building and buy the contents. What a gamble!

A few days later, the first truckload left Camden for Riverside. We arrived at the new shop; I unlocked the door and went in. I couldn't believe my eyes. It was empty. Nothing was left but the welding machine.

I drove down the street to Chaccio's office. "Where are the contents of the building that I paid you five hundred dollars for?"

"You bought the welding machine, that's all," he said.

I thought to myself, "You lying S.O.B."

This went back and forth for 10 minutes. I saw that I was dealing with a crook. I was getting nowhere. I walked out and slammed the door. It took almost two weeks to make the move.

On the first day of the month, old Chaccio would be at our door for his rent money. If the track was open, he'd be there within the hour.

THE SEAFARERS

Blacky Cordillo was an old head knocker for the unions. He started out as a strong enforcer. Blacky's phone call went something like this: "McCarthy, meet me at the Cherry Hill Inn, Tuesday at twelve-thirty sharp."

"Blacky, I'll meet you Thursday at one o'clock. That is the only time I have open." I thought I would put this turkey in his place.

"O.K., one o'clock Thursday." he said.

I'd been a member of the telephone company union and the Operating Engineers Union 829, but now I was on the other side of the street. What I had in my favor was that I knew how these guys thought.

Our meeting at the Cherry Hill Inn was a little more threatening than I expected. When Blacky and his three goons finished their third martinis, they put on their tough act.

"McCarthy, I can do this to your little boat company," he said, putting his thumb on the edge of the table and rolling it in a left to right movement, just like the mafia does when they want to get someone murdered.

When the four of them started to walk out of the restaurant, I said, "Blacky, I'm going to give you a lesson in life. Never mess with anybody until you know who you're messing with."

The union bosses kept their boats at the Atlantic City State Marina. Another old union head knocker, Tom Battles, ran the restaurant and bar at the marina. When I got back to the shop after our lunch meeting, I got on the phone and called the union bosses I knew. First was Ray Cohen of the Teamsters union. "Ray, I had lunch today with Cordillo of the Seafarers. He's trying to get into my shop. Can you help me?"

"I'll do my best," Ray said.

Next was Lou Lanny who ran the liquor union. I said the same thing, "Can you help me?" And, "I'll do my best," Lou said.

I called everyone I could think of, even the guy in Lewes, DE who ran the baker's union.

On ten o'clock Monday morning, Blacky Cordillo came to my office. Now it was "Mr. McCarthy," not just "McCarthy." The first words out of his mouth were, "Were you ever in union affairs?"

"Blacky, that's none of your business. Have you gotten any phone calls lately?" I asked.

"Yeah, how do you know all those people?"

"Like I said, Blacky, it's none of your business."

The majority of the workers at Sea Mac had already signed the "I want a union" card. That afternoon I saw the employees outside the building with the union people. This was not the first time they'd been there. I was a little hurt that the shop leaders did not tell me about the union invasion. Now it was too late to do anything, just make the best out of it.

We hired an attorney who specialized in the employer's side of union takeovers. At the federal building in Philadelphia, PA, we met with the union under the supervision of a federal referee.

The attorney and I entered the meeting room. At a long, wide table were the federal man sitting at the head and five men representing the union on the left-hand side.

Before sitting down, the lawyers on both sides said hello to each other, using each other's first names. "Hi, Bill," "Hi, Joe," "Hi, Sam," just like they were going to have dinner together.

After we sat down, our attorney said, "What do you guys want?"

The federal man at the head of the table said, "Now, gentleman, we're past this stage…" but before he could finish the union guy said, "Get lost."

The federal man walked out of the room.

Our attorney repeated, "What do you people want?"

The union man carried on about more money, longer vacations, more holidays, plus many other things.

Our attorney stood up and said, "Follow me. Fred." We walked into the hall. "Well, Fred, that's what they want. What are you willing to give them?"

"Not a god damn thing. I'll close the place up first," I said.

"O.K., we'll go back in and tell them that."

Next the union people went into the hall. When they came back in, we'd go back out. This went on for an hour or so. Finally, the union man returned and said, "A nickel an hour raise, and the day after Thanksgiving off. That's it."

We went back into the hallway. "I think we did pretty good, Fred," our attorney said.

"It sounds O.K. to me," I replied.

We returned and the our attorney said, "O.K., we'll buy the deal."

The union guy said, "It's a deal, but McCarthy has to put on a show."

On our way out, I asked, "What's this show thing they are talking about?"

"It goes like this," he said. "Monday the union guy will come in your office with the new shop steward and a couple of employees. Once inside your office, the union will demand all the things they asked for this morning. You're going to say you will shut down the company and pound on the desk. You and the union will argue and holler at each other. When the show is over and the smoke clears, it's a nickel an hour raise, and the day after Thanksgiving off. That is the end of the show."

THE PAINTER IS SICK

After three months of the union, the workers realized that it was not all it was cracked up to be. Several people asked me if I could get them out of it. My answer was always the same: "You got yourself into the union, now you'll just have to live with it."

PARTNERSHIPS

They elected John Proth as shop steward. From that day on, Mr. Proth never did a day's work. When I walked into the shop, he tried to look busy, but I could tell he was just pretending to be working.

At the time we had the most unique paint shop in the industry. The large filter door would open and a boat would be rolled into the spray booth. After the door closed, the exhaust fan started. Clear varnish was pumped from a 50-gallon drum and circulated through a heater. To spray the thick varnish, a temperature of 190 degrees was needed. The painter would blow the dust off the boat with an air hose and wipe it down with a dust-removing tack cloth. The next step was to spray the inside and deck of the boat with several coats until the surface had six millimeters of clear varnish. This equaled 10 brush coats of varnish.

The boat entered the spray booth with a 60' drying tunnel. The air moved at five miles per hour at a temperature of 90 degrees. At the end of the tunnel, the boat returned for a final application of clear varnish. The process took 20 men to prepare the boats and only one painter to spray them.

One Monday morning, the painter called in sick. He and I were the only ones who knew how to operate the system. I changed my clothes, put on the spray outfit and replaced the sick painter.

The first day was uneventful. The next day, the painter called in sick again. So, I changed my clothes and returned to the paint department. I was spraying my third boat when the big filter door opened. Standing in the doorway was a man dressed very casually.

I said, "What in the hell do you think you are doing? Can't you read: 'Do not open doors'? Now, close the doors very slowly."

"YOU can't paint these boats," he said.

"Close the damn doors and get the hell out of here!" I said. I was going to give him a shot of paint, but I was afraid if I hit the doors it might stir up some dust. "Who the hell are you, coming into my shop like this?"

"I'm the union representative."

"So what?" I said.

"You are management and not in the union. Therefore, you cannot do union work," he said.

"Look Mister, this is my shop, and I will do anything I damn please. You and your union are not going to tell me what I can or cannot do. Now get the hell out of here!"

"If you don't do what I tell you, I'll call a walk-out," he threatened.

"You know, mister, I think you are chicken shit. Follow me," I said.

My dad came up with the name Sea Mac.
If you want to buy a boat, "See Mac."

Sea Mac production at the Riverside, NJ factory

I walked over to the main power panel. In a LOUD voice, I said, "Everybody stop what you are doing and come over here."

Slowly, the men gathered around me. They all had a "what's this all about" look. I said, "As you all know, Bill the painter is out sick. Your union representative says I'm management and if I keep painting he will pull a walk-out. So what this means is that we are shutting down the shop until Bill gets better and comes back to work."

The men went into a huddle. The next thing I knew, the workers were escorting the union representative out the door. I'm quite sure it was John Proth who blew the whistle.

A month or two later, I asked the union representative to come to my office. "Your shop steward John Proth is costing me a lot of money. He's not doing his job. In fact, he's not working at all. I'd like you to spend some time in the shop, then come back and tell me if you would keep him on the payroll. His actions are rubbing off on the rest of the shop. And I trust you will not tell Proth what you're doing."

A few hours later, the union rep returned to my office and said, "I see what you mean. Proth is really taking advantage of being the shop steward."

"Look," I said, "I'll get Proth into the office and lay it on the line. If he doesn't get on the ball, he's out. Do you agree?"

"Yeah, I'll go along," he said.

A few days later, I got Proth in the office and said, "Either shape up, or you're out the door."

All this time, Proth had a look that read, "You can't fire me. I'm the shop steward."

I finally said, "John, you're not listening to me, are you?"

"I'm the shop steward. You can't fire me," he said.

"Sorry, John. You just talked yourself out of your job. You can pick up your pay on Friday."

THE WAREHOUSE

Back in the late '50s and early '60s, we didn't sell many boats from September to March. But after March, we couldn't build enough boats to fill the demand. This meant we only had a six-month season. We had to come up with a solution to the problem—fast. Then the light bulb went on! We'd get a warehouse. We'd borrow money from someone and build boats in the off-season. Then we'd sell them in the spring and summer months. Great idea.

Sea Macs on the truck at the Riverside, NJ factory

A Sea Mac on the TV show, *The Price is Right*, hosted by Bill Cullan, 1961. The winner was the contestant who came closest to guessing the price.

The Philadelphia National Bank wanted our banking business. They could be the money source. Before we could do anything, we had to have a money commitment. First, money; second, storage. With these two things we could put the plan in motion.

Bill Smith was the sales representative for the Philadelphia National Bank. He'd call on us once a month, trying to swing our account into his bank. I called him the next day and asked him to stop by the office around 2:00.

At 1:45 Bill walked into the office. We shook hands and sat down. I explained our problem and how we thought we could solve it.

"How much money are we talking about?" Bill asked.

"Probably up to one million dollars," I said—a lot of money in 1959.

"Let me take this to the bank and see what they say," he said.

The following week Bill came to our shop with two big shots. "This is Mr. Smith and this is Mr. Jones," he said. "They have a proposal for you to consider."

Mr. Smith said. "Our bank is willing to give your company a line of credit for up to one million dollars. The first step would be to get your warehouse bonded by American Express. Every time a boat enters this warehouse, our bank will give you 80 percent of the boat's value."

"Sounds fair to me," I said.

"American Express will check the inventory in your warehouse every two weeks," said Mr. Jones.

"That's only fair," I said. We shook hands. Mr. Smith said, "We will draw up the papers and get back to you."

After the bankers left the building, I went into Etta's office. "Etta, it worked. The bank is going to lend us money as we build the boats," I said.

"Sounds great. How much will they lend us?" Etta asked.

"Up to one million dollars," I said.

"That's a lot of money. Do we need that much money?"

"I don't think so, but it's nice to know it's available," I said.

We talked Mike Chaccio into building a warehouse next to our building, with connecting doors. By October we were ready to roll.

As the boats were finished, they'd be piled on top of one another in the warehouse. There were six boats in every pile. By the following March, we had over 600 boats, ranging from 14 feet to 21 feet, in the warehouse.

Around April 15, Bill Smith called and said he wanted to have lunch with me. I said, "I don't go out to lunch. I bring my lunch with me in the morning."

PARTNERSHIPS

Now Smith got very demanding. "I want to have lunch with you tomorrow, say at the Golden Dawn diner at one o'clock?"

"O.K., Bill, if you put it that way. I will be there," I said.

That night I told Etta what happened with Bill the banker.

I got to the diner about 1:05, and there was Bill sitting in a booth waiting for me.

"Hi, Bill, how's it going?" I said.

In kind of a nervous voice, Bill said, "Not too good, Fred. The bank wants their money, all of it."

"You must be kidding me. I don't have that kind of money. How am I going to pay it all back? I kept my part of the agreement. As soon as we move the boats, we pay the bank. That's just what we're doing," I said.

"That's true Fred, but you're not paying it back fast enough."

"Wait a minute, Bill. The time frame was the boating season, not half the season," I told him.

"Fred, the bank wants the money and that's that," he said.

"Bill, I don't care what the bank wants. I don't have the money. It's all tied up in the boat inventory."

"I'll show you how to pay the bank back," he said. "You're going to sell your house, car and airplane."

"Stop right there, Smith. I'm not selling one god damn thing. If that's how your god damn bank operates, then here's the key to the shop. Your bank is now in the boat business," I said, getting up and walking out of the diner.

THE BEGINNING OF THE END

One thing I learned over the years is never ask a banker for anything. Just tell the banker what you want. If you ask a banker for a loan, he will put you through hell before you get one dollar. Let's say you want to borrow $5,000. You call the bank and ask for the banker you've been dealing with.

"Hi, Bill. How are you? Bill, put $5,000 in my account. I'll be in to sign the paper this afternoon. Thanks, Bill, I gotta run."

This tells the banker that he might lose you as a customer if he doesn't follow your instructions. It works most of the time, but not always.

The Philadelphia National Bank was getting nervous. They wanted to renege on our agreement. They wanted their money now. Our agreement had been to pay the bank as we sold our boats. Things did not look good.

The reason the boats were not selling was very simple. The boat dealers were not buying our boats to show in their showrooms. Why buy our boats for inventory when we have a warehouse full of boats. That old saying, "You can't buy from an empty wagon," was coming true. I never thought the boat dealers were so shortsighted.

In the spring of 1963, these two guys came up, from where I don't remember, Bud Dolmer and Ernie Bler. They were cooking up some kind of deal. When they saw all the boats in our warehouse, the wheels started to spin. "Let's buy a marina and go into the boat business", one of them said. "Good idea," the other one said.

Along Route 130 was a marina that had an Evinrude outboard motor franchise. The three of us got in my car and drove up to the marina, owned by a builder named Smith facing Route 130. The Rancocas Creek was behind it and there was a launching ramp along the north end of the property. In the small showroom only one outboard motor was on display.

Mr. Smith had lost interest in the business and was very happy to get the place off his hands. Bud and Ernie went to work on Mr. Smith. When the smoke cleared, we bought the place for next to nothing. I was now one-third owner in a marina.

We needed a name for the marina. Someone said, "Big D," for "Big Deals." Sounded O.K. to all of us. This was the start of Big D.

By the end of that summer, Big D was one of the largest Evinrude dealers in the country. Big D also sold the entire inventory of the Sea Mac Boat Company. This got the bank off our back.

A few days after our meeting in the diner, the bank had gone into our personal savings account and took all our savings. I went to a lawyer friend of mine and told him what the Philadelphia National Bank had done to us.

His comment was, "What they did to you and Etta is legal, but not ethical."

When I finally got the bank off my back, I made a vow to never take a loan from another one.

THE END OF SEA MAC

About every ten years, the boat business hits rock bottom. 1963–64 was one of those years. Sales were way down and the union did not help matters. Before closing the doors for the last time, I was looking around for something to replace the Sea Mac Boat Company.

PARTNERSHIPS

Then one day I realized the answer was looking at me right in the face. Norwalk was the answer. Sea Mac had been making the planking for their boats, and Gordon Keenan ran the Norwalk Boat Company. All their templates were available, the union crew was still around; what more could you ask for?

I had never had a partner before, but I thought it might be nice to have someone to share the load and help with the big decisions.

Gordon Keenan and I met at Compton's Log Cabin Restaurant in Haddon Township on Cuthbert Road. We sat at the bar and I told him my idea. Gordon did not share my excitement. He did not think it was such a great idea to join forces. I tried to win him over that night, but could not. We parted company and went our separate ways.

Our rent was paid up to January 1, 1964. This gave me about 60 days to put this thing together, and move all the equipment out of the Riverside building. Gordon finally gave in and said he would join forces with me. I guess he got tired of all my phone calls.

We rented a building at the Burlington County Airport, in Lumberton, NJ, and started moving the equipment from Riverside. I asked Mike Chaccio if I could have a couple days past the January 1 deadline to finish moving the inventory out of his building. Chaccio said, "Sure, take as much time as you want."

On New Year's Day, I went to the building and started loading our pickup truck. These cops came charging into the building with their guns drawn. That S.O.B. Chaccio called the cops and said someone had broken into his building and was stealing his stuff. I told the police that Chaccio said I could finish moving after our lease ran out on January 1. The police were very nice about the matter. There was nothing they could do, because I had nothing in writing and they knew what kind of man Mike Chaccio was.

Our lawyer in Riverside told me one day that Chaccio had made all his money by serving prison time for some big-name gangster. I am sure the lawyer knew what he was talking about. We'd intended to clean the inside of the building, but now it was a different story. Chaccio could keep the sawdust, 50-gallon drums, and scrap lumber.

We rented a building at the Burlington County Airport owned by the Cohen brothers, who also had a business in structural iron A few years prior to this, Etta and I kept our Ryan Navion on their airport. But now it was tied down at the Morristown Airport, which was closer to our house in Cinnaminson.

I met with Dave Cohen and told him we were starting out with very little money. We might be late with the rent money at times. Dave said he'd work with us and he turned out to be a man of his word. A few months after we moved into the airport building, Dave stopped by for a visit. "How's it going, Fred?"

"Well, Dave, it's coming along, but like all new projects, cash flow is our big problem," I said. "I'm sure you will work it out," he said.

We continued to talk about everyday things, and Dave walked out and left in his car. A few days later, we got a letter from his iron business. Gordon always opened the mail and wrote out the checks.

"Gordon, I hope that letter is not an eviction notice," I said.

He opened the letter. We couldn't believe our eyes. There was a check for $5,000 and a short note saying, "Pay us back when you can." Five thousand dollars then was like $50,000 now—maybe more. It really helped us out.

I called on every boat dealer I knew in Long Island, Connecticut, New Jersey, and Massachusetts. My main question was "What kind of boat do you need to fill out your inventory?" Nine out of 10 people said a 26' to 28' sedan cruiser that could sleep six people.

The first two boats we built were 27' sedan models that slept six adults. Ted DeGarmo, a boat dealer in Long Island, bought the first two. The boats had lap streak sides and a smooth bottom, both made out of half-inch plywood. They were the only two sedan cruisers we ever built. We just could not sell the style of boat that the boat dealers had asked for.

The third boat we built was a 28' sport fishing model. All the dealers said this boat would not sell. There were too many boats like this on the market. We put our first sport fishing boat in the New York Boat Show. Ted DeGarmo and his sales people ran the show.

In those days, the boat show ran for 10 days. By the fourth day, we had to tell Ted to stop selling the boat. In four days, Ted and his crew sold all the boats we could build, at the rate of two boats a week. We were off and running again. The Jersey Boat Works was born.

*We were off and running again.
The Jersey Boat Works was born.*

PARTNERSHIPS

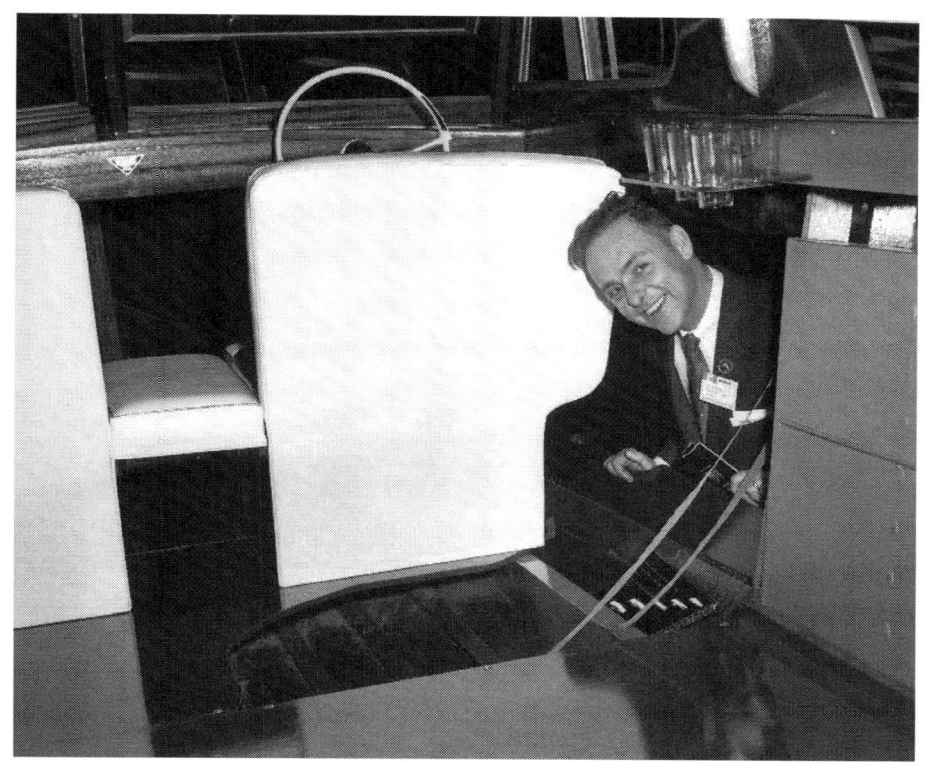

Inside the cutaway section

Sea Mac, with a cutaway section in the side
for viewing, at the New York Boat Show

Jersey Boat Works / Jersey Yachts

GORDON KEENAN, NORWALK BOATS

Gordon Keenan and I had met in a local restaurant with Ray Bouley, the rep from Harbor Sales, our plywood supplier. Gordon had come over to say hello to Ray. Gordon worked for the Genary Brothers who owned a machine shop that made cannon shells for the U.S. Army. Ralph and Wilbur Genary also owned large powerboats. Due to their size, they could not find a place to dock their boats. To solve this problem, they bought a small boatyard in Mays Landing, NJ. A dock was built to accommodate the two boats.

The docking problem was solved, but what should they do with the boatyard and the four employees that came with the boatyard? Ralph asked the leader of the four men, "Can you guys build a boat?"

He said, "Sure we can build a boat. Boatbuilding is our trade." This was the start of the "May Craft" boat company.

The following year, the Genarys put one of their May Craft boats into the Philadelphia Boat Show. To their surprise, the boat was a big success. They sold more boats then they could build in a year. May Craft was on its way, and Gordon Keenan ran the show.

For some reason, May Craft Boat Company did not last very long. There is no way I can find out why because all the people involved in the company have passed on.

It was several years before I saw Gordon Keenan again. After May Craft closed down, Gordon started building boats for a man in Norwalk, CT. The boats were called "Norwalk Boats." They were 26' wood boats with oak frames. The skin was fir plywood, and the rest of the boat was Philippine mahogany (which is really Philippine cedar).

Gordon was also involved with Egg Harbor Boat Company and Cherubini Boat Company. Both companies were building 36' or 38' Norwalk boats and that's about all I know about the larger Norwalk boats.

Gordon walked into the Sea Mac office in Riverside one day. "I understand you have a scarfing machine that can make long pieces of plywood out of half-inch four-by-eight-foot fir plywood."

"Yes, I can make a piece of plywood from here to Philadelphia," I answered.

PARTNERSHIPS

"I'm building 26' plywood boats, and I would like someone to fabricate the side planks and the bottom, and deliver the parts to my shop in Mount Holly, New Jersey."

"Sure, Gordon, we can handle that. Do you want us to finish the plywood?" I asked.

"That would be great," he said.

"Gordon, do you have the full size templates for all the parts?"

"Yes," he said.

I gave Gordon a price for the parts we were to make. The price was O.K., so we started making these 30-foot long parts, and we would deliver them on our twelve-wheeler. Our rig was long and the loads were heavy, so we needed twelve wheels to carry our loads. The truck was one of the first cab-over-engines that the Ford Company built. A very short time later, Norwalk Boat Company went out of business and never paid us for all the parts we made for them.

THE PARTNERSHIP

Gordon and I were partners from 1963 to 1979. We started Jersey Boat Works together. The 16 years we were together we never had a quarrel or argument. I guess if we did have an argument, we would probably have killed each another. Gordon did things that I did not like, and I know I did things that he did not like.

The men we hired were mostly Gordon's Norwalk people. The only Sea Mac person was Chuck Bonnick, who came to work for me right out of high school and stayed with the company for 27 years.

We slowly outgrew our building at the Burlington County Airport and began looking around for a new location. Every piece of ground had some type of drawback. Dave Cohen, our landlord, came into our office one day, and Gordon told him we were looking around for a new location. We were going to build fiberglass boats and we needed higher ceilings and more square feet.

Dave said he and his brother owned four acres right next to the airport. The land had frontage on Stacy Haines Road and he would give us a good price per acre. "Let's talk," we said. Dave and his brother were nice people to deal with.

Several months prior to this meeting, Dave and his brother had some money problems. We lent the brothers the money they needed. This was our chance to say thanks for helping us out when we were starting Jersey Boat Works. We did not ask the brothers for the money; they just gave it to us because they could see that the money was needed.

We bought the four acres from Dave and his brother, and we started to make plans for our new boat factory. It was decided to make the fiberglass shop a single building. For fire protection, the fiberglass shop would be sixty feet behind the assembly building.

How great it was back in those days! We did not have all the laws and rules that people have today. We did not have all the parasites that feed on the planners and dreamers, like we have today.

On an 8 1/2" x 11" sheet of yellow lined paper, I drew the outline of the two buildings we planned to build. Gordon took the drawing up to Town Hall to get a building permit.

Mr. Gaun, who gave out the building permits, looked at my drawing for a few minutes, and said, "Everything looks O.K. I'll have Betty type out a building permit, but remember, you must follow our building code to the letter. Bill Allen, our building inspector will come down on you if you do not follow our codes."

Gordon agreed and returned from Town Hall with the building permit and a copy of Lumberton's building codes.

I have forgotten how the state of New Jersey got wind of our building project, but they found out somehow. We were told that the state of New Jersey would require a sprinkler system. The state considered fiberglass boatbuilding a fire hazard.

A sprinkler system would be a nice thing to have, but we had two problems. First, we did not have the money. A sprinkler system is a very expensive thing to install. Two, we had no city water supply. How can you have a sprinkler system without water?

We tried to reason with the state of New Jersey, but they did not want to hear about our problem. Barry Parker was the Speaker of the House for our state senate. He was a fishing friend. I called Barry and told him my problem. He said he'd look into it. Barry called me back three days later. "I've made an appointment for you with Mr. Smith in the Newark Office of the Engineering Department that's requiring you to install the sprinkler system in your new building. I'm sending you a letter of introduction to give to Mr. Smith that should open some doors."

I drove to Newark to meet Mr. Smith. As soon as I walked into his office, I could see he was burning up inside, and he did not care if his temper showed.

"Mr. McCarthy, I see you have some very influential friends in our state."

"Not really," I said.

"Speaker of the House and maybe our next governor is not influential?" he said.

"Oh, Barry Parker? He's just a fishing friend," I said, handing him the letter of introduction. This just added fuel to the fire. Barry Parker's letter was very complimentary.

Smith finally stood up and said, "Do what you want. We won't interfere with your new construction. But if you don't install a sprinkler system, you are very foolish." He turned around and walked out of the room.

I walked out of Mr. Smith's office, got in my car and drove back to Lumberton.

THE POND

We started to plan our new buildings. To get the proper elevation, we'd need lots of fill dirt. If the floors were too low, the building would be under water after a heavy rain.

To keep the ceiling in the fiberglass shop under 20 feet, we decided to put the 40' hull mold down in a four-foot deep pit. When the overhead crane lifted the hull out of the mold, the bottom of the hull would be at floor level. We heard there was an underground stream running in front of our building. If this was the case, we could dig a pond for water and use the dirt for the fill we needed.

We hired a backhoe to dig some test holes. The first hole that was dug hit water at three feet. Now the sprinkler water problem was solved. We had all the water we needed.

We brought in a drag line and the pond was dug to a depth of 10 feet. The pond also gave us 3,000 cubic yards of great fill dirt. Now all we had to do was find the money to install a sprinkler system.

We hired a sprinkler company to design a system that would be approved by the state of New Jersey. Three weeks later, they submitted their design with drawings.

Going over the drawings, I could not believe what an undertaking was ahead of us. A 150 horsepower, 1,000 gallon-a-minute fire pump had to be 10 feet underground, in a concrete vault. Every contracting company we asked to bid on the job just looked it over and walked away.

I remembered two brothers in Oaklyn, NJ, who would do most anything. They were smart and would try anything. The big problem was that the water table was only three feet underground. How can you dig a 10-foot hole in the ground, when you hit water at three feet?

The brothers looked the job over and gave us an estimate. We didn't ask how they would do the job; we just wanted them to do it. It was a simple job, if you knew how to do it.

The brothers drove 15 feet into the ground at several well points, and hooked them up to a diesel pump. The well pump ran 30 days and 30 nights. At the end of the 30 days, the water table was down 15 feet in a 70-foot radius. Now the brothers had 10 days to dig the 12' by 12' hole in the ground, 10 feet deep, and then pour the concrete house.

The six-inch suction pipe ran 30 feet from the pump house out into the pond. This was only the beginning. The cost for the pump and the things that went with the pump, like a starting switch, pipe, and sprinkler head almost broke us.

Several years later, we had a fire that started around 3:00 a.m. The sprinkler system put the fire out before the volunteer fire company got to the scene. The Lumberton volunteer fire company did a great job. I thought they'd put out the fire and just leave, but the volunteers stayed until all the water was swept out of the building and everything was put back in order. A great bunch of men.

Two men in the paint department caused the fire. Rather than putting their dirty rags into the proper container located in the paint department, they put their dirty rags in this 50-gallon trash drum in the tool room. Spontaneous combustion set the balled-up rags into a roaring fire. I guess the sprinkler was worth all of our sleepless nights.

WOOD TO FIBERGLASS

Things were going pretty well. We were building eight boats a month and selling them. Gordon was opening the mail and signing the checks, while I ran all over the East Coast selling boats and working the boat shows.

We bought 10 acres on Route 38, with the plan to build a new boat-building plant. Route 38 was a main road in Lumberton with a lot of traffic and turned out not to be a good place to build boats, but it turned out to be a good investment, even though we used it to build. Every time we needed money, we would hock the 10 acres.

When I was not traveling, I spent my time in the plant. The shop foreman, John Cartwright, had been with Gordon at the Norwalk Boat Company. John knew I could run the shop without him. Whereas Gordon was not a boatbuilder, and without John he'd be lost. John and I just tolerated each other. I put up with him just to keep the peace.

Gordon and I went out for lunch every day. This was new for me. I was always a brown bagger. One day during lunch, I said, "Gordon, we have to go into the fiberglass boat business. Wood boats will be a thing of the past very shortly."

"Yes, we have to think about it," Gordon answered.

"Gordon, thinking about it is not the answer. We've got to do it now, not next month."

"What do you know about building fiberglass boats?" he asked.

"Nothing, but we've got to learn how to build them or we'll go out of the boatbuilding business."

Well, one thing led to another. We found a resin supplier that was willing to let their top salesman spend time with us and show us how it was done. Joe Cherubini and I were the students. It was decided our first fiberglass boat would be a 31' sedan.

To build a fiberglass boat, the first step is to make the plug, which is a full-size model of what you are going to produce. Whatever the plug looks like, the mold will look the same. A good plug will look like a beautiful boat, only inside out.

After the plug is finished, a mold is created over it. Many coats of fiberglass mat are laid up on the plug. When the fiberglass mat is proper thickness, a steel grid of 1" to 1 1/2" steel pipe is welded and connected to the mold by fiberglass strips, leaving a half-inch space between the grid and the mold. The grid is on 18" by 18" centers.

The next step is to remove the mold from the plug. Many coats of highly polished wax are required to keep it from sticking to the mold. If things go right, the plug will not be damaged as the mold is lifted off. If the mold sticks to the plug, it's a disaster. This is a rough idea of how a fiberglass mold is made.

The hull mold is only one part of the finished boat. Next come other large molds—the deck, cabin, cockpit and bridge molds. There are also many smaller molds. The tooling to make a fiberglass boat is quite an undertaking and very costly.

Joe Cherubini built all the molds for our new 31' sedan. Joe was like all the Cherubinis, very gifted, smart, and loaded with talent.

I was out on the road for three days, and when I returned I could see nothing had been done on the 31' hull plug.

"Were you out sick?" "It looks like no work was done on the plug," I said.

"Every time you're not here, Gordon takes me off the glass boats and puts me on the wooden boats," Joe said.

One morning I went into our little storeroom for something, and I saw a five-gallon bucket. Out of curiosity, I looked into the bucket and could not believe what I saw. On a 28' wooden boat, the side planking is called a lap strake, which means that one plank is lapped over another plank. Where the planks overlap they are fastened together every four inches with copper rivets. When the rivet is sent through the rivet hole, the man on the inside of the boat slips a half inch copper washer over the rivet, and then cuts the rivet to the proper length. The cut-off piece is $1/8$" in diameter and about $1/2$" long.

The five-gallon bucket I found in the storeroom was filled to the top with these cut-off rivets. Can you imagine the hours it would take to pick up all those tiny cut-offs that would fill a five-gallon bucket?

I told Charlie Goshey, who worked on a bench next to the storeroom. "Charlie, let me know who takes that five-gallon bucket out of the shop," I said.

"O.K.," Charlie said.

A few hours later, I went into the storeroom. The bucket was gone. "Charlie, who took the bucket?" I asked.

"I didn't see anyone take it," he said.

Charlie would not cover up for someone; he was that kind of guy.

I went out in the parking lot and looked into all the cars and pickup trucks for signs of the lost bucket. Some of the men took home sawdust in cardboard boxes. They would spread the sawdust in their gardens, although back then I didn't understand why. Then it hit me. I reached into the sawdust of the top box and pulled out a handful of copper rivet cut-offs. I went to the office and told Gordon what I had found. Whoever puts that sawdust into their car is the culprit.

As the workers drove off, I was surprised that no one took the cardboard cartons. The last one to leave was John Cartwright, our foreman. John got into his pickup truck and to my great surprise he drove right over to the cardboard cartons and started to load them into his pickup truck.

PARTNERSHIPS

"Gordon, I've found our crook. Come on."

When Gordon saw it was Cartwright, he was so mad he spit out his dentures when he tried to talk.

The boxes had other things besides copper rivet cut-offs. Things like deck hardware and running lights. Gordon gave John a real tongue-lashing. He told him to clean up the other boxes and return the parts to the storeroom.

Back in the office, I said to Gordon, "Here is a man that has been with you for a long time. We catch him stealing and you give him a talking to. I would have run his ass out of here, but quick. This is not the first time Cartwright has pulled this."

The truth of the matter was Gordon was afraid we would lose Cartwright, and Cartwright knew that.

Finally, in 1966, the 31' sedan was completed and put into production. After that we decided to make a 31' sport fisherman. The two-sport fisherman boats had a very low cabin top. I thought that looked great, but the dealer wanted a higher roofline, like those of other boat companies. A new cabin mold was created to make the boat dealers happy.

Sometimes it is better to be a follower than a leader. You can only be a leader when you've got lots of money and time.

HOW THE JERSEY BOATS EXHAUST SYSTEM WAS BORN

For years diesel-powered boats had problems with diesel exhaust, turning the boat's transom black after a day's run. The faster the boat ran, the more exhaust built up on the transom. This is sometimes called "the station wagon effect."

After a long, fast run, the transom would be covered with diesel exhaust smoke. For years I tried to come up with a way of overcoming this problem.

Once I put very large air scoops on each side of the cabin. The idea was to drive air into the cockpit and the air would hold back diesel smoke from entering into the cockpit. It was a great idea; the only problem was, it worked in reverse. The station wagon effect sucked the exhaust into the cockpit and out through the side vents. Now you had a smoky transom and a smoky cabin side. All in all I tried several different ideas, but without success.

One day we were coming back from the Wilmington Canyon, where we were fishing the Atlantic City Marlin Tournament. The Continental shelf runs north and south along the East Coast. Every so often the Continental shelf goes east and comes back to the west. The opening along the shelf could be several miles wide and several miles long, and very deep. This is called a canyon. It is something like the Grand Canyon on land; only it's much deeper. The big fish swim in the deep waters of the canyon. When it's time to feed, the big fish cross over the drop-off into shallow water where the smaller fish hang out. The idea is to go up and down the canyon drop-off and hope for some marlin to notice your bait. There are several canyons off our coast. North is the Hudson Canyon, going south is the Wilmington Canyon, followed by the Baltimore Canyon, and so on.

On this day, my son Freddy and I were coming home from the Wilmington Canyon. On a good day, it's a nice trip. On a bad day, it can be hell. This was a good boat ride day, but not a good fishing day. Our boat had no fish. It was a long, 170-mile boat ride (round trip).

Freddy was driving the boat and I was standing in the back of the cockpit watching the water flying by the transom. I'd done this many times, but today was different. The water was telling me something, but what?

I walked away from the back of the cockpit and climbed the ladder to the flying bridge to talk to Freddy. We were doing an honest 26 knots. The 47' Jersey was doing her thing. After a few minutes, I went back down to the cockpit. What was it telling me?

After a few minutes, it started to come together. As the boat was being pushed through the water by the propellers, the water or wake coming off the bottom of the boat was pushed outward. It does not hit the side of the boat. Why not send the exhaust into the wake? Send it not just straight into the wake, but at an angle of about 40 degrees. By shooting the exhaust into the side wake, the exhaust would be carried away by the wake. Simple. I couldn't wait to try it.

On the next boat we built, the exhaust pipe ran straight back to the transom, like all the boats. But this time, before the exhaust pipe reached the transom, we put a 42-degree turn in the exhaust pipe. This put the exhaust pipes closer to the outboard corner of the transom, and now, rather than a round exhaust pipe coming out of the boat, we ended up with an oval exhaust pipe discharge. On the sea trials, the new exhaust design worked perfectly, no station wagon effect, whatsoever. The exhaust shot into the boat's wake and was gone.

I guess you just stumble on new ideas; you don't just invent them.

By the way, as you walk through a marina, count how many oval exhaust pipes you see.

THE FIRST JERSEY 40'

The fiberglass 31' was doing well. Sales were good and mechanical problems were nil. It was time for a bigger boat—something like 40' would be great. On the drawing board the 40' looked good, so we went to work making the plugs. From the plugs, we would make the molds. We started the project in August 1968 and had the first boat finished by the following January.

Our dealer in Florida bought the first boat and wanted it as soon as possible. To save a buck, he did not want a generator, air conditioning and heating, and no flying bridge enclosure. He said he could install those items in Florida. After dealing with this guy for a couple of years, we realized he was a real fruitcake, but that's another story.

Riverside Marina made the boat ready and put it overboard. To ship the boat from our shop to the marina, the flying bridge had to be removed to lower the boat on the trailer. We had to get the overall height below 12 feet.

Dave Rigley, who ran the Riverside Marina in New Jersey, supervised the operation. Soon the boat was put back together and both engines were running. It was time for the big test. How would she run?

Dave and I were on board with a deckhand and two mechanics with tools.

"Dave, you run the boat. I want to see how she feels," I said.

We worked our way out the channel to the open Delaware River. In the river, Dave took both engines out of gear. One more check, before the big speed run. Everything checked out O.K.

"Dave, I guess it's time to face the music; put the pedal to the metal," I said.

Dave eased both throttles forward. As the engine's rpm increased, the boat moved faster, and the boat lifted out of the water. At full speed, we were really flying.

"Dave, put her in a nice easy turn," I said.

The boat now went into a nice easy turn, and was laying over about 10 degrees. The turn felt good.

"Dave, tighten up the next turn."

"O.K.," he said.

"Nice," I said. "Feels real great. Run with the tide for awhile, and then give me the tightest turn you can."

As the boat ran with the tide, the faster she went. She felt like this was all it could do. I said to Dave, "Give me the tightest turn you can."

My dad aboard a 31' Jersey Yacht, 1972

Etta and Marie Homan on the cockpit of the first
48' Jersey Yacht near Atlantic City, NJ, 1972

Without a word, Dave spun the wheel to starboard as fast as he could. The boat slowed down as she went into the tight turn, just like she should.

"Dave, that was perfect," I said.

"You can't ask for anything more than that," he answered.

We spent another hour putting the boat through everything we could think of. What a relief. After all these months of hard work, it looked like we have a winner. All we had to do now was drive the boat to Miami and get our money for the first 40' Jersey Yacht sold.

Driving a boat to Florida in the dead of winter is bad enough, but without a generator, heating system, and bridge enclosure this is pure madness. A radio and radar would have been nice, also. But the old saying, "You gotta do what you gotta do," sums it up.

We ran the boat back to the marina, and checked for any oil, water, or fuel leaks. Everything was O.K. My good friends, Russ Homan, who was our photographer, and Jim Reilly, my neighbor in Cinnaminson, said they wanted to go along for the ride.

"I think you guys are nuts, but you are certainly welcome," I told them.

Our dealer, Charley Bidgood, in Great Bridge, VA, was one of the best boat critics I knew. He really knew his stuff. I asked him if he would take a ride with us when we reached Great Bridge to tell me what he thought of our new boat. "For real, Charley, you can't hurt my feelings. I want to know what you really think of the boat."

"Fred, things are very slow here this time of year. If it's O.K. with you, I'd like to go all the way to Miami with you."

"Nothing would make me happier, Charley, but before you commit yourself, you should know that there is no generator, no heat, no bridge enclosure, plus no lower steering station," was my answer.

"When you get to Great Bridge, I'll be ready."

"O.K., Charley."

It took a couple of days to get the boat ready. We planned to stay in motels every night, and eat in restaurants, so we didn't need a lot of gear. We got an early start and reached Great Bridge, VA, the first night out. Charley met us at the dock. I showed him the boat. "Are you sure, Charley, you want to go with us? It's a really cold ride without a heating system."

In South Carolina, during the night, we got over an inch of solid ice. We were lucky we could walk from the hotel to the boat, which was 15 feet lower than the street level.

We went down the embankment, rather than the ice-covered stairway. Charley Bidgood slipped, fell down on the ice, and rolled down the entire hill. He looked so funny rolling, that we couldn't stop laughing. It was lucky that he wasn't hurt. It took us an hour to chop the ice off the steering wheel and the control panel.

We were in a motel in Georgia one night. I was talking to Etta on the telephone. A loud horn went off and a voice came over the PA system. "Everyone evacuate the motel! There may be a bomb in the motel. Everyone evacuate the motel!"

"Get out of there as fast as you can," Etta said.

"Are you kidding? This is the warmest I've been in a week. I'm not moving out of this room until tomorrow morning," I said. There was no bomb and no one got blown up.

Etta, Marie Homan and Barbara Reilly flew down to Jacksonville, FL, to meet us. The day they arrived on board, the temperature was 18 degrees. Needless to say, I will never make that trip under those conditions again.

All during the trip, Charley Bidgood never said a word about the boat. I was getting nervous. Did he like the boat or not? Just before we were ready to leave Florida for the flight home, I said, "Well, Charley, you have spent the last 10 days on our new boat. What do you think of her?"

There was a short pause, then he said, "You can't expect any boat to do more than your boat did. She's going to be a winner."

With that, we all said our good-byes and left for home.

DIESEL 31' FUEL COOLERS

Our sales were pretty good. The 31' was doing well, and so was the 40', but we had to keep ahead of the competition.

We thought a diesel 31' would be a good idea. We contacted our local GM dealer and asked what was a good engine in their list. We were told their 3-53 series would be a great engine for our 31' sport fisherman. 3-53 stands for three cylinders and each cylinder was 53 cubic inches. The size and weight were O.K., but the horsepower was a little low. But, what the heck, the price was right. So we ordered a pair—one was right-hand rotation and the other was left-hand rotation.

They fit the 31' sport fisherman perfectly; no modifications were needed. The cockpit floor was just the right height and didn't need to be raised. One reason no modifications were necessary was because we installed the engine differently than any other boat company. Most builders at the time set the engines on top of engine stringers or engine beds.

We set the engines inside the stringers on four large aluminum angles bolted to the stringers and bedded in a quarter-inch neoprene. We called them stringers because they ran from the bow to the stern, the full length of the boat's bottom. The neoprene helped stop the noise and the vibration from being transmitted through the boat.

By putting the engines inside the stringers, it gave several inches between the engine and the stringer. When an engine needs a major overhaul, you have to drop or remove the crank pan. The crank pan is on the bottom of the engine and removing it is a major job. The propeller shaft must be disconnected, the fuel lines, the wiring, the exhaust system and so on, before the engine can be lifted off the engine beds. This is very time-consuming and very expensive.

When the engines are set inside the stringers, the technician has enough room to reach under the engine. The crank pan can be removed and a complete engine overhaul can be achieved without the costly parts removal.

The engines were delivered from our GM distributor. The truck was unloaded and the engines were rolled into our engine department. When I looked at the two engines I was shocked. They were not new. The paint was chipped and they were not what we'd expected.

It was winter and too cold to do the sea trials in New Jersey; so we shipped the boat to Florida. It would be a lot nicer to work and photograph in the bright sun, not the gloomy winter up north.

Russ Homan and his wife, Marie, accompanied Etta and me to Florida. By the time we arrived in Ft. Lauderdale, the boat was in the water and ready to start sea trials.

The first run was great. The boat ran well and did all that we had hoped for. We were really pleased with her performance. The speed could have been a little faster, but it was acceptable. Later on, we went to the 4-53 engines. These engines had four cylinders, not three like the first boat. Russ took a lot of photos, running shots, stills, etc. As usual, we used Etta and Marie as our models.

The diesel sport fisherman went into production. In 1970 it sold for $27,610 retail. Today you can't buy one engine for that price.

The second pair of engines looked much better. I guess our GM distributor got on the ball. I did not find out until later that the GM distributor had sold these engines to another boat company and they had installed them on their boats. I have no idea how long they were used. The engines had been returned to the GM distributor, who in turn sold them to us as new.

That summer we fished a 31' sport fisherman in several tournaments.

The engines were a pair of 4-53 GM. When we ran out to sea in the early morning, they were full of life and snappy. When the boat went into a head sea, the engine's governors pumped more fuel into the engines, and the boat came to life and plowed right through the head sea.

Coming home in the afternoon, the engines lost their pep. When the boat went into a head sea, the engines just died. The rpm (revolutions per minute) dropped by several hundred. GM tried their best to find the problem, new injectors, new fuel filters, etc., but nothing worked.

After a fishing trip one day, we were tied up in the Atlantic City State Marina in Atlantic City, NJ. (This was several years before the casinos, and Trump did not have control of the marina). On a 31' sport fisherman, the engine sat between the fuel tanks in the engine compartment. The reason for this setup: As the engines burned off the fuel, the boat kept the same trim.

I lifted the engine hatches and climbed down into the engine compartment, to just look around and make sure everything was O.K., any water leaks, oil leaks, etc. When I reached over the starboard engine, I leaned on the starboard fuel tank for support with my hand. I was amazed by how hot the fuel tank was.

Like most GM engines at that time, the fuel pump circulated the fuel through the engine and back into the fuel tank. The engine picked off only what it needed. Ideally, the engine didn't need much fuel. At full speed, it consumed a lot. The fuel pump circulated about 50 gallons per hour, but the engine at full-load only used 10 gallons per hour. This was a way to cool the injectors.

The next day I went to see the GM distributor. I met with Jimmy Louis, the company's best diesel brain.

After the handshake, how are you, and so on, I said to Jim, "What does hot fuel do to a diesel engine?"

"It kills them, that's what."

This could be the answer to our problem. When we left the dock in the morning, the fuel was cool. Coming back in the afternoon, the fuel was hot from all the times the fuel had circulated through the hot engines.

We purchased two heat exchangers and installed them on the two engines. Now the fuel was cooled before it entered the engine. It worked. The fuel cooler was born. Today every diesel engine installed in a boat is equipped with fuel coolers.

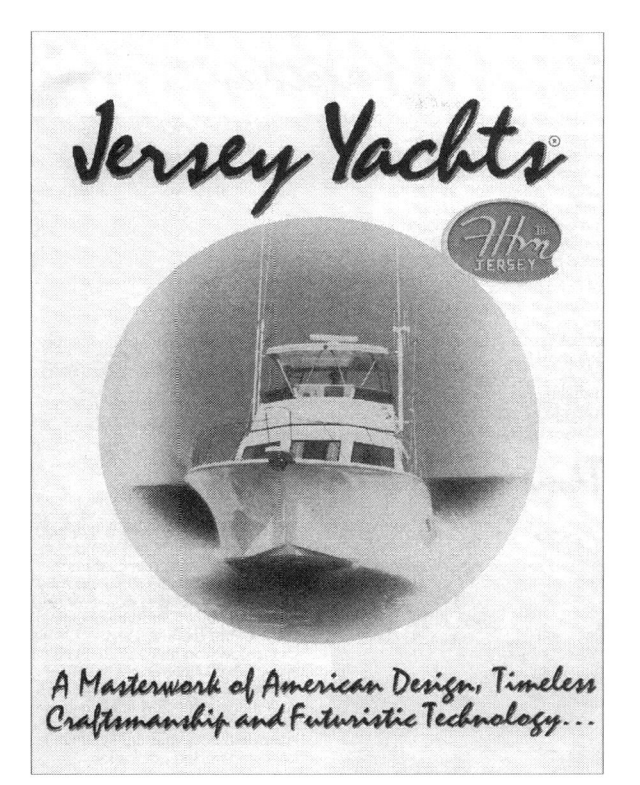

Jersey Yachts sales brochures

THE BREAK-UP

In August 1978 the boat business was very slow. Gordon and I went to the bank and borrowed $50,000, using the 10 acres on Route 38 as collateral. On the way back from the bank, I gave Gordon a little lecture. "Gordon, you really have got to spread this money around, a little here and a little there. You cannot just give this money to a couple of suppliers. It has to go around to all our suppliers."

"O.K., O.K.," Gordon, said.

We drove back to the shop, and I phoned our dealers to try to get some boat orders. Fall was coming, and we needed orders to keep the shop working over the winter months.

A week later, Gordon was out and I needed a check for a truck delivery. I went into our office, opened the safe and took the checkbook. When I opened it, I could not believe my eyes. The $50,000 was gone. Just like before, a few suppliers got paid, and the bulk of the suppliers got nothing.

When I got home that night, I told Etta how upset I was. "I can't take it anymore. I have to do something," I said. We talked and talked and talked. Finally, we came up with a plan.

Our vacation started the following Friday. At lunch that Thursday, I said to Gordon, "We go on vacation tomorrow. While you're on vacation I'd like you to think about something, and come back after vacation with an answer."

"What do I have to think about?" Gordon asked.

"You have to think about three items, and pick the one you like the best, " I said.

"What are the three choices?" Gordon asked.

"One: You buy me out. Two: I buy you out. Three: We close down the company and walk away."

"I can give you my answer right now," Gordon said.

"No, Gordon, not now, after the vacation," I said.

The first day we returned from our vacation, Gordon said to me, "I am not going to buy you out, and I think you would be crazy to buy me out. My answer is close the place up."

"We've worked too hard and for too many years to just close up and walk away from it all," I said.

"You're nuts," said Gordon.

"You are probably right Gordon, but I have to try," I said.

A price was set and a pay-out program was made. The paper was signed and sealed.

The inventory was down to nothing. If we didn't get some orders, where would we get the money to buy the materials and pay the men?

A few days later, Dick Davies a boat dealer from Brielle, NJ, walked into the office. He liked our boats and wanted to be our dealer for the south end of New Jersey. How lucky could we get!

He didn't have a floor plan with any bank. Therefore, he said, he'd like to pay for the boats as they were built, providing full payment after the boats were completed. We were back on track, and the boats started to roll.

A few days after Gordon and I signed the papers, he came to the shop. Gordon said Lahn, a real estate friend of his, wanted to buy our 10-acre lot on Route 38.

"That's great, Gordon," I said.

"Yes, it is. I want to turn all my things into cash."

"What's his offer?" I asked Gordon.

"Sixty thousand."

"Sixty thousand! He's not our friend. He's your worst enemy," I said. "If we sell the ground for 60,000, you get 30,000 and I get 30,000, right?"

"That's right."

"Gordon, I'll buy your half for 30,000, O.K.?" I said.

"O.K., you can have my half for $30,000," was Gordon's answer.

"Gordon, this is the dumbest thing you could do. Please tell your wife it was your idea, not mine. I do not want people to say I cheated you out of the ground on Route 38."

"Good deal or bad deal, I want out," was Gordon's answer.

I just could not talk Gordon out of selling the ten acres on Route 38. If I didn't buy Gordon's half of the ground, he wanted to sell it to Lahn Real Estate Company.

The deal was set. Etta and I bought Gordon's half of the boat company and the 10-acre piece of ground on Route 38. Etta and I were sole partners again, just the way we'd started.

MY SON FREDDY

Freddy and I have one big thing in common: We both hated school, and we both got poor grades. If I got a "C" on my report card, it was a good day.

My eleventh-grade English teacher, Mrs. Melinger, told me in front of the whole class that I was going to grow up to be an ignoramus. She told me to diagram a sentence on the blackboard. At the blackboard, I picked up a piece of chalk and wrote the sentence the way I thought it should be written. Mrs. Melinger looked at me and said, "Why did you change the sentence around?" I told her that I didn't know.

"What do you mean, you don't know?" she said.

"That's the way it should be. That is all I know, and I don't know why."

On my report card, I always got "D's" and "F's."

Freddy came to work at Jersey Boats in 1977, after his eleventh-grade class, and never went back to school. He and I both ended up with GEDs. I told Freddy when he was 10 years old that when was 12, he could come with me on the fishing tournaments. We always had a company demo boat, which went to the boat shows and competed in many fishing tournaments. I took Freddy to his first tournament when he was 12 years old. He was 28 years old when he fished his last one.

Freddy worked in every department at the boat company: the mill, fiberglass, mold room, engine department, etc. When he worked in the mill department, I was so worried he would get hurt. The big ripsaws made a lot of noise and gave off a lot of sawdust, but they were not the dangerous machines. Due to the noise, everyone gave them lots of respect.

The quiet machines, like the band saws, were the most dangerous. Because they were quiet and ran smoothly, people thought they would not hurt you. Metal working machines have a tendency to throw your hands out of the cutters, and the woodworking machines have a tendency to pull your hands into the cutters. I was told many years ago that wooden boatbuilding was more dangerous than bartending. At that time, bartenders were very high insurance risks. From the mill, Freddy went into the engine department. It covered engine installation, general installation and all that goes with the mechanical things on the boat.

On December 28, 1988, we sold Jersey Yachts to two brothers, Bill and John. Freddy stayed on, and Etta and I bought a 53' Hatteras. It was a very comfortable boat, and we had a lot of fun on her.

On all the fishing tournaments with Jersey Yachts, Freddy never left the flying bridge. When the boat was underway, he was always on deck. He never told me until after we sold the company that whenever he went below deck at sea that he got seasick. I could not believe it. All those years, he never said a word about getting sick.

PARTNERSHIPS

Freddy in Ocean City, NJ, 1964

Fredric Hamilton McCarthy III, on the bridge of a 47' Jersey Yacht sportfisher, 1988

Etta and Freddy with his grandparents, Genevieve and Fred, Sr., 1964

Freddy working on the bridge of a 61' Real Ship in Riverside, NJ, 1999

It was not until 2002, the year we built our last boat, I found out Freddy hated building boats.

When we started building steel trawlers in 1990, Freddy ran the show. He was my right-hand man. The smallest trawler we built was 61', and the largest was 73'. They were all very plush and comfortable with four staterooms, each with its own head and shower, galley, large salon, bridge, and stand-up engine room. The range varied from 3,000 to 5,000 miles non-stop.

Etta came up with the name of our new steel boat company, Real Ships. "Don't buy a boat, buy a Real Ship."

It is hard for me to believe all the years Freddy worked and fished with us, that he never told me that he got seasick or that he hated working on boats. He always gave us the feeling that he loved what he was doing. It's easy to fake something like that for a short time, but it takes a great man to do this day after day, year after year.

I take my hat off to my son, Freddy. A real trooper!

DON'T TURN YOUR BACK

About two or three years before Gordon and I parted company, we were having lunch at the Flying W Ranch Restaurant. Gordon had met the restaurant's bookkeeper, Pat Toner, and he told me that he'd hired her to run our office. She would answer the telephone, keep the books and be a girl Friday. It sounded O.K. to me. Why not? The company was growing and we would need such a person sooner or later.

After Gordon retired and John Cartwright was gone, I was the whole show: I sold the boats, designed them, and ran the shop. I had my hands full. I just did not have the time to sign the checks. Someone had to be on hand all the time. Signing checks would hold me down. I needed to be loose to cover all the bases. To solve the problem, I authorized Pat Toner to sign the company checks.

I walked into the office one day. No one heard me enter the room. In the back office, I saw Pat Toner standing in front of the file clerk. Pat was holding a pile of invoices. There must have been 20 to 30 payables in her hands. Next I saw her throw the pile of papers in the clerk's face. The girl began to cry.

When Pat Toner saw me, she turned bright red. "Get your coat, Pat. We're going out to lunch," I said.

PARTNERSHIPS

Pat did not say one word on the ride to the restaurant. We sat down at the table and ordered.

"Pat, we're going on vacation and will be back four weeks from today. I want you to go home and when the four weeks are over, come back to work with your head screwed on right. Your job will be waiting for you."

"O.K.," she said.

Then I said, "All the time you're home, your paycheck will be in the mail every week."

We went back to the office after lunch, and Pat gave the girl a half-hearted "I'm sorry."

When we returned from vacation, Pat Toner did not show up. We were so busy that the weeks just flew by. April 15 came and went. The books were closed, the taxes were paid, and all was well.

In May, I was served with papers. Pat Toner was suing me: One million dollars for sexual harassment and one million for breaking my promise to keep her job forever.

It turned out that Toner had been stealing from us big-time. Not hundreds of dollars, but thousands of dollars. In fact, not long before this all happened, I said to Etta, "I must be doing something right. We are starting to make real money."

Toner had all kinds of little tricks. One was to make out a check to "cash," type in some supplier's name, and go to the bank and cash the check. At that time, the bank had private banking for their big customers. You went into a private room and the cashier sat behind a desk. This made it easy for Toner to cash company checks made out to cash. This was before the computer, when the bank still gave all your cancelled checks back to you.

At the time, I was on the Lumberton Planning Board. Our chief of police sat next to me during the meeting. At the next monthly meeting, I told the chief the whole story. "What do you think a judge would do in a case like this?" I asked him.

"He would give her a good talking to and say don't do it again, case dismissed."

I had our attorney, Wes Manuel, call Toner's attorney and tell him the whole story. Jersey Yachts had lent Toner money for a down payment on a condominium. Toner was told to sign over the condo to Fred McCarthy. If this were done, then I would not file charges against her.

Toner turned over the condo and left town.

Another day in the life of boy boatbuilder.

THE BIG BOSS

It was now 1981, and it came to me one day that it was time once again to think ahead. The 31' mold was getting tired and the 40' mold was showing some wear. If something happened to me, Etta could carry on for only a couple of years. It was time for a whole new line of sport fishing yachts.

We replaced the 31' boat with a new 36' boat. The plan was to make the boats lighter, faster, good-looking, and to make a dry running boat. First came the styling. I spent a long time on the drawing board, but I just couldn't get the right look. Then one day, the big boss upstairs moved the pencil for me, and a new look was born. This was the start of the Jersey 42'.

Step one was completed, now for step two, a dry running hull. George Homan, Russ's cousin, and Joe Pleckia were making the hull plug. "George, make the chine about six inches into the bottom, perfectly flat," I said.

The chine is where the bottom of the boat meets the side of the boat. So what I told George to do was where the bottom meets the sides of the boat, make the bottom flat for six inches before you start to make the bottom shape. At the stem or bow of the boat, taper the six inches down to nothing at the stem. After I saw the six-inch chine, I said, "George it doesn't look right. Let's make a nice fillet between the chine and the bottom. You know George, like a good-looking radius."

George said, "O.K."

This was stage number two on the way to a dry boat.

Now the light boat stage: Our fiberglass lay-up and stringer design was very successful. From day one, we never had a hull failure, so let's not mess with that. The only thing we could do was to try to take out some weight in the interior; this did not amount to very much.

We covered all the bases that we could. The styling looked pretty good. The six-inch chine should make the boat run very dry. We fell down on the weight reduction, and as for the speed, we would have to wait for the sea trials.

Finally, all the molds were completed. It was time to build a boat. We could start making our new 42'. The styling for the new 42' boat had been easy. All I had to do was to make the boat look like the 36' boat, her little sister.

My big mistake: Cummings Engine Company came out with a new engine. It was a straight six-cylinder diesel. We had a newly designed boat and a newly designed engine.

The new boat was picked up by Riverside Marina and trucked to their yard. Dave Rigley always did an outstanding job in making our boats ready for shipment or delivery to our dealers. Riverside Marina also did all our trucking. In all the years Riverside trucked our boats, we never had a problem. Not one boat was ever scratched.

The boat was picked up on a Friday and the following Friday we were having our dealer and Jersey Yacht owners rendezvous at the Harrah's Marina and Casino in Atlantic City—just a little tight for time.

I had a pretty good idea about the boat performance, but I had no idea about the newly designed diesel engine. The Big Boss moved in again and I had a good idea. "Call the Caterpillar engine dealer up and tell them to have a pair of engines on the loading dock, ready for shipment on a moment's notice."

Riverside worked over the weekend, and the boat was launched on Monday. Monday afternoon, the Cummings Engine Company man showed up. He did not put any type of gauges that would tell him how the engines were performing, such as: Are the engines putting out the designed horsepower, or were they overloaded? Are they running hot or cold?

The diesel man started both engines and said, "Let's go." I went up to the flying bridge and said to my guys, "Throw the lines off," and we started out of the harbor.

Five minutes into the sea trial, both engines started to smoke. The cooling water was air-bound and both engines were cooked. Back at the dock, I got my three guys together. "As you know, our dealer meeting is next Friday in Atlantic City. Along with our owners get-together. A lot is resting on this boat getting there by Friday." I said. I had a hunch this might happen, so I had Cat get a pair of engines on their loading dock, ready for pickup. I can have the engines here by four o'clock. I know it is a big job, but I know you can do it."

Chuck Bonnick said, Do you have any idea how much work it will be to change engines?" "Yeah, Chuck. I know exactly how much work it will be to swap engines."

Bonnick was always the one to say it can't be done.

"Look, Chuck," I said. "Don't say it can't be done. We'll never know until we try."

Everyone just stood there with long faces.

A little more help from the Big Boss, I said this without thinking about it. "If I leave here on Thursday morning with this boat completely finished with the Cat engines, I'll give you $5,000 to split between the three of you. Now tell me it can't be done."

Things started to happen. The boat was ready for sea trials on Wednesday afternoon. At 3:00 we left the dock and headed out to the Delaware River. On the river, we ran the new boat at full speed, did all the maneuvers, tight turns, backing down, and others.

We were delighted with the results. She was very fast and tracked like an arrow, and was very dry running. All the things we wanted were there. I was surprised with the boat's speed, because it was a lot heavier than we thought it would be.

Most boatbuilders mount the engines on top of the fore and aft engine stringers. I have always mounted the engines inside the fore and aft engine stringers. One advantage to this method is that you can replace the engines more easily. The engine mounts are 6" x 6" x ½" aluminum angles. It is just a matter of unbolting the engine mounts, moving them to the new location, and drilling new ½" bolt-holes.

We could never have met our deadline if the engines were mounted in the normal way. On Friday at 12:35 we pulled into Harrah's Marina in Atlantic City, NJ, with a winner.

THE NEW LINE

The 36', 42' and the 47' all looked alike. In fact, it was difficult to tell the 42' from the 47'. The only way to tell the 36' from her big brothers was by her size.

All three boats had large fillets that connected the bottom to the same flat chine. The only difference between the three chines was their size. All three boats were very fast for their size and horsepower.

For the longest time, I couldn't figure out why the boats were so fast. Was it the streamlining? It couldn't be weight, because the boats were heavy for their size. It was not due to a clean bottom shape, because all three boats had thick keels. Between the top of the engine stringers to the bottom of the keel, the boats had a 36" backbone. The large, deep keels were a lot of drag, but what they did for stability and propeller protection overpowered the drag factor.

Then one day the light went on. The answer was where the bottom met the big, flat chine with a radius between. The shape of the chine was the same as a blade or bucket on a steam or gas turbine. As the boats ran through the water, the shape of the chine turned the flow of water. This change of water flow helped to lift the boat out of the water, which cut down on drag. The drag reduction made the boat run as if it was much lighter. Lighter boats go much faster and burn less fuel. We called this "the turbo lift bottom." Another plus for the three boats was the interchangeable fiberglass parts.

We were unable to fill the orders. Our fiberglass shop did not have the room or the manpower. This was the bottleneck. One day a man from Pearson Yachts walked into our office. Pearson was a big name in the sailboat industry. At this time the sailboat business was really down.

We talked about this and that, and finally got around to why the man was here. "I'm looking for work," he said.

"Would you be interested in making our 47' hulls?" I asked.

"Sure, we'd be very interested."

One thing led to another and Pearson was going to be our 47' hull builder. Pearson's plant was in Rhode Island. If you drove, it was a six- to seven-hour trip. Riverside Marina trucked the 47' mold to Rhode Island.

All this sounds very quick and easy, but it was not. First, we had to supply Pearson with a list of all the fiberglass material they would need for each hull. Second, we had to furnish Pearson with templates of all the stringer parts. Third, was their price in line with our costs? Fourth, how much would it cost us for Riverside to pick up the hulls in Rhode Island? And could the hulls be nestled three at a time? And finally, how could we inspect the hulls under construction? It took a lot of doing, but we got it together. It was very clear that we needed an airplane to make it all work. An airplane that could carry six people, including the pilot, is IFR equipped, and cruises at 175–200 knots and was in good condition.

All the airplanes we looked at were too big and fuel hogs. One day we got a call from a dealer in Georgetown, MD.

"I have just the plane you're looking for," he said." It's a 1982 Cessna Crusader with only 210 hours on the airframe and engines. For the last year, the plane had been hangared in Phoenix, AZ. The engines are turbocharged and fuel-injected. The 303 had a service ceiling of 25,000 feet, and a cruising speed of 200-plus knots. I think you'll really like this new plane."

"Well, it sounds good. What make are the engines and what is the fuel consumption at 70 percent power?" I asked.

"The engines are 300 horsepower Continental engines, with 70 percent power and they burn 28 gallons per hour," he said.

"What's the asking price?"

"One hundred fifty thousand dollars and the owner will not take a penny less," the broker answered.

We bought the plane and it turned out to be great.

THE BUY-OUT

One afternoon in 1986, a man came into the office and asked Patty, our office manager and daughter-in-law, if he could see the owner of the company. Patty called me on the intercom.

"Send him up," I said. My office was now on the second floor, along with a large conference room.

"I have a client who'd be interested in buying your company. Are you interested in selling?

"I really don't know. I never thought about it," I said.

"Would you like to meet my clients?" he asked.

"What do they know about the boat business?" I asked.

"Their father always had a large boat, and they were raised around the water," he said.

"Let me think about it. I'll call you in a few days and let you know how I feel about it."

When I went home that night, I said to Etta, "How would you like to sell the boat company and retire as a millionaire?"

"That sounds good to me. When is this dream going to come true?"

"A guy came into the office this afternoon and said he had some people that were interested in buying Jersey Yachts."

"Is he for real?" she asked.

"I don't know," I said. "Etta, you know, the boat business runs in 10-year cycles. Right now we are getting close to the eighth year," I said. "We have a year's backlog of orders. We're building almost one boat a week, and averaging a net profit of $30,000 per boat. It can't get any better than that," I said.

This was over 20 years ago.

I called the broker, "We can't promise you anything, but we'll listen to what you have to say." The broker brought in his two clients the following Wednesday, two brothers, Bill and John. Their father had left them his business, something to do with banking. It wasn't doing well and they were looking for something else. I was really up front with the brothers. I told them how demanding the boat business was, and how you had to be on top of everything every minute. I could see in their eyes they were fascinated with everything they saw: the noise, the people climbing all over the boats and such. When a boat company is running good, you can feel the rhythm, the pulse. It sounds like music, and at this time, we were a concert.

I got the family together and told Etta and Freddy about the offer. Freddy said, "Dad, it's your company. Do what you think is best." I could see a little disappointment in their faces. "O.K., let's do this. Freddy, you are the new company president. The only thing I want is for you to tell me if there are any big changes to be made."

As I think back, this move was not fair for Freddy. I did not spend enough time with him to teach him all the ropes. It wasn't until several years later that I found out that Freddy did not like working for the boat company. For all those years, he did his job and never complained once. He is a real dedicated son. I am very proud of him.

The months passed and things went quite well, but Etta and I had the same old problem, we were on call 24 hours a day. I finally said to the family, "We're reaching the peak of the 10-year cycle. It's now or never. If we wait much longer, it will be too late. Now is the time to get the best price for Jersey Yachts."

The next day, I called our accounting firm and asked them to call the two brothers and see if the door was still open. The door was still open. Our lawyers met with their lawyers. Our accountants met with their accountants, and so on. The selling price was $6 million, and we let them rent the buildings. The first thing they wanted was a complete inventory: every nut and bolt, and every stick of lumber.

The brothers were interested in the company because Jersey Yachts had no debts. Invoices were paid every two weeks, and there were no bank loans. Etta and I had agreed years ago: "If we can't pay for it, we don't buy it."

When you bring the so-called pros into the works, you end up with meetings and more meetings. You had meetings to decide if there should be a meeting. One of the reasons Jersey Yachts was so successful was the employees. They were paid well and they had good benefits, such as profit sharing, hospital insurance, two weeks summer vacation and two weeks Christmas vacation. Our work week was 45 hours, and the men were paid for 48 hours. They were the highest paid workers in the entire boating industry.

We were very fair in taking the inventory. The out-of-date items were omitted. We could have pumped up the inventory by 15 percent and the brothers would never have known, but fair is fair.

The sale price had been agreed upon some time ago. At settlement the brothers would give Etta and I a certified check for $6 million. Remember, this was over 20 years ago, and they would rent the property for $17,000 a month. Not bad.

At the meeting in our dining room, I sat on one end of the table and brother Bill sat at the other end of the table. His brother John, their accountant, and the broker sat across the table from Etta and our accountant. Things were going well until the brother's broker dropped a bomb. He said, "We would like to negotiate the selling price."

"Are you joking?" I asked. "Not really," he said.

I sat there for a few minutes boiling. I got up from the table and stood there for a few seconds and said, "I can't believe you would pull a cheap shot like this. The game is over. Jersey Yachts is not for sale." I then walked out the door and headed for the barn.

One of the brothers caught up to me and said, "The broker did this on his own. It wasn't our idea. We're very sorry."

"O.K., I'll buy that, but no more tricks." I was bluffing, too.

After that episode, everything ran very smooth. On December 28, 1988 we went to settlement and signed the papers and walked out of the room with a certified check for $6 million. The very next day we had to make out checks to the government for 38 percent of what we received, for taxes to the federal government, plus another check to the state.

THE CHANGING OF THE GUARD

After the two brothers took over Jersey Yachts in 1988, the first thing they did was to give everyone a credit card. I really wanted the brothers to be successful. The deal included retaining my services and for every hour in my contract, I gave them three hours. If only John had been in charge, I think they would have had a chance. Bill, a retired cop, was the president. He sat in his office and when a customer came in the front door, he went out the back door. I think he was afraid of people.

After several months, Bill said to me, "You know, Fred, this isn't what I thought being the president of a boat company would be like."

"What did you expect, Bill?" I asked.

"Something like, come to the office, read *The Wall Street Journal,* then lunch. After lunch, a little golf."

"I don't know where that tune is playing," I said. "If you remember, I told you both how tough the boat business is. It's a 24-hour-a-day job."

I'm sorry now that I wasn't more of a businessman, instead of a fatherly type man. When we turned over the business to the brothers, everything was going great: good sales, good cash flow. The first three months the rent money was there. The fourth month the brothers said, "Can we just pay the interest on the rent." A good business man would have said, "Hell, no. You made a deal, stick to it." But no, Father Fred said, "O.K." The interest only was paid twice. Total of five payments: three full payments and two interest-only payments. I just hated to see the Jersey Boat Company go down. It was like losing a friend. All those years of work and worry! Sure, we got a good price for the company, but money is not everything.

Several months passed and things went from bad to worse. The company just could not carry the burden the brothers put on it. John tried to keep the company going, but the family drag was too much to handle.

Etta and I decided to buy a motor yacht. Yes, a motor yacht, not a sport fishing boat. Etta had an idea. "Before we buy one, why don't we charter a motor yacht and see if we like cruising?"

"Great idea. Sounds like that is the way to go."

We went to a yacht broker in Fort Lauderdale and chartered a 61' Hatteras with a captain and a girl hand who cooked. We asked Etta's cousin Nancy Klumpp and her husband Ed if they'd like to come along. We chartered the boat for a weekend. We boarded the boat at Pier 66 in Fort Lauderdale, around 10:00 a.m. on Friday. We stowed our gear and headed north up the Intrarcoastal Waterway, or ICW.

The ICW was built during the Great Depression to allow travel from Texas to Key West, and then from Key West to Boston, in protected water 90 percent of the time.

We spent the rest of the day heading north. There were several bridges that had to open to let us pass. Around 5:00 we pulled into the Australian Pier in Palm Beach. Our deckhand cooked up a great dinner that night. We just hung out on the boat that evening.

Hey, this cruising is not too bad, I thought. The boat was very comfortable: living room, dining room, kitchen with a dinette, four bedrooms, three bathrooms, known as "heads" on a boat. In the old sailing ships, there were no bathrooms. If you had to do your duty, you'd would go to the bow of the ship, climb down on the netting under the bow spread, and relieve yourself. In other words, you went to the head of the ship.

We ended up in Fort Lauderdale late Sunday afternoon. It was really a great weekend. I thought selling boats was a difficult job. I never realized buying a boat was a lot more work than selling a boat. After looking at several boats, Etta and I bought a 53' Hatteras Motor Yacht. Etta and I flew back to New Jersey, while the Hatteras was getting ready for her long trip back to New Jersey.

Hey, this cruising is not too bad, I thought.

Aboard the *Mystic Lady* on a trip from Atlantic City, NJ to Bellhaven, NC, 1998

The *Mystic Lady*, our 53' Hatteras, in Jupiter, FL, 1991

Etta christening the *Henrietta*, in Oriental, NC, August 28, 1993

Etta came up with the name of our new steel boat company, Real Ships. "Don't buy a boat, buy a Real Ship."

The first Real Ship ever built, the 61' *Henrietta*, which carried a two-passenger, amphibious airplane as a tender

When we returned to New Jersey, Jersey Yachts was still running. Why I let the brothers continue without paying rent, I will never know.

On October 19, 1992, the brothers had run the company for approximately two years and eight months. I walked into an empty office. When I opened the factory door, there was Bill standing on a box with all the workers in front of him. The end of his talk was, "We're going into Chapter 11 and closing the company down."

As the workers left the room, I walked up to Bill and said, "Thanks, Bill, for letting me be the last one to know."

"Sorry about that. You better get a good lawyer," he said, then turned and walked away. Why did he say that, I wondered?

THEIR TRUE COLORS

I hadn't understood what brother Bill meant when he said after they laid off all the employees, "You better get a good lawyer."

The brothers owed Etta and me over a half million dollars in back rent, and I should get a good lawyer? I was right in one thing. The 10-year cycle bottomed out 18 months before the brothers closed their doors, or should I say, our doors. The killer came in the form of a 30 percent luxury tax.

What our great politicians did not understand was yes, some people had enough money to pay the sales tax and now the luxury tax, but they could not justify the taxes in their minds. So they did nothing.

One day we received a letter from some hot-shot lawyer in Philadelphia stating that the brothers wanted the money they paid for Jersey Yachts back. All the money, they said, not just some of the money. Can you believe that? They buy our company, run the company for two years and eight months into the ground, owe us half a million in back rent, and now they want all their money back.

I will say one thing, Bill was right when he said, "You better get a good lawyer." All the time I was helping these guys, they were just planning how to get their money back and walk away from the mess they created.

Their hot-shot lawyer from Philadelphia dug up a law written by the Department of Environmental Protection that said something like this: If you buy a company that has any type of contamination that you were not told about, the seller must give your money back. We never had any contamination or spills of any kind. So the way they got around this was that someone got our oldest employee to sign a sworn statement that "Before the brothers bought the company, the company had a massive acetone spill."

PARTNERSHIPS

I could not believe that a man who had worked with us for over 25 years would do such a thing, but there's that old saying, "Money talks."

Thank God the brothers and their slippery lawyer didn't realize that their scheme would never work. First, we'd never had an acetone spill. Second, the acetone was stored in a 250-gallon tank. If acetone did spill, 250 gallons would not be considered massive. Third, if we'd had an acetone spill, it would have been absorbed by the earth and dissipated, because acetone is a degradable chemical.

The next several months were hell. The brothers brought in the Department of Environmental Protection (DEP) and showed them this statement about our massive acetone spill. The DEP thought they had a great case. They decided to dig a hole in the factory floor and drill a deep well. They'd monitor it for 30 days, then send samples to their lab. Every time a well was drilled by the DEP, we had to drill a well next to their well so that our lab could make sure that their lab was on the up-and-up.

Then there were the trips to the bankruptcy court. The 36-year-old judge had no idea what was going on. At one hearing, the judge asked one brother, "Are you trying to sell this company?"

"Yes, Your Honor, we are trying very hard to sell the company," brother John said.

"Are you advertising that the company is for sale?" the judge asked.

"Yes, Your Honor. We have spent quite a bit of money advertising," John said.

Now, if you were the judge, wouldn't you say, "Show me some of the advertisements you have run and the paid receipts for those advertisements." Sure you would, but not this judge. He just said, "O.K."

By this time, Etta and I are getting sick of the whole thing. Every week the bills would come in, $2,000, $8,000, $12,000.

The brothers were now trying to get ownership of the factory. They just wanted their money back. One day, after weeks of paying the big bills we would get every week, Etta said, "Let's give them the factory buildings. I am getting tired of all the pressure week after week."

When I told our attorney, Wes Manuel, that we were considering giving the brothers the factory, he said, "No. Let's not give them anything. They can buy the factory for $50,800. That's a giveaway, but at least you will get something." "Let's do it," Etta said.

When we sold the boat company to the brothers, everything was written in stone. We found out later that stone can turn to clay very quickly.

My Friend Russ

RUSS THE PHOTOGRAPHER

I met Russ Homan in 1942. His father was a sheet-metal worker, or as it was called back then, a "tin banger." Mr. Homan could make anything out of sheet metal, and his brother, George Homan, could do wonders with wood. Between the two of them they could make almost anything.

Russ Homan Jr. hung out with us on Newton Creek in spring, summer, and fall. One winter, his father made him a beautiful 10' boat out of galvanized sheet metal. It was a work of art and made to last forever. After it was retired from Newton Creek, it was planted in Mr. Homan Sr.'s front yard as a flower box. It stayed there for years, dirt on the outside and dirt on the inside.

One day, a man came to the door and asked Mr. Homan if he could buy the flowerpot boat. The boat was at least 20 years old and the new owner restored it to its original condition. The old boat had a new life. They don't make galvanized sheet metal like that anymore.

Russ's father gave him a used "speed graphic" camera that cost $25 for his birthday. When you see an old-time movie and all the newspaper men are taking pictures with big boxy cameras, with a big light bulb sitting on top of the camera with a shiny round reflector behind the light bulb, that's a speed graphic camera. It had a lens that made the subject jump out of the picture. Russ could never find a camera that could take pictures as good as his old $25 speed graphic. In the early days, Russ took pictures for weddings, high school proms, and any other things he could find. Plus, he took pictures of all the Sea Mac boats.

Pictures that went into our brochures and advertising, still shots or running shots, were right up Russ's alley. As time passed, Russ picked up more and more marine accounts. In that time frame, Hank Bowman was the most respected boat test author in the country. To have your boat written up in a Hank Bowman test article, with a good test result—you were made. Even to be asked by Mr. Bowman for an interview was an honor.

One day, I was told a Mr. Hank Bowman was on the phone. "Hi, Mr. McCarthy. I'd like to do a test on your new 21' Sea Mac. My only stipulation is, when I test a boat, the builder doesn't see the results until the magazine is on the newsstand," he said.

Russ Homan with his Speed
Graphic camera, 1950

Russ as the process photographer on the Walt Whitman Bridge, 1950

With Hank Bowman (left), test author, on a Sea Mac, 1961

Hank Bowman testing the Sea Mac

Russ Homan on the *Miss Terri*, 1958

I thought for a minute and said, " I will think about it and let you know, Mr. Bowman. What is your telephone number?"

I thought about the test. What makes this guy so damn smart? He might like the way I do some things, but he might like things done his own way. Who said he's right? If he gave us a bad report, it could hurt us for a long time. What to do?

A few days passed and all I could talk about was Hank Bowman. Finally, I said, "The hell with it. We build a good boat; let this Bowman guy try to take our boat apart." I called Bowman and we set up a day for the boat test on the Delaware River, in Riverside, NJ.

On the morning of the test, we fueled the 21' Sea Mac and ran it for 30 minutes or so. I told Mr. Bowman I'd supply a photographer named Russ Homan, and a boat for the photo shoot. I also said I would not be present during the test.

Three of our men would be present to help in any way necessary. Russ and Hank Bowman hit it off right off the bat. From that day on, Russ traveled all over the country with Hank Bowman as his official photographer.

Russ did such great work that all the boat companies tested by Bowman wanted Russ as their company photographer. With over 15 boat companies under his belt, Russ ended up as the leading marine photographer in the country, all with his $25 speed graphic camera.

THE *MISS TERRI*

We'd been in the building in Riverside about three months and things were working out nicely. The 14' and 16' boats were in full production. We had about 20 to 25 boats under construction at all times.

The writing was on the wall. We needed a bigger boat in the line, but what size? We talked with our dealers and friends and came up with the 21'. We could handle 21' with the equipment we had and wouldn't have to buy any new tooling.

One model was open like our 14' and 16' boats. The second model had a hard top over the steering station. The first boat with the hard top went to Russ Homan. Russ came into the shop one day when his boat was being built. "Fred, I've been thinking about my boat. I'd like you to cut two large hatches in the hard top, big enough for a person to stand up while underway."

"Gee, Russ, I don't know. I can make the hatches. That's no problem.

But it might look a little funny with a boat running and your head sticking out over the hard top," I said.

"I don't care how it looks," Russ said.

"Hey, it's your boat. I'll do whatever you want."

I think that was the first boat with a cabin top hatch that you could stand up in while steering the boat. Now there are thousands of boats running around with heads sticking out of the cabin top.

Russ named his boat the *Miss Terri* after his first child, Terri Homan.

One day, Russ, his brother Bob and I were out fishing off of Atlantic City in the *Miss Terri*. We were about 20 miles offshore when the weather started to change. Back then, the only electronic device we had was a radio receiver. We could listen to other boats, but could not talk back to them. But we did have our trusty compass.

Soon, we were engulfed in a fog that had almost zero visibility. We started back to the Atlantic City State Marina. I took the distance and divided it by our speed, and estimated our running time to the beach. This could be off by 30 percent or more; it was mostly a guesstimate. We put Russ's brother Bob out on the bow with a mouth-blown foghorn and told him to blow the foghorn every three minutes. Russ turned on his radio.

We could hear all the boats with radios talking about the heavy fog. We heard one captain say, "Hi, Bill. How are you doing?"

"O.K., I guess."

"Bill, do you have any idea where you are?" The captain asked.

Bill said, "I know exactly where I am, Joe. I'm at 27th Street in Ocean City."

"Bill, how the hell do you know that?"

"I ran up on the beach and the lifeguard told me," Bill wisecracked.

When I felt we were getting near the beach, I had Russ stop and shut the engines down. We listened for the surf, but heard nothing. After about 10 listening stops, we finally heard people playing in the small surf. It had to be Atlantic City.

We headed north at a very slow pace just outside the small surf. Without any warning, this gigantic object appeared a few feet ahead of us. Russ slammed the engine in reverse and our boat stopped. My heart was pounding like a drum. We inched back to see what this huge object was that had scared us so much. When we were a few feet away from the thing, Bob yelled out, "It's the Steel Pier." Now we knew where we were. We went around the end of the Steel Pier and worked our way up the coast to the Atlantic City Inlet. Inside the inlet there was no fog.

Russ kept the *Miss Terri* for many years. On a Sunday, he would go off shore to the Atlantic City Bell Buoy by himself. He would shut down the engine and just drift and listen to the Bell Buoy. This was Russ's church.

OUR FIRST FISHING TOURNAMENT

The year was 1959. We thought that entering the Atlantic City Tuna Tournament would be a good way of getting some exposure. Mercury Marine motor company had a branch one mile down the street from our shop. George Pidcock was the branch manager. I met with him one afternoon and told him about the Atlantic City Tuna Tournament, and I asked if Mercury Marine would work with us in some way. George said he'd talk to his boss and see if there was any interest. To my surprise, the Mercury Marine motor company thought this was a great way to promote their engines. We were going to use two boats: Russ Homan's *Miss Terri* and our company boat. Both boats were the same size, 20 feet down the center line. The only difference was the *Miss Terri* had a hard top, and the company boat had a canvas top. The idea of the two boats was very simple. If one broke down, the other would tow the sick boat home.

The founder of Mercury Marine was Carl Kiekhaefer. When Kiekhaefer heard about our idea of two small boats powered by outboard motors, fishing against big inboard powered boats, he went crazy. He thought this was the greatest thing he ever heard of and went all out. The first thing he did was to put two new Mercury engines on each boat. The engines were checked and rechecked. They had to be flawless. Next he put another Mercury engine on the boat with enough spare parts to rebuild all the engines. Then he put a P.R. man at the marina to send out news reports to the press. Hamberger was his name. Some years later, Hamberger ended up as president of the largest jet ski company in the United States.

On the Sea Mac boat were four people: the Mercury engineer, our advertising agent, a boating magazine reporter and myself. On the *Miss Terri* was the boat's owner, Russ Homan; his younger brother, Bob Homan; and his cousin, George Homan. Russ was our company photographer, and his brother, Bob, was learning the art under Russ, who later also taught his son, Mark.

The week of the Atlantic City Tuna Tournament finally came around. We trailered the Sea Mac boat to Brigantine, NJ and the local boatyard put it in the water. The run from the boatyard to the Atlantic City State Marina was only a few miles. The marina sat out in the middle of nowhere. The hotels and casinos were many years away.

The *Miss Terri* was berthed at the Atlantic City State Marina year-round, winter and summer. I guess we looked like a rag-tag outfit. Two little 20' outboard boats, with wooden swivel captain chairs from an old ferry boat. The only navigation equipment was a compass and a watch. Can you see the boat people today going 65 nautical miles off shore, fishing for six hours and going 65 nautical miles back to the marina with no ship-to-shore radio, no depth finder, no GPS, no bunks, no air conditioning, no head, no flying bridge?

RCA came out with a new Citizen's Band radio and a radio direction finder. RCA was one of Russ Homan's accounts. When they heard about the Atlantic City Tuna Tournament and that Russ was a contender, they really got interested. They asked if we'd use their equipment. Russ asked me if we should take the offer. "Why not Russ! We can use all the press we can get. Ask them if they'll put the story in some of their publications."

Russ picked up the two Citizens Band radios and the two radio direction finders, and brought them to our shop. This equipment sat on a flat surface and there was no installation involved, just turn them on, and they were ready to work.

We checked into the little motel across the street from the marina, and stowed our gear. Back then, the tournaments were fair and the prizes were small, maybe a little television set, a fishing rod, things like that.

The boats had to stay inside a set of boundaries. This gave the slower boats an even chance. A weather boat would go offshore and check the sea conditions. If the weather was too bad, the weather boat would call in, "No fishing today. No fishing today."

Our little boats would not have a chance in hell to compete in today's fishing tournaments. First, the costs are out of sight. Second, there are no boundary lines. That means the fast boats can run off shore 100 miles out and still be back to the dock on time. Third, the big boats can handle bigger seas. Fourth, the prize can run in the millions. What it boils down to is that the money people have a big advantage over the little guys.

Well, back to the good old days. The first day of the Atlantic City Tuna Tournament was a day to remember. At first, no one bothered to look at the two little outboard boats tied up in the marina. But when we pulled up our tournament flags with our tournament number (#50) flying off one of our outriggers, some heads turned. They just could not believe these two little boats were for real.

PARTNERSHIPS

With Bob Homan (right) at The Atlantic City Tuna Tournament, 1959

Tournament flag number 50

The weather couldn't have been better. The wind was blowing 10 to 15 knots, and the sea ran around three to four feet. The three days of fishing were very slow, and there were few tuna caught. Out of all the boats, only six boats caught tuna, and by good luck we were one of them. It was not much of a tuna fish, but it was a tuna!

The last day of the tournament when we pulled into the weighing dock, flying our tuna flag, there were a lot of hard feelings. The next meeting of the Atlantic City Tuna Club, several members got up and said, "We want to pass a rule that to enter the Tuna Club Tournament, a boat must be over 30 feet and powered by inboard engines."

The dock master stood up and said, "You people are just poor sports. These two boats came in, fished the tournament, ending up in second place. They never gave me a minute's trouble. Which I can't say about some of you people! They came, they fished, they left, like real sportsmen."

We received really great press. This one fishing tournament put Sea Mac on the map; we were now on our way. The following year, the Atlantic City Tuna Tournament was one of the largest in the country. You could hear the boats going out of the inlet for miles. It was like a traffic jam.

This tournament started to drop off after a couple of years. There were fewer boats every year. One day, in early spring, the mayor of Atlantic City came to our house, and asked if we'd consider coming back to his tuna tournament. "I'm very sorry, Mr. Mayor," I said. "We were barred from this tournament a few years ago by the Tuna Club, and I do not want to go where I'm not wanted."

The truth of the matter is this: We went into their tournament once. We had great weather, no engine or boat problems, caught fish and had great press. If we went back, we might destroy all that we'd gained in the first tournament. You know that old saying: "Quit while you're ahead." Those tuna club members who stood up and said, "30 feet and no outboards" couldn't have done more for us. Thanks, you great sportsmen!

A PHOTO TRIP

Over the years, Russ Homan and I did many photo sessions together in places like Puerto Rico, Ecuador, and Mexico. In 1972, when our first Jersey Yacht arrived in Puerto Rico and was made ready by our new dealer, Russ and I flew there for a photo shoot. The dealer furnished us with a 60' Andy Mortenson with a crew of two men.

The boat had the highest tuna tower I had ever seen. Heights never bothered Russ, but they bothered me.

When the Walt Whitman Bridge was built, Russ was given the job of progress photographer. This meant he'd climb to the top of the towers on the cables. The only thing under the cables was air.

Russ was on top of the tower on the Pennsylvania side of the river. A cargo ship was going under the bridge. The roadway was not built at this time. The picture Russ shot showed the cargo ship passing under the two cables. It was a great picture and showed what it felt like to be standing on top of the tower with no bridge under you.

Russ also photographed some radio towers that were several hundred feet high. Better him than me.

As we headed out of the inlet and into the ocean, the 31' Jersey passed by the old Fort in San Juan, Russ and I were up in the tuna tower. The sea was getting pretty nasty as we entered the ocean. Finally, I said to Russ, "I've had enough of this, I'm getting off this roller coaster."

To get down from the tuna tower, you had to lie down on your stomach and let your feet dangle in mid-air until you found the ladder. When your feet were placed firmly on the ladder rung, you would stand up and proceed down the ladder. I lay down on the flying bridge floor, and then slid back until my feet were dangling looking for the ladder. I could not find the ladder step. "Russ," I yelled.

Still shooting pictures, Russ said, "What?"

"I can't find the ladder rung." I was still hanging over the edge and trying not to show the fear in my voice.

"I guess not," Russ said.

"What do you mean by that?" I asked.

"You're going off the front of the tower. The ladder is in the back of the tower, not the front," he said.

That shows you I'm not at home when I'm more than three feet off the ground. But when I'm flying our airplane, I don't get the feeling of height.

That night after dinner Russ said, "I'm going for a walk. You want to come along?"

"No, Russ, I'm beat. You go yourself," I said.

About 10:30 p.m. I woke up and Russ was not back yet. Now, I was getting a little concerned. I hoped he hadn't gone into a bad neighborhood and gotten robbed! Half an hour later, Russ walked into our hotel room.

"Where have you been, Russ? I was getting worried about you."

"You won't believe what I just did," he said. "About four blocks down the street from the hotel, I saw an open-air hot dog stand. The smell of the hot dogs cooking made me hungry. So I sat down on the nearest stool. The cook walked over and said in a broken English, 'What can I get you?' 'One hot dog,' I said. He took one hot dog off the grill, put it in a bun and put it on a paper plate, and came over to where I was sitting."

"What's so great about eating a hot dog?" I asked.

"Across the street a teenage dance was going on in the school gym. The music was so loud, I felt like I was eating my hot dog inside the gym. About four stools down from where I was sitting was a teenage kid watching me eat my hot dog. He wouldn't take his eyes off of me. About halfway through my hot dog, I turned and said to the kid, 'Would you like a hot dog?' His eyes lit up and with a big smile he said, 'Si, senor.' I said to the waiter-cook, 'Give my friend here a hot dog.' The kid ate the hot dog like he was starving."

"So, you bought a kid a hot dog. What's so great about that?" I asked.

"In a matter of minutes, the little hot dog stand is bulging with kids from the dance, and I'm buying them all hot dogs," he said.

"Why did you do that?" I asked.

"I don't know. I guess they looked poor and I didn't think they had any money. The look on their faces was worth every penny. I really loved every minute of it. The smiles and the laughing, it was just great."

That's my Russ, and that is just what kind of a person he is.

THE HADDONFIELD FISHING CLUB

The Haddonfield Fishing Club was founded by Charley Durray in the early 1970s. Every year the club went on a fishing trip. The club was limited to 50 members but only 30 usually went on each trip because the type of places that the club visited could usually only handle 30 people.

Russ Homan and I were members. Our first trip was in 1972. We were going to fish for striped marlin in the Pacific Ocean, off of Salinas, Ecuador. We flew from Philadelphia, PA to Guayaquil, Ecuador, stopping in Mexico City for fuel. From Guayaquil, we traveled in an old bus with no air conditioning, 80 miles across a desert to Salinas, Ecuador. We arrived in Salinas before noon and some of us die-hards went fishing that afternoon.

Salinas was like the end of the world. We were told to stay in groups and not to wander off alone. The government outlawed headhunting, but not everyone obeyed the law. The average wage, back in those days, was only a few dollars a year. When people found out they could get $100 a head, and $1,000 for a white man's head, no white person was safe. Gulf Oil had a plant five miles down the road from us. All the white workers lived in a compound with 15-foot walls around it.

Russ and I spent a day taking photos of the place. We entered a native village. No one was around. The place looked empty. The first person we saw was an old woman with something on her head. She had only two or three teeth, and wrinkles all over her body. Russ said, "I've got to get a photo of that woman; she would make a great picture."

"I don't know, Russ. You may get someone upset. Is it worth it to take the chance?"

"I will do it so fast, no one will see me do it."

No sooner had Russ taken the first shot than a big old man came around the corner of one of the huts. If looks could kill, I think we would be dead. "Think fast," I said to Russ.

Russ walked over to the chief. He placed the camera around the chief's neck and motioned for him to take Russ's picture. The chief was grinning from ear to ear. People started coming out of their huts, and before you know it we were in the middle of a big party—dancing, laughing, and acting like it was the fourth of July. That's how our photo shoot ended.

When the Gulf Oil people found out there were 30 or so Americans five miles down the road, they invited us over to their compound for a cocktail party. They picked us up at 5:00.

Having been in the boat business for many years, I've been to many cocktail parties at boat-show time and this cocktail party, in a compound in the middle of nowhere, was by far the very best.

I said to our group, "Let's leave the party before any of our people get out of hand." Before we left the compound, I asked our host, "Is it true what we hear about headhunters?"

"It sure is," he said.

We returned to our hotel at about 9:30. The people from the compound were heartbroken that we were leaving so early. They enjoyed our company so much, that they showed up at our hotel and partied most of the night.

For some reason, I left for home two days before anyone else. I took the old open-air bus 80 miles across the desert to Guayaquil. From Guayaquil, I got a flight to Panama. When I entered the Panama airport terminal, all I could see were soldiers carrying automatic guns. They kept looking at me in a way that made me very uncomfortable. They were not smiling!

I finally got a direct flight to Miami. I'd been wearing a khaki jungle jacket and pants the whole trip. When I was walking through the terminal in Philadelphia, a big young black man walked up to me and said, "Man, you look really cool. Where did you get that outfit?"

After three days without a shower, I did not feel very cool.

On the trip I caught three large striped marlins and won the big trophy. This trophy was on display in Compton's Log Cabin Restaurant in Haddon Township. When the restaurant burned down, there went my big trophy.

HADDONFIELD FISHING CLUB, CABO SAN LUCAS

Our fishing club decided to go to Cabo San Lucas, at the very bottom of the Baja Peninsula in Mexico. The biggest problem was getting there. The nearest airline flight was to La Paz, Mexico and Cabo San Lucas was about 100 miles south. The only road was not paved; it was just two ruts in the sand.

We flew out of Philadelphia and landed in La Paz's tiny airport. There were some charter planes, an old DC-3 and an old Twin Beechcraft. The DC-3 had 24 seats and the Twin Beech could carry eight, including the pilot. After a walk around, I told the pilot of the Twin Beech that I wanted the right seat, the co-pilot's seat. After I showed him my multi-engine license, he gave me a big smile.

When we arrived in Cabo, I asked the pilot, "Where's the airport?" He tipped the left wing down, and pointed down to what looked like a sand road. I gave him a little smile and looked away. All I could think was that I was glad that this is not my airplane. The pilot did a nice job getting us on the ground, or should I say the sand?

There were no docks or marinas in Cabo. The small fishing boats would pick us up in a cove. You took off your shoes and waded out to the boats. The first three days the fishing was stinko. On the fourth day, Russ and I decided to go on a photo trip, which we realized would be difficult. The boats returned to the cove around 4:00. By that time the hotel bar was about to open and soon everyone would be drinking pina coladas and margaritas. A 10- or 12-piece mariachi band, dressed in black-and-white fancy clothes with big black-and-white hats played until dinnertime. Dinner was served in a beautiful dining room at 7:30. That was the problem. Four-thirty to 7:30 was just too long for cocktails. By the time dinner was served, half the crew was ready for bed. There was a large punch bowl in the dining room, just in case you did not get enough margaritas. The owners of the hotel sat off in a corner, four men and four women, talking quietly. The rumor was that they were big-time mafia people.

On the fifth night, during dinner, one of our guys threw three cherry bombs into the punch bowl. With the stone walls, the sound was deafening. It sounded like mortar shells. When we looked over in the corner, all six people in the owner's party were under their tables.

The next day Russ and I went on our photo trip. We went down to the beach and took pictures of a big hole with the sea flowing through it. I think over the years, I must have carried Russ's camera case over a thousand miles, and it never got any lighter. We got so involved taking pictures that we didn't notice the incoming tide. By this time, the tide had shut off our way back. After a little panic, we decided to climb over the 200-foot rock wall that was holding us trapped with the incoming tide.

"I don't know, Russ. That wall of rocks looks awful high to me," I said.

"We don't have a choice, Fred. It's climb or drown. I think we should take the climb, don't you?"

"O.K." "You go first."

"Me, go first? You're the high-wire guy. You go first," I said.

"If you're ahead of me and need help, I'll be there to help you," Russ said.

"Yeah, when I stick my hand in one of those holes and some big rattler snake clamps down on my hand, you hit the snake with a rock," I told Russ.

"Ah, come on. We can make it."

We started the climb. It was very hot and very steep. About two hours later, we were about 20 feet from the top. I stopped climbing and said to Russ, "This is it, I can't go another foot."

We stopped climbing and held onto the rocks and rested. The rest did the trick. When we finally reached the top, sat down, and got our breath, Russ took my picture.

When we got home and Etta saw the picture of me sitting on the rock, she said, "That trip was really good for you, Fred. Look how rested you look in this picture."

I was completely exhausted. Russ and I never caught a single fish.

At Cabo San Lucas, 1971

With Russ Homan (to my left), and my winning marlin catch, in Solis, Ecuador, 1972

MARK HOMAN

Mark Homan was born in September 1960, the son of my good friend, Russ and his wife, Marie. Mark followed his dad in the photography industry. After Mark learned the nuts and bolts of the industry from his dad, he moved to New York City to learn the art of photography. He rented a room and bought a bicycle to get around the city.

Money was nil and Mark had it tough. He finally got a job with a good, or should I say, a well-known studio. Mark saved his money and bought great photography equipment. It wasn't long before the studio borrowed Mark's equipment to do their photo shoots.

After a few years, Mark got homesick. He missed his family and friends and moved back to South Jersey. After a few years, he got his own studio with the latest equipment and his clientele grew.

Mark had a client who was a book publisher and he took authors' photos. Some of the authors went like this: Chuck Yeager, the first man to break the sound barrier; Lee Iacocca, the auto man; President Carter; the Watsons, father and son of IBM; and on and on.

While Lee Iacocca was getting his portrait taken for one of his books, he got upset. So did Mark. The people running the show would not listen to anything he said. Mark realized that he was about to lose the $8,000 fee. He decided to just let them do what they wanted.

After the last picture was taken, he took another camera and walked toward the exit door. He waited for Iacocca to leave his office. When Iacocca started walking down the hall, Mark was ready. When Iacocca raised his arm, Mark took a couple of quick shots. One of those shots ended up on a cover of Lee Iacocca's book. What the hotshots could not do in over an hour, Mark did in 30 seconds. What a great talent!

Mark really loved life. He liked riding his motorcycle, mountain climbing, boating, and just about everything you could think of. Mark asked me to teach him how to fly an airplane.

"I don't have an instructor's license and I'm not a good teacher. Go to some airport that has a good flight school," I told Mark. "Another thing, if you go to a flight school, fly as much as you can. If you only fly once a week, you'll never learn how to fly an airplane.

Mark took my advice. He started flying lessons and did well. He made two long solo flights. He had two friends also named Mark who were pilots from SmithKline Beecham. They flew an old Cessna 310, a twin engine, low-wing airplane, with retractable landing gear. To enter the aircraft, you had to climb up on the wing and slide into the four-seat cockpit. The 310 was replaced in 1982 by the Cessna 303, which held six people, and was cabin class, which meant you entered the cabin by a door in the back end of the aircraft and walked up to the cockpit, as you would do on a commercial airliner. Jersey Yachts had a 1982 Cessna 303 as a company plane. It was well equipped and with her fuel-injected, turbo-charged engines, the 303 could climb to 25,000 feet. With autopilot, all you had to do was punch in the numbers and the 303 would fly safely.

On the afternoon of September 2, 1994, Mark One called Mark Two and asked him if he'd take his place that night on a trip to Pittsburgh with eight or nine stops on the way. Mark Two agreed and called Mark Homan looking for someone to keep him company. He thought it was a great opportunity, night flying, multi-engine aircraft, flying IFR (Instrument Flight Rules). The flight was just routine. Fly to such and such airport, pick up specimens, and take off to next airport.

Two days before Labor Day in September 1994, the two Marks boarded the old Cessna 310 for their pick-up samples flight. Mark Two settled in the left seat (pilot's side), and Mark Homan settled in the right seat (co-pilot's side), and they were ready to go. The trip had eight stops in Pennsylvania. Mark slipped into the right seat. In two weeks he'd have his private pilot's ticket and he'd be sitting in the left seat.

Things went well, just routine pick-up and go. Just before the eighth stop, the old Cessna broke up in midair and came down in pieces. The only thing they know for sure is one wing came off. The main body of the airplane ended in a small body of water upside down, an hour west of Harrisburg, PA. For the next few days, the local townspeople did all they could to help the Homan family with their terrible loss.

What really happened? No one knows for sure.

From laboratory tests:

1. There were no drugs found on the 310.
2. The pilot had smoked marijuana within the last one and a half hours.
3. Mark Homan tested clean (this was found in two different tests, by two different laboratories).

Mark Two's boss said at Mark Homan's funeral that he flew with Mark Two once, but would never fly with him again. On his one and only flight, Mark Two put the airplane in a nose-dive, straight down. His boss was terrified. This brings up the question. Did Mark Two put the old 310 into a spin that night to show Mark Homan how great a pilot he was? If his boss had been that frightened, why did he keep Mark Two on the payroll? Good question! Just think if the boss fired Mark Two the night he put the plane into a dive, maybe both men would be alive today.

More Planes

PIPER APACHE

My friend Paul Canton had a Ford dealership in Riverside, NJ. He owned a Beechcraft Bonanza. The Bonanza was a four-place, low-wing plane with a V-shaped vertical tail. It was much faster than the Navion, but not as forgiving. If you made a dumb maneuver or pulled a no-no, the Navion would overlook it.

We both had our planes based at the Moorestown Airport. Paul, by the way, was a flight instructor in WW2. He was based in Florida and flew B-24s or B-17s. One day in a conversation, Paul said, "Fred, I've got an idea. Why don't you sell the Navion and I'll sell my Bonanza and we'll buy a twin-engine plane?"

"I don't know Paul. I don't have a multi-engine rating."

"That won't be any trouble for you," replied Paul.

"Let me think about it for a while," I said.

"In the meantime, I'll look around for something," Paul said,

"How are we going to sell our planes, Paul?" I asked.

The next time I saw Paul he told me about a deal with the Flying W Ranch. The Flying W had a 3,400-foot runway; half was in Lumberton, NJ and the other half was in Medford, NJ. The "W," as it was called, had a 1962 Piper Apache that we could work some kind of a deal with. Before I knew it, I was half-owner of a twin-engine Piper Apache.

The plane was painted red with white trim and white wings. The Apache was powered by two 150 horsepower engines and carried four people. After the deal was made, I took the Navion on my last flight from Moorestown Airport to the Flying W (a total of eight miles) and gave the papers to the "W."

Later on down the road, a fellow I went to high school with bought the Navion. He was married and had a daughter who was deaf. I don't know if she was born that way or it happened later on. The new owner of the Navion took his daughter up for her first plane ride. When they landed, his daughter said, "Daddy, I can hear!" Can you believe that?

Well, that was over 50 years ago and the Navion is still sitting on the field, falling apart. If you call the owner and ask him if you can buy the airplane, he gets very nasty and his answer is "no, not now, or ever."

I found a good instructor and started working on my multi-engine rating. The hardest thing about the Apache was learning to fly on one engine. Every foot of altitude you lost was gone forever. You didn't have the power to get it back.

On one of my lessons, I took Henry and Daryl, my two nephews, along for a ride. The instructor shut down the right engine and said, "You just lost your right engine." The Apache did not have counter-rotating propellers. They both turned in the same direction. When an engine was dead and the propeller was windmilling, it was like cutting a piece of plywood in a circle with the same diameter as the propeller and putting the plywood in front of the engine. The idea was to feather the dead engine ASAP. When the engine was feathered, the leading edge of the propeller was facing into the wind. This cut down most of the drag and the propeller stopped windmilling.

A few seconds later, my nephew Daryl said, "Uncle Fred! Uncle Fred! Uncle Fred! Look quick. The propeller is standing straight up. It's not turning!"

The instructor said, "I think your Uncle Fred broke the engine. That's why it's not turning."

Daryl just turned 50 years old. Back then he could stand behind the pilot's seat.

Today you're not allowed to shut the engine down. Instead you throttle the engine to about 1,300 rpm and you pretend the engine is not running. But you never know if you can handle a situation until it happens for real. Then it could be too late.

After a bit, the instructor said I was ready to take a flight test for my multi-engine rating. I flew the Apache to North Philadelphia Airport. I had a 1:30 appointment. It turned out the guy who was going to give me the check ride was also named McCarthy. The first thing he said was, "Where is your 10-hour instrument certificate?"

"I didn't know that was necessary for a multi-engine certificate."

"Sure it is," was his answer. That was a real kick in the head.

I took the 10 hours of instrument instruction and later found out that this McCarthy guy was all wet. You didn't need 10 hours of instrument instruction. By the time I found out it wasn't necessary, I'd taken the full 10 hours. It was pretty difficult, because back in those days, you didn't have all the goodies that make instrument flying a lot easier.

The last plane Etta and I had was a Cessna 303 Crusader. The autopilot would take you down the glide slope, right down to the runway. There were only two things it would do: pull back the power and make the flair out onto the runway.

I made another appointment for the flight test to finally get the multi-engine rating. I drove down to Moorestown Airport, where we kept the Apache, and got her ready for my test ride.

Before I tell you what happened, let me go back and tell you what happened during the winter of that year. Etta's sister lived out on Long Island, about 70 miles east of New York City. The way Etta and I flew the Navion to the nearest airport was quite simple. Take off from the Moorestown Airport, climb to 1,200 feet, head for New York. When we saw the bay, we'd drop down to 300 feet, fly across the bay and when we reached the west end of Long Island, we'd make a right turn and fly along the beach, passing Fire Island and on to the airport.

This route took us out of all the Idlewild's air traffic. (Now called Kennedy Airport) The owner and operator of the "W" was the kind of guy who thought that whatever he did was O.K., but he'd blow the whistle on anyone else. I was getting the Apache ready for a trip to Long Island to stay with Etta's sister for the weekend. Mr. "W" walked up to me and said, "Do you have your multi-engine ticket?"

"Mr. 'W,' I don't think that's any of your business,"

"If you take your wife with you, I'll turn you in," he said. "You bastard."

"Take an instructor with you. He can fly back by himself."

"How much?" I asked. "Twenty dollars an hour," was his answer. "Give me your best price for the trip."

We made the deal. The instructor, named Milo, was from Norway. We all climbed into the Apache. Etta got into the back. Milo and I were up front. He was in the right seat, I was in the left. We took off. When we reached 300 feet, I leveled off.

"Why are you staying at 300 feet?" asked Milo.

"Milo, this time of the year the weather on Long Island is too unpredictable. It can change in only minutes. I know if I stay under the clouds, I'm safe."

"You're flying a big plane now and it should be flown like a big plane. Climb to 5,000 feet."

"But, Milo... ."

"Climb to 5,000 feet."

I leveled off at 5,000 feet, heading east. The clouds were starting to form under us.

"When we get to the airport, how are we going to go down through the clouds?" I asked Milo.

"Do a 180 and we'll find a hole and let down through the hole."

We headed west. After a time, Milo says, "There's a hole over there. We'll go down through that hole."

"Milo, do you have any idea where we are?" No answer.

"Milo, I'll tell you where we are. We're right over Idlewild Airport. That's where we are. That's it! We're going home."

Milo grabbed the yokes and started descending through the hole in the clouds.

"Milo, you're going to kill us, you big show-off. You just can't drop out of the sky over a big airport like Idlewild."

Sure enough we broke out almost on top of Idlewild Airport. At 600 feet, Milo turned to an easterly heading, and as we went east it started to rain. Within minutes the rain had turned to sleet.

"Milo, turn this damn airplane around, now!"

"We'll make it," he said.

We started to take on ice. The Apache wasn't equipped for what's called "known-ice." The windshield was covered with so much ice, we couldn't see. Finally Milo spotted the runway and landed the plane.

While taxiing to the airport office, I said to Milo, "Stay here for the night and go back in the morning."

Milo said, "No, I'm going back as soon as possible."

"Milo, the plane is insured. If you want to break your ass, go ahead."

Etta and I got out of the Apache and walked to the office. The weather was really stinko. If the Apache were fully equipped for "known-ice" conditions, it would still be very foolish to fly in this kind of weather. We heard the Apache's engines come to life. We turned around and there went Milo down the runway. Is this the last time I'll ever see my airplane, I wondered.

Etta and I entered the office. The airport manager walked over to us, "Your sister was here to pick you up, but I sent her back home. I told her no one would be flying in this kind of weather, other than a damn fool."

"It's a long story," I said, "and I don't want to talk about it."

We called Etta's sister, and one hour later she picked us up.

We finally got to Cliff and Gloria's house. My brother-in-law was a line chief at the Suffolk County Air Force Base. After we settled in, I gave both boys a toy that Etta had bought. I forget what Henry's was but Daryl's was a small electric speedboat. I happened to walk into the living room while Daryl was eating a greasy piece of chicken.

PARTNERSHIPS

"Daryl, get in the kitchen with that greasy chicken," I said. His hands were full of grease.

Daryl has a deaf ear.

"Daryl, get in the kitchen or I'll tell your mother."

No response.

"Gloria, Daryl's eating greasy chicken with greasy hands in your living room."

Enter Gloria. "Daryl, get in the kitchen with that greasy chicken now and wash your hands!"

On Sunday morning, Daryl came up to me and said, "Here's your boat. I don't want it."

"O.K., Daryl. I'll take it back." I took the boat and put it in our overnight bag.

After lunch, we all got in the car and headed for the airport. Fifteen minutes before we reached the airport, Darryl called from the backseat. "Uncle Fred, I really love you. Honest, I do."

Boy, what a con job to get that boat back. "I know you do, Daryl."

A long silence.... "I really love you, Uncle Fred."

I let him sweat it a little more.

"Do you want your boat back Daryl?"

"Sure I do!"

I had the boat with me in the front seat and said, "Here it is, Daryl. Take good care of it."

We arrived at the airport. Paul was going to pick us up with the Apache. An hour passed and no Apache. A little later, a Piper Comanche landed and taxied up to the airport's office (as you can see, Piper aircraft were named after Indian Tribes). Who steps out of the Comanche? Paul.

"Where is our Apache?"

"Just after take-off from the "W" I lost an engine. It's in the shop, so I rented this Comanche."

"What's wrong with the engine?"

"Don't know. It started to lose power and when I leaned the fuel mixture, it picked up power. The power held until we landed. Fred, you might as well fly the Comanche. You're paying for it."

Back at the "W," we went into the office and Mr. "W" handed me a bill for the Comanche rental that was really out of line.

"Look, " I said. "You make me take a daredevil flight instructor. Then the airplane you just sold us breaks down. And now you want a big profit on this rental. No way!"

After 30 minutes of bickering, we finally made an adjustment.

The problem with the Apache's engine was very simple. A mechanic had left a tieback used to hold back wires while he worked on the engine. Somehow it had been sucked into the carburetor. This choked the engine and it was getting too much fuel, more than it could handle.

Well, back to where we'd been. I made another appointment to take the multi-engine test. The day I returned to the airport, I thought I'd do a little more practicing. At 11:30 Paul drove up with some VIP from Ford Motor Company. He introduced me and said, "I'm taking Mr. VIP to the 'W' for lunch. Want to come along?"

"I'm taking my multi at two o'clock. But, yeah, I've got time to go with you. Tell your friend to sit up front. I'll sit in the back. I've never been in the back." Flying six miles for lunch is called a "$50 lunch."

On our final approach to the "W," I realized that sitting in the backseat, you had no feeling of speed. In fact, it felt like the plane was getting ready to stall. And then it STALLED! We were 10 feet off the ground and in a stall. We hit the ground just before the blacktop runway, with a big jolt. The plane really shuttered, but we were O.K. We rolled down the runway and parked.

After a nice lunch, we climbed back into the plane. I was still in the backseat looking out the window. I tapped Paul on the shoulder. "I think you better pull over and check the left wing." Paul looked over his shoulder, "Looks O.K. to me." I told Paul to pull over again.

He pulled off the runway, stopped and shut down the engines.

We got out of the plane and checked the left wing. The skin over the wheel was wrinkled. I got down on the grass and looked up into the wheel well, the place where the wheel goes in the up position.

I couldn't believe what I saw. The main wing spare was cracked in half. The wing spare is like the backbone of the wing. Paul taxied over to a parking space. We tied the plane down.

There it sat for months. I didn't get my multi-engine rating and stopped flying for a long time—but flying is like riding a bike. You never forget.

PAUL PRINCE, CAMDEN AIRPORT FLYING SCHOOL

In the late 1960s, Etta and I lived in Cinnaminson, NJ. A few years earlier, Etta and I had been fishing in Puerto Rico and I caught a blue marlin that set the record for Puerto Rico. The record stood for over 20 years.

We had friends down the street, Jim and Barbara Reilly. Jim had a brother-in-law who loved fishing. Jim asked me, "Could I bring my brother-in-law over to see the blue marlin hanging on your rec room wall?"

"Sure, Jim, any old time."

His brother-in-law, Paul Prince, was a captain for United Airlines. One night, around 11:00, the doorbell rang. When I opened the front door, there were Jim and Paul standing on the front porch. Paul looked at me at said, "Freddy, how the hell are you?" Jim asked his brother-in-law, "How do you know Fred?"

"We went to flying school together," he said.

In the house, I showed them the mounted fish in the rec room. I made some drinks and Paul said, "I know what happened to the people in our flying class, all seven of them."

"I can't even remember their names," I said. "Did you ever see any of those beautiful airplane paintings? The details are fantastic."

"Well, _____ was one of our classmates!" Paul said.

"His work is great," I said.

"Do you remember when Mike Todd, the husband of Elizabeth Taylor and the producer of *Around the World in Eighty Days* was killed in a plane crash?"

"Sure I do," I said.

"The pilot of that plane was _____. You remember him, don't you?"

"Not really," was my answer.

The next morning, Jim went to work in his machine shop and Paul Prince went back to Washington, D.C., and United Airlines. Maybe someday I'll be able to fill in the names.

THE 303

Etta and I bought our Cessna Crusader in 1982 from an airplane broker in Maryland. Etta and I had discussed the 303 at great lengths. Several years ago, we'd decided not to take out any loans. If we did not have the money to buy something, we did not buy it.

I called the airplane broker and said, "If the Cessna 303 is what you say it is, we would like to see it. How do we see the plane?"

"I had a ferry pilot fly it here two weeks ago from Arizona. Come down and take a look. I know you'll like what you see," he said.

"We will be there this Saturday, around 11 o'clock," I said.

"See you then."

On Saturday, Etta and I took off for Georgetown. We found the airport and the only large hangar. A man was standing outside the hangar door. He was the broker we'd come to see. We shook hands and said our hellos, then he showed us inside the hangar. All the lights were on. In the middle of the floor sat the only airplane in the hangar. What a beautiful sight. All the hangar lights were reflecting off the highly polished plane. The plane looked like it just rolled off the factory floor.

The broker opened the rear-entrance door. "Climb aboard."

Inside, on each side of the passenger compartment were two seats, facing one another, with a folding table between each. Forward of the four seats, was the cockpit. I walked up the aisle and sat down in the left seat, the pilot's seat. Everything was first class: auto pilot, LORAN, for long-range navigation, two radios. This baby was made for us. The only disappointment was minor. All the switches were on the pilot's left side. All 20 of them had nameplates to tell the pilot what they were for. There were two missing switches, but they had the name plates "No smoking" and "Fasten your seat belts."

We looked at the log books and everything looked O.K. A couple more walk-arounds, and I was sold. Etta gave the broker a deposit and said the balance would be paid in full when the plane was delivered.

The 303 was delivered the following week. The delivery pilot was Stanley Johnson's stepson, a retired navy pilot. I still did not have my multi-engine license, so I had my friend Paul Canton get checked out on the 303. Then, at a later date, Paul could check me out.

This all happened at the Flying W Ranch in Lumberton. Nobody could get over what a wonderful flying machine we'd bought. I gave Stanley's stepson a bank check for $150,000. The 303 was now ours, and paid in full, no loans.

A plane came and picked up Stanley's stepson and we spent the rest of the afternoon checking out the 303. I never thought we'd own a one-year old airplane equipped like this one

GENE GIEHL

I first met Gene Giehl when he was in his mid-30s. He was working for Paul Canton in his Ford Motor dealership in Riverside, NJ. Gene was a good-looking man with lots of charm, a real catch. He was married to a lucky girl from French Canada. Monica spoke French frequently, but she had no French accent whatsoever when she spoke English. They were a handsome couple. I lost contact with Gene for several years. During that time, Gene was a passenger in a serious automobile accident. Gene survived the crash, but he lost the use of both his legs and had been in a wheelchair ever since.

One night, Etta and I were walking out of the Hideout, a local restaurant, when a voice called, "Hi, Fred." I turned around. Gene and Monica were sitting in a booth finishing their dinner. We hadn't seen them in 20 years.

"Come over and sit down," Gene said.

It was the same Gene Giehl; he just looked a little older. We sat with them for a good half hour, maybe more. "Are you still flying?" he asked me.

"No, Gene," I said.

"Why not?" he asked.

"I haven't flown at all since we lost the Piper Apache. With the boat business and Gordon Keenan retiring and all, I just don't have the time. Plus, I have no place to go."

"That was a long time ago, nearly 20 years. I wasn't in this wheelchair then," he said.

I thought Gene would have stopped flying now that he was in a wheelchair, so I didn't want to say anything.

"I have a Cessna RG Gene said. "I've got a partner but he never flies, so it's like I have my own private airplane."

"That's great, Gene," I said. "But how do you work the rudder and push peddles?"

"I can push my feet down, but I can't control them. I made a contraption to solve that problem. I throw the wheelchair in the backseat and strap my feet to the peddles with Velcro. The contraption has two arms that I can pull backwards to apply the brakes, nothing to it."

He was a flight instructor, and his contraption fit a Cessna 150 and 152, both good training airplanes.

Gene said, "Go get your physical, and I'll get you current."

"I don't know Gene, it's been a long time since I quit flying," I said.

"Let's do it, Fred."

So I went and got my physical. I passed without any problems.

A few weeks passed. The phone rang; it was Gene. "Fred, I have an instructors license now. Let me give you a check ride in my Cessna RG Cardinal, and I'll bring your license up to date."

"Gee, Gene, I don't know."

"It'll be fun. I'll pick you up on Saturday around 11 o'clock," and he hung up the phone.

At 10:45 the following Saturday, Gene was sitting in his Jeep in my driveway. The sky was clear, but the temperature was below freezing. We drove to the Burlington County Airport. We passed through the main gate and drove over to Gene's hangar.

To get the Cessna out of the hangar, we had to chip the ice on the bottom of the sliding door. The RG Cessna was a very nice airplane. It was a high-wing, four-place, single-engine plane painted red. Like everything Gene Giehl owned, it was immaculate, not a speck of dirt anywhere. The thing looked like it just came out of the factory.

By the time we reached the runway, the cabin heater had us nice and warm. We went through the checklist. Gene read the list, and I did the checking. It went something like this. Gene: "Gear down three green." I would put my finger on the three green lights and say, "three green." When the three wheels were down and locked, the lights were green. When the wheels were in the up position, the lights were red.

My problem was that I couldn't find the ground. On landings, I didn't know when to pull the yoke back to raise the nose and make the flare just before touchdown. I was either too early or too late pulling the yoke back to stall the plane for a nice gentle landing. I tried several landings; each one got worse. Finally, I remembered what an instructor told me many years ago. "Pretend there's a garage door at the end of the runway. Can you see it? O.K., now fly."

That worked. It all came back to me. The only difficult part about getting back into flying was all the new rules and the radio work. The old basic instruments were still there: needle and ball, airspeed, etc., but there was a lot of new stuff that was really great. The transponder tells Traffic Control where you are, and at what altitude. The Ground Positioning System (GPS) replaced the LORAN. Tell the GPS where you would like to go, and the GPS will tell the pilot how far it is, how long it will take to get there, how fast you're going, etc. Now, if you're equipped with an autopilot, push the button to connect the GPS to the autopilot, and all the pilot has to do is sit back and the two will fly you there. All the pilot has to do is work the radios. If John F. Kennedy Jr. had these two items on board his airplane, he and his passengers would probably be alive today.

Gene signed my logbook, and I was again legally a single-engine pilot.

Gene was a born pilot. There are lots of pilots, but very few born pilots. For the next several years, Gene and I spent many hours together.

PARTNERSHIPS

Co-pilot Etta in the Cessna 303, 1984

With the Cessna 303, 1984

YOU GOTTA HAVE BALANCE

Paul and Gene had some great ideas for the Cessna 303. When it was built, all the flight instruments were on the pilot's side of the instrument panel and powered by a vacuum pump. Gene had a set of flight instruments installed on the co-pilot's side of the panel, which were powered by electricity. Now two different types of power powered the instrument panels: vacuum and electric. I believe this was the only Cessna 303 with this setup.

Gene designed a pair of clamp-on rudder pedal arms for the toe breaks problem, which I made in our home's basement machine shop. Next we took off the aluminum engine spinners of both propeller cones. Jim Reilly had them gold-anodized. Those really made the 303 look sharp.

Both engines ran a little rough, so Gene replaced all 24 spark plugs with a better type. This did the trick. Now, both engines ran very, very smooth.

Our first trip to Pearson's in Rhode Island almost turned into our only trip. We had subcontracted our fiberglass hulls to Pearson Yachts. Not being the pilot in command or the co-pilot, I did not check the plane for weight and balance.

Paul was in the pilot seat; Gene was in the co-pilot seat. In the cabin was the fiberglass boss, the plant supervisor, Dick LaCates, our in-house decorator, Lauren, and last, but not least, me and two big propellers in the luggage department. I sat in the last seat on the left side of the cabin.

Paul taxied to the active runway and stopped. Paul and Gene went through the checklist: About 20 to 25 items had to be checked before takeoff. When that was completed, Paul pushed the button on the yoke and said, "Cessna 5497 Burlington County Airport."

He taxied out to the center of the runway and applied both brakes, and pushed both throttles to full power. When the turbos reached 32 inches of boost Paul released the brakes, and down the runway we went.

The next thing I heard over the sound of the engines was, "I can't get the tail up!"

The first thing I did was go to the luggage compartment, pick up the two propellers (one at a time) and run up the aisle. I put them both behind the cockpit and stood over them. Shifting the 200 or so pounds from the rear of the plane to the front of the plane did the trick. Now Paul could get the tail of the plane to lift. If the runway had been longer, Paul could have just pulled back the power and landed. But when you are doing 85 knots and there is no runway left, you have a big problem. We were all very lucky we did not crash.

If one of the engines had failed on this take-off, we would, as they say in the airplane world, have "bought the farm." This was the closest I ever came. After that, I was very conscious of the weight and balance of the 303.

The 303 was like all twin-engine airplanes. They will lift more than the weight and balance that the specs call for as long as they have both engines on the line. If the plane is overloaded and one engine quits, you are going to buy the farm. That goes for speed, too. If on take-off, you do not reach your VMC speed, and one engine quits, you must pull back the good engine. If you do not shut down the good engine, that engine will turn the plane upside down, and another farm is sold.

After we landed in Connecticut, I got off the plane with the two propellers. We had a customer there who said that his boat was not running like it should. The information he'd given me over the phone led me to believe that his propellers were the problem. I told him to have his boat out of the water and to pick me up at the Chester Airport, which was just a few miles down the road from the boatyard. Needless to say, he was overjoyed with this kind of service.

Chester Airport was not the greatest place to land the 303. The runway was only 2,500 feet and there was a large oak tree dead-center on one end.

When we arrived, the boat owner was waiting for us. Paul did not shut down the engines. I just opened the back door, got out, and someone handed me the two propellers. I closed the door and off they went to Rhode Island.

When we arrived at the boatyard, the boat was out of the water and the old propellers were on the ground. The yardmen installed the new propellers and the boat was back in the water in 45 minutes. The boat owner started both engines, and we headed out to Long Island Sound where the boat owner put the boat through her paces. A smile came on his face; his problem was gone.

The 303 was not going to pick me up until 4:30, so we went out for quite a long lunch. After that, the boat owner drove me back to the Chester Airport.

Everything went as planned. He was happy, our people enjoyed the trip, and now each side knew the other side. We landed at the Burlington County Airport just a little before five o'clock. A lot was accomplished in one day. The Cessna 303 was a real winner.

A New Life

Our Home In Lumberton

LOOKING AROUND

It was a normal Saturday afternoon. I locked the boat shop up at a little after 1:30 p.m., got into my red, four-door Cadillac, and drove home to our Cinnaminson house. It was a beautiful day. The sun was shining and the weather was hot, but not too hot. The year was 1973.

I parked the car in our driveway and walked into the house. Nobody was home. Then I did something that I had never done before or since that day. I put on my bathing suit and walked out to our backyard swimming pool with a magazine under my arm. After swimming a few laps, 10 to be exact, I sat down with the magazine and started to read an article about people moving in and out of the cities. This really got me thinking. We'd lived in an upscale neighborhood in Cinnaminson with nice neighbors and well-kept homes for 13 years. I hadn't driven around the neighborhood in years. I decided to check it out.

I soon realized that the neighborhood had gone downhill. I saw houses with driveways in need of repair and lawns that needed care. That night at dinner I told Etta about the magazine article and what I'd seen while driving around the block. I said, "Etta, I think it's time to look around for another area, one that has a future. And, by the way, our own house needs a new driveway, which is a big job, and a new roof." Etta joked that I was making it sound as if it would be cheaper to move than make the repairs.

"Gee, Fred, I don't know. This really is such a wonderful house. It has everything you could ever want. A big swimming pool, four bedrooms, five floors, a poolroom. I just don't know," she said.

"You're right, Etta. I can't argue with you about the house. It's the future that worries me."

"Why don't we just look around and see what's available," Etta said.

Well, we did look around. In fact, we looked around for almost four years. We'd go to a real estate office and it would go something like this:

"My name is Fred McCarthy, and this is my wife Etta. We are looking for about 10 acres of ground, with some open area and some woods. Do you know of such a piece of land in this area?" I'd say to the broker.

"Would you like a small stream running through the property?" The broker would answer with a smile.

"Sure, that would be great," Etta would reply.

After talking with several of these clowns, we decided brokers were not the way to go. We began looking around on our own, stopping at farmer's houses and asking if we could buy a piece of land from them.

At the time we didn't know how subdivisions worked. If a farmer had 100 acres, he could divide it into three pieces under the subdivision code. If the farmer sold us 10 acres, the remaining 90 acres could only be divided one more time.

If the land were divided more than three times, this would be called a major subdivision. That changed the rules and the cost went through the roof—streets, sidewalks, landscaping, and on and on. This was why the farmers couldn't cut us a 10-acre piece of ground.

On the weekend, we kept on driving around the countryside looking for what we wanted. One afternoon, we ended up way in the Pine Barrens. If we moved out this far from the boat company in Lumberton, Freddy would be on a school bus forever.

THE RIGHT SPOT

After looking all over the place for a small piece of land to build on, we gave up. Three years and hundreds of miles of driving was enough. We'd found out that small farms were few and far between. But finally we found a family in Lumberton with a 10-acre plot for sale. It was just what we were looking for—it had a small creek; trees bound the north side of the property and the remaining eight acres were farmed.

I called the owners. The land cost $30,000, about $3,000 an acre. That sounded like a fair price to me. In fact, it was a great price if it was like the seller said it was. Etta and I drove out to see the place that day.

The 10 acres were easy to find. They were on Eayrestown Road, now called Landing Street, and inside the city limits. The 10 acres looked very big. We could not understand why this beautiful piece of land, the first farm out of town, was only $3,000 an acre. Something had to be wrong. The land was 20 feet above the creek, so it was not wetland. The soil looked good. The location was great. What else could it be? We walked back to the car, and drove back to our house in Cinnaminson.

The next day we met with the broker and drove out to the farm. He told us that the owner had two parcels of land—the 10-acre plot and another connected, 30-acre plot, which was not for sale.

We walked around and when we reached the creek, Etta said, "This is a nice piece of land. Why is it so cheap?"

There was a short pause, and the broker finally said, "The ground is landlocked. There's no way to get on the property from the road."

"Boy, that's a bummer," I said.

"What good is a piece of ground you can't get onto," Etta said.

"I don't know," the broker replied.

On the way home Etta and I could not stop talking about the 10 acres: location, size, county, and creek. What else would you want? We drove all around the property looking for a 15' by 30' piece of land owned by somebody else that we could use as a road to the property. It did not take long to find out that Louis Russo owned that little piece of ground. He lived on the farmhouse on the other side of the creek. Etta and I drove up his lane and saw a very good-looking girl, who turned out to be his daughter, Rose Ann Russo. A couple of minutes later, her father, Louis Russo, came out the back door. After we introduced ourselves, I told him that we wanted to build a house on the 10 acres on the other side of the creek. "The property is landlocked by your land, and we wondered if there was anyway we could solve the problem."

Mr. Russo thought for a few minutes, and said, "You want an easement from me?"

"I didn't know there was a name for it," I said.

"It's common out in the country," he said.

The meeting lasted about 30 minutes. Louis Russo gave me an easement to cross his land.

He made our day. Now we could buy the 10 acres and build our new house.

MAKING PLANS

It looked like the 10 acres was going to fly. If Louis Russo kept his word and came through with the easement, it would be a done deal. We had a lot of work ahead of us: design the house, sell the Cinnaminson house, and prepare the land for the new house.

Etta and I sat down and laid out our plans. The Cinnaminson house was paid for, so whatever we got from the sale we'd spend on the new house. That way we wouldn't have a mortgage on the new house. To do this, we'd have to do a lot of the work ourselves. That was our basic plan.

We called the broker and told him we would buy the 10-acre lot. Draw up the paperwork, and we would come to his office and give him a deposit on the 10 acres.

After signing the papers and giving the deposit, all we had to do was go to settlement. We went to the 10 acres many, many times after that. Where will we build the house, the barn, and the driveway? All this had to be done before we could start.

A friend of ours, Frank Tippen, was a great builder. He'd done many projects for us in the past and we wanted him to build our new house. Another friend, Russ Young, had a house in the Pocono Mountains that we liked, designed by an architect in Haddonfield, NJ.

We spent a weekend at Russ Young's house with Jim Reilly, his business partner, and his wife, Marge, who was Jim's sister. It was big, but not too big. Etta and I went to the same architect. He knew the house, so it would not be a start-from-the-bottom job. We came up with a similar plan, changing it to fit the 10 acres, but the overall look was the same.

We were very lucky to have Frank Tippen as our builder. The building plans had many mistakes that Frank found and corrected. Sorry, I'm getting ahead of the story.

THE EASEMENT

Things were coming together. The money for the land was in the bank, and the certified check was made out. The settlement was on Friday. We were putting a lot of faith in Louie Russo, but he had not given us the easement in writing yet.

On Friday we were in the office waiting for the sellers to show up. Twenty minutes after the meeting time, the wife showed up. After another 30 minutes, still no husband. We set another closing time for next Tuesday at 11:00.

This time the seller's wife didn't show up. Were they telling us something or were they just nuts? This time I told the husband to set up a time for the settlement, and if either one of them didn't show, I would take them to court for damages.

The third settlement time came around, and finally they both showed up. We signed the papers and handed over the check for $30,000. Before we went home, we stopped at our new land and walked around for an hour or so. It was a great feeling to know we owned this farm.

The next day, I went to see Louie Russo and told him we'd bought the ground, and would not do anything more until we had the easement he'd promised to give us. He said he was too busy right then but would do it next week.

"What's so important right now," I asked.

He had a job that had to be finished that day and his helper hadn't shown up.

"Well Louie, I'll tell you what. We'll drive to the courthouse in Mt. Holly in my car, get the easement on records, and when we get back here, I'll be your helper until we get the job done."

Louie didn't know what to say. I kind of put him behind the eight ball. If he didn't go now, he'd probably never go.

Louie looked down, shuffled his feet a little and didn't say a word. "Come on Louie, you promised me you would give us an easement; and I know you are a man of your word."

We finally got the easement and returned to Louie's farm. "So, what's this job we have to get done today, Louie?" I asked.

"We have to dig potatoes. It's a two-man job. One man drives the tractor that digs the potatoes, and the other man drives the tractor that pulls the potato hopper. The potato digger will shoot the potatoes into the potato hopper."

"Lead the way." I said.

We walked out in the field where the tractors were. "You drive the hopper and I'll drive the digger," Louie said. "You see how the hopper is next to the digger?" Louie said. "Keep the hopper the same distance. The only thing you need to do is move the hopper forward or backward so that the potatoes fill both ends."

I climbed up on the hopper and started the engine. Louie started the digger. We both put our tractors in second gear and started going up and down the field digging potatoes.

I was amazed at the number of potatoes we dug in each direction. We worked very well together. He knew what I was thinking, and I knew what he was thinking without saying a word to each other.

This would not be the only time we worked together. From that day on, Louie and I became good friends. He was a good farmer and a nice guy.

This turned out to be a great day. I got to know Louie, and we got our easement. What more could you ask for?

THE BOY SCOUTS

The easement was on file at the courthouse and we were ready to go to work on our new project. There was so much to do; we didn't know where to start.

We'd commissioned the architect to start on the plans. Frank Tippen, our builder, was on standby. We knew where the location of the house would be; the next step was to get the location ready.

Years ago, there was no trash or garbage collection. The farmers would find a place away from their house to dump their trash and garbage. On our new farm, we found this dumping place was 60 feet east from our new house location, along a path near the creek that was covered with vines, bushes, and types of growth so thick that we did not see the bottles, cans, tires, buckets and every other thing you could think of. How the hell were we going to get rid of this trash? Good question.

I heard that the Boy Scouts had a service to do yard work to make money for their troop. It went something like this: the township would drop off a dump truck on the site on Friday afternoon, and would pick the truck up early Monday morning.

The Boy Scouts would work all weekend to put the junk into the dump truck. Great idea. It took four weeks to do the job. The first weekend, the boys filled the whole dump truck up with glass bottles right to the top.

The price was fair and the boys did a great job. We never did get all the trash out. But, it's 100 percent better then it was.

A neighbor wrote an ad for the *Courier Post* that made the Cinnaminson house sound like a mansion. That day, a young couple called and made an appointment to see the house.

They arrived around 4:30. They had a nice car, dressed and spoke well. Their names were Bob and Betty. We spent a couple of hours with them, and when they left I said to Etta, "They're going to buy this house. You wait and see."

"I hope you're right," Etta said.

A week went by. No Bob or Betty. I guessed I misjudged them.

After a few weeks went by, we were getting very disappointed with the people looking at our house. Just a bunch of tire-kickers.

Saturday rolled around and at lunch we decided to put the sale of our house into the hands of a real estate broker. I drove up Route 30 to the office of a real estate agent who had a pretty good reputation. His commission was seven percent. I signed the sales agreement and left for home, a five-minute drive, and a total of four blocks.

I parked the car and went into the house through the garage like always. Etta was in the kitchen as usual. When she heard me open the garage door, she came and met me at the top of the stairway.

"You were right again," she said.

"Right again about what?"

"The couple, Bob and Betty who you said were going to buy the house just called."

"And...? I said.

"They said, if our house is still for sale, they would like to buy it."

"I can't believe it! I cannot believe it!"

"Why not? You said they were going to buy the house the first time they were here," Etta said.

"I can't believe they called 60 minutes after we signed a contract to pay a broker seven percent to sell the house. That is what I can't believe," I said.

"What do we do now?" Etta asked.

"I'll go back to the broker and see what kind of a guy he is, Etta. What took these people so long to make up their minds to buy our house?"

"The day they looked at our house, her mother had a stroke and died. It's taken her that long to get over the shock."

"I can see why they forgot the house," I said. "I'll see what we can work out."

I drove back to the broker with my fingers crossed.

"Back so soon," he said.

"You're not going to believe this, but when I was here signing the papers for you to sell our house, my wife was home and she sold our house. What can we work out?"

The broker thought for a few minutes. "I will do all the paperwork, and make the settlement and whatever else has to be done for three percent.

"You're an honest man and a gentleman," I said.

We shook hands and I went back home and told Etta how lucky we were to be dealing with a square shooter.

THE OLD ADZE

Frank Tippen started the job by clearing the site: cutting down the trees that were in the way of the house. The site was on a small incline or hill. This would put the basement floor even with the ground in the back of the house.

In the back of the house, facing the creek, you could see the basement wall. It had a double door and one window on the left side, and a standard door and one window on the right side. Inside the basement were a wall and a stairwell separating the two basements. The side with the double doors had the heating system and our machine shop. With the double doors and an eight-foot-high ceiling, we could drive our mowing tractors into the basement for repairs.

The other side of the basement was going to be a recreation room and wine cellar. We built the wine cellar, but never the recreation room.

Lumberton has had a number of floods over the years. The last two were bad enough that they made national TV. With our house 20 feet above the creek, we will never have flood damage.

The living and dining rooms have four, 8" by 8" beams that run from the foundation up to the 8" by 26" beams that support the roof. They are truly working beams. The side beams that are 4" by 6" are just for looks.

I looked all over for the beams. Everywhere I could think of, but no luck. Then one day, someone said, "Why don't you go over to Philadelphia and ask one of those dock builders?"

The first dock builders I came across had everything we needed, even the 8" by 26" by 32' beams. All the beams were delivered the Friday before the Fourth of July weekend.

I told Tippen I was going to adze all the beams, just like they were aged two hundred years. I took the old adze that was given to me by Dick Thompson to the boat shop and made it razor sharp. Dick Thompson owned the Lewes Boat Yard, located in Lewes, DE.

When Frank Tippen heard I was going to adze all the beams for the living room and the dining room he said to me, "This is the Fourth of July weekend. The crane will be here on Tuesday morning. That gives you four days to adze all those beams. I don't think you can make it. It is too big of a job, and if they are not done in time what can we do with some beams adzed and some not adzed?"

"I don't know Frank. Just hope we get the job done in time."

"If you don't, we will have to pay the crane anyway."

Frank was not too happy about the whole thing, but he did not say another word about it. After Frank and his crew left for home, I went to the car and got the old adze out of the trunk.

I thought I would start on the 8" by 8" beams. It was 5:00, and I thought I could get a couple of hours in before heading for home. I climbed up on one of the 8" by 8" beams, and started chipping away with the old adze.

The beams were made from Western Fir trees, and they were the hardest fir trees I've ever seen. They felt more like concrete than wood. A little before 7:00, I headed for home. It was a long day.

Saturday morning rolled around and I was on the site by 7:30 a.m. My hands were very sore from yesterday's adzing. With adze in hand I climbed up on the 8" by 8" beam and started adzing where I left off last night.

My hands were sorer than I thought. I should have worn gloves last night. I climbed off the beam and walked over to a tree stump and sat down. Back then I was into meditation in a big way. After a few minutes I closed my eyes and started to meditate.

I could see in my meditation the chips flying off the fir beams. There were chips all over the place. The chip piles were starting to get higher and higher. The 4" by 6" beams were finished and were piled up in one neat pile. The working beams were too heavy to lift. They were rolled over in order to adze all four sides, and left where they were. Now, I could see all the beams finished and ready to be lifted into place. Frank Tippen in my meditation got out of his car, took one look at all the beams and said, "How the hell did you do all those beams in three days?"

I opened my eyes. I was still sitting on the tree stump and the superhard fir beams were still laying in the same place. After a few minutes, a car drove in and parked. I was surprised to see my brother-in-law, Hank, step out of the car.

He walked over to the my stump seat and after saying good morning and all that stuff, he said, "What can I do to help?"

"How would you like to learn how to use an adze?" I asked.

"I've been swinging a body and fender hammer all my life. This will be something new." Hank said.

After showing Hank how to use the adze, I went back to my tree stump and sat down. Not long after, my nephew Daryl drove in. "What can I do to help you, Uncle Fred?"

"Hank, show Daryl how to use the adze."

I did not have time to get back to my stump when Etta drove up with Freddy.

Freddy said, "Dad, can I help out?"

"Sure, Freddy, you can learn how to use the adze."

People came and went all weekend, taking turns using the old adze. The chips kept flying in all directions, just like I saw in my meditation. By the time Tuesday rolled around, the beams were all ready for the crane crew to put them in place.

My meditation was so real it was spooky. Frank Tippen even said, "How the hell did you do that?" Why I stopped meditation, I don't know. Just lazy I guess.

THE STAIRS

The house was coming along nicely. The roof was on and shingled. The windows were on. Now the new house was watertight. Etta and I were working every night and all day Saturday and Sunday staining and varnishing the doors and windows, and any trim that was installed. We picked black walnut.

Frank said he had a great stair builder. The stairs that ran from the living room to the second floor would be quite large and would be visible from the kitchen, dining room, and living room. If the stairs did not look good it would spoil the house.

The two stair builders came out to the house with Tippen a few days later and took notes for the new stairs. When they were finished I said to them, "Give me your lumber list, and I will furnish all the lumber. Is ash O.K.?"

"Ash would be fine," one of them said. A few days passed before we heard from the stair builders.

The stairs would run from the living room to the second floor with a landing one-third of the way up. At the landing, the stairs made a 90-degree turn up to the cantilevered balcony floor. The stairs have no risers; you can see between every step. This took away the big bulky look. All the stair materials would be 2 1/2" thick, except for the balusters, which would 1 1/2" by 1 1/2".

The drawings from the builders were quite impressive. I asked the stair builder, "Do you always make such detailed drawings?"

"Yes, we do. Ninety percent of our work is either churches, courtrooms or that sort of thing," he said.

After that answer, I was afraid to ask the price. I turned and said to Frank Tippen, "What do you think, Frank?"

"A stairway like that would really make the house one-of-a-kind," Tippen said.

"All right, Mr. Stair Builder, give me the bad news. How much?" I said as I looked over to Etta.

"With you supplying all the lumber and doing all the finish work, our price for building the stairs, railing, etc., installed and ready for finish, would be $5,000."

"You get what you pay for," Tippen said,

"Yeah, Frank, but for $5,000, you can buy a Cadillac," I said. A pause.

"I don't think it's too much money. Look at the size of the opening. Where are you going to buy ready-made stairs that will fill it?"

"I think we should go ahead with these stair builders," Etta said.

"There is your answer, gentleman. Give me the lumber list as soon as you can."

Etta made out the deposit check and everyone left, except Etta and me.

The lumber list finally arrived, and we lost no time in getting an order out to Rex Lumber Company in Englishtown, NJ. Rex Lumber was a supplier of Jersey Yachts, and we were told the ash we wanted, with beautiful knots in it, was in stock. The shipment was to go directly to the stair builders.

While waiting for the stairs to come, Frank had an old 12-foot ladder nailed to the upstairs floor. The ladder was a little shaky, but it did the job.

Etta and I were sanding, staining, sealing, and varnishing the inside doors and trim. The house was now watertight, which made painting, etc., a lot easier. The hard part for me was the 8" by 26" beams supporting the roof that had to be stained.

The rigging that the sheetrockers used to sheetrock the ceiling was still standing in the living room. This was my chance. On Sunday morning, we went to the house and moved the scaffolding around so that I could reach the beams and stain them. We were quite happy when the job was over.

Finally, the stairs were completed and ready for delivery. We set up a time to meet the stair builders and to see the beautiful ash stairs. The truck backed up to our front door and the men started to unload the stairs, which were wrapped in heavy brown paper.

First came the lower set of stairs, then came the landing. The long set of stairs from the landing to the second floor was last. Those three parts were the only thing sub-assembled. Everything else was just cut-to-size lumber.

I kept looking at all the parts, and something just didn't look right, but what? Etta and I just stood there and watched the men working. What am I missing? Then it hit me like a ton of bricks. I can't believe my eyes.

"What is wrong?" Etta asked.

She walked with me over to one of the stair builders. He must have seen I was not happy. He met us halfway and said, "Is something wrong?" He asked.

"Where are my beautiful knots?" I asked.

"Did you say knots?" he said. "Yes, I said knots," I said.

"Oh, we always cut the knots out of the lumber and glue the pieces back together," he said with a smile.

There went our beautiful small knots we were so proud of. This house is going to drive us knotty

THE MACHINE SHOP

The house was coming along great. The time had come to think about moving from Cinnaminson to Lumberton. The house items were no problem. The big problem was moving the machine shop in our garage. The machine shop had been a very busy place. I had built scale-model trains there, fixed some farm equipment, and sometimes machined parts for my boats. The biggest things to move were the milling machine and the 12-inch-gap bed lathe. Between the two of them, they must weigh a couple of tons.

I called Jim Reilly, my neighbor in Cinnaminson, and asked whom he'd used to move his machinery around. He gave me his rigger's name and phone number. His name was Worthington, and he was a real pro.

The path that ran along the creek, and the two-door opening into the basement saved the day. The path was wide enough to back the big truck right up to the basement door. The crane on the truck just picked up the machinery and set it down on the dollies, and rolled the machinery into the shop. The unloading took less than 45 minutes.

Moving from half of a two-car garage into a 20' by 30' shop was like heaven. The large machines used 220-volt, three-phase current. We did not have that power in Cinnaminson. There we only had the old house current, 110 volts single phase, so we used a converter. The converter we had would take 110 volts single phase and convert it into 220 volts three-phase. The converter did the job, but it was not the greatest way to go.

A few months passed before we could think about building trains in the machine shop again. In Cinnaminson, I had built a scale model 4-4-0 locomotive and a 2-6-0 Mogul out of scrap metal. A 4-4-0 has four small pilot wheels in front and four driving wheels in the center and no wheels in back of the driving wheels. This was the engine that won the West.

The 2-6-0 Mogul had two small pilot wheels, six big driving wheels in the center and no wheels behind the driving wheels. Both engines burned coal and ran on tracks that were seven and a half inches inside the rails.

Because of my interest in trains, I had looked up Tom Marshall in Yorklyn, DE, and we became friends. He had several Stanley Steamer automobiles and several steam locomotives in his museum, "Magic Age of Steam." One day he called and asked, "Fred, do you know that Northern I have in the museum?"

"I sure do."

"How would you like to buy the Northern?"

"I would truly love to buy your Northern, Tom; but, we've just built a new house and money is kind of short," was my answer.

"This is not transferable. It is for you only. No one else. If you'd like my Northern delivered to your house, the price is $1,000," he said.

"At that price it's not a sale, it is more of a gift. Are you sure you want to do this?" I asked.

"That's the deal. It's up to you," Tom said.

"Sure, it's a deal. It's a wonderful deal," I said.

To build a locomotive like this, if you had all the casting from the foundry it would take 7,000 to 8,00 man-hours. A Northern is a 4-8-4, which has four small pilot wheels, eight big driving wheels and four trailing wheels behind the driving wheels. A full-size Northern could pull over 100 carts at 80 miles per hour-plus.

Clearing trees

Adzing beams with my brother-in-law, Hank

Hank taking over

Hank and I taking a break

...we'd have to do a lot of the work ourselves.
That was our basic plan.

A few weeks later, Tom Marshall and his right-hand man, Stump, drove up to our house with the Northern in the back of his truck. They backed the truck up the path alongside the creek. When they reached the shop's double door, they were twenty-feet higher from where they started from at the bottom of the path.

After unloading the engine and the coal car into the shop and onto the two stands they brought with them, Tom told me some of the history about the Northern. The man that built the locomotive was a WWI airplane fighter ace. After WWI, our engine builder started a newspaper comic strip called "Rusty Reilly." Around 1953, our builder passed on.

After his death, his wife got in touch with Tom, and Tom bought the Northern from her and put the Northern in his museum, "Magic Age of Steam." The Northern was on display for about 25 years.

The night after Tom and Stump went back to Delaware I started to look the old girl over. The workmanship was very good. The big problem was the engine was built right to scale. To have a good running steam locomotive, you must go out of scale in many areas. For example, if you made the piping to scale the pipes would be too small and the pipes would be plugging up all the time.

I was sure that other things must also be out of scale. As a result, the Northern had to be completely dismantled, and many, many parts had to be re-machined and many parts had to be replaced. The undertaking took over one year, but it was worth it.

POWERING THE SHOP

I called Public Service Electric & Gas, and told them I wanted a three-phase 220 service for our machine shop. After being handed off from one person to another for 20 minutes, I finally got the right man. We set a meeting for next week at 10:00 a.m.

At 10:15 a PSE&G car drove up our lane, and parked in front of our garage doors. The man was in his late 40s and was not Mr. Nice Guy. He did not mention his name. He just said, "I'm from PSE&G." Like I did not know who he was when he drove up my lane in a car with a big PSE&G painted on both side doors.

My feelings were right. I took him down to our new workshop and showed him the different machines. He said, "I'm sorry, but you do not qualify for a three-phase service."

Etta and I were sanding, staining, sealing, and varnishing…

"Why don't I qualify for three-phase service? I have more than 25 horsepower of equipment," I said.

"The rule says you must have at least one motor over 25 horsepower," he answered back.

"If I had 200 sewing machines in service, you're telling me I could not get three-phase service, because I don't have a 25-horsepower sewing machine? Where are you coming from?" I asked him.

"No three phase, and that's that," he said as he started for the door.

"O.K., you want to play games. We will play games. I guess you can find your way out," I said.

Now it is game time.

Over the years I have bought some machine tools from a company in Blackwood, NJ. A nice young man who really knew his stuff owned it.

A few days after the PSE&G clown's visit, I drove down to Blackwood to see him. I walked around the shop just looking. The owner walked up to me and said, "I know the face, but not the name."

"Fred McCarthy from Lumberton, NJ."

"You build boats, don't you?" he asked.

"That's right."

"What can I do for you?" he asked.

"I know you will think I'm a little crazy, but I have reasons for what I'm doing. I would like to rent a 30-horsepower, three-phase air compressor for a few weeks. I don't care if it runs or not. I would like it shipped to my garage in Lumberton, and later to be picked up and brought back here. Sounds crazy, but I have my reasons. What do you think it would cost?" I said.

"I don't have a 30-horsepower, three-phase air compressor on the floor right now. Would a 50-horsepower be O.K.?" the shop owner asked.

"No problem!" I said.

"It's really just a delivery and pick-up. If the air compressor sits in my garage or your garage, what's the difference?"

"If the air compressor sits in my garage, you can't sell it," I said.

"This one is going to the scrap yard. What's the difference if it goes now or in a couple of months from now? It will cost you $300 bucks for the whole job," Mr. Good Guy said.

A few days later, this big truck drove up our lane with this very big compressor sitting on the back. In a very short time the big compressor was off the truck and sitting in the back of our machine shop. The truck driver was very happy when I gave him a nice tip.

After the truck left, I washed the air compressor down and cleaned and polished it. The air compressor did not look like new, but it was impressive.

The following Monday, I called PSE&G. This time I had the right telephone number, and I could tell it was the same guy who had come by earlier. I said who I was and I had the right horsepower to have three-phase, 220-volt service in my workshop. His voice told me he was still not a happy camper. Boy, this guy was something else.

He finally set up a date to come see the new addition to our shop. On that day, the same PSE&G car drove up our lane. Mr. PSE&G got out of the car and said, "I am from PSE&G."

Like I didn't know.

I opened the overhead garage door and there sat this big, 50-horsepower air compressor. I said to Mr. PSE&G, "That's a 50-horsepower, 220-volt air compressor. Now, do I qualify for service to run my air compressor?"

A few seconds passed, and he said, "Yes, you qualify for our three-phase service." He went back to his car and came back with the paperwork. He measured the distance from the street to the house at 1,800 feet for the location of the meter box. After all the paperwork was done, he turned to me and said, "What are you going to use that big compressor for?"

"Mr. PSE&G, all you have to do is make that thing over there make noise. The rest is none of your business."

With that Mr. PSE&G just turned and walked to his white PSE&G car. We now have three-phase, 220-volt power in the shop.

GEORGE HOMAN

It was a Saturday in 1978, and we'd been living in the Lumberton house for a very short time. Someone knocked on the back door that leads into our mudroom. Most farmhouses have mudrooms. Anyone coming in from the fields had to have a place to take off their muddy boots before going into the kitchen.

When I opened the mudroom door, to my surprise George Homan and his wife were standing there. "I hope I'm not bothering you," George said.

"Not at all, George. It is nice to see you and Ruth. Come on into the house. Etta is in the living room," I said.

"You're just in time for coffee," said Etta, giving her hand to Ruth.

"I hope we're not interrupting you," Ruth said with tears in her eyes.

"Not at all," said Etta.

While we were waiting for the coffee to perk, we sat at the dinning room table.

I could feel the tension in George and Ruth, but I did not say anything. Finally, George said, "Fred, I need some advice. I don't know what to do."

"What's the problem George?"

"Are you sure you have the time?" George said.

George Homan was Russ Homan's cousin. "Sure, George, I'm willing to listen. I don't know if I can give you good advice, but let's hear it."

George told us how he and his brother-in-law, Jim Gilem had started Productive Wood Company, making patterns out of wood, in his father's basement. They each started out with 50 shares of stock. When Jim's son, Hal, got out of college, he went out on the road as a salesman. As an incentive to sell more, they both gave him two shares of stock.

"When I went into work this morning," George continued, "Jim called me into his office and said 'My son and I own 52 percent of the company stock, and you only own 48 percent of the company stock. Hal and I had a meeting last night and we voted you out of the company. We want you off the property, and take your personal things with you.'"

By this time, George had tears in his eyes.

"I'm not surprised by what you've told me about Jim Gilem. Only a snake would do to you what he did. You're his brother-in-law. Your sister works in the office. She must have known what was going on."

"I really don't know," George said.

"George, they all planned this scam together, over a long time. I'm glad your dad and mother aren't here. It would break their hearts to know what they did to you."

"What can I do about it?" George asked.

"I'm no lawyer, George, but I think you can't do anything about it. You signed over your two shares of the stock of your own free will."

"I don't know what to do," George said.

We had our coffee and talked about the whole mess. Finally, I said, "George, you never worked for anyone in your whole life, but why don't you come to the boat works for a month? I don't know what you will be doing, but it will be better than just sitting around the house doing nothing. Give it some thought, and let me know," I said.

We sat around the dining room table for another hour or so talking about how rotten Jim Gilem and his son were. It was getting late, and George and Ruth were getting ready to go home. They were both a little calmer, but still in shock. On the way out, George turned around and said to me, "I still can't believe what my family did to me. Some people will do anything for money." On the way out the mudroom door, George said, "What time should I come to work on Monday?"

FHMC

George Homan was at the front door of Jersey Yachts at 7:45 a.m. Monday morning. Over the weekend, I kept thinking about George and where to place him. What can a master pattern maker do in a boat factory?

I introduced George to Dick LaCates, our plant manager, and told Dick that George would be with us for about a month or so. We talked for a short time, and then Dick left my office.

"Sit down, George, and let's talk about your stay here," I said, as I picked up a pad of paper. "George, my dad had a way of signing his initials. It went something like this." I took the pad of paper and drew my dad's initials in big letters: FHMC, the way my dad signed his initials. The letters stood for Fredric Hamilton McCarthy. I handed the drawing to George, "Can you make a pattern three times that size?"

"That's easy. Do you want to cast them in bronze?" George asked.

"Does the kind of metal make a difference in making a pattern?" I asked.

"Every metal has a different shrink rate. Some metals shrink more than other metals. To compensate for this, we use a shrink rule. A standard rule, one inch is one inch. On an aluminum shrink rule, one inch may be one and one-eighth inch to compensate for the aluminum shrinkage as it cools down," George said.

"I'm learning already, George. What do you need to make a pattern?" I asked.

"I have all the tools. The only thing I really need is a layout table that is eight feet by eight feet, very strong, level, and smooth," George's said.

"Boy, that's some table, George."

I took George out in the shop, and up on our lofting floor that was over the mill and down the north side of the building. To build a boat, everything must be drawn full-size. This is called "lofting." "Is this area O.K., George?" I asked.

"This will do fine."

"I guess your first job is building a layout table. Whatever you need, just tell Dick LaCates and he'll get it for you.

George made the layout table and the mold to cast the logo. Now every Jersey Yacht had my father's initials on it, and it brought me luck for the rest of my life. George did a lot of other things, too. His 30 days of working at the boat works turned into 14 years.

Trains

THE 4-4-0 LOCOMOTIVE COMES TO LIFE

Until I was 10 years old, my family lived in Maywood, IL. After that, we moved to New Jersey where my father and two other men started the RCA service company. Our house in Maywood was one block from the Chicago North Western Railroad. The railroad carried passengers and freight. In the morning and late afternoon, the passenger trains ran about every 15 minutes carrying people in and out of Chicago.

As a child, I wanted to be a railroad engineer. I would dream of driving one of those fast passenger trains. My mother had two or three brothers killed on the railroads, and she always made me promise that I would never work on the railroad.

One block down and one block over was the Melrose Park Train Station where lightweight passenger trains picked up and dropped off passengers. You could stand close enough to touch these coal-fired Greyhounds with steam-driven air compressors that panted as if the engine was a breathing, living thing.

A few blocks over were "the hills." A spare track ran from the local steel mill to the hills. The slag from the mill was piled up on both sides of the track. The track between the two hills made a great shelter for the hobos. It was another hangout for us kids. The railroad was our playground up until I was 10 years old in 1936.

Some 20-plus years passed before I started to think about trains again. In 1970, I was laid up with disc problems in my neck and spent lots of time in traction. I asked Etta if she could get some information on large-size model steam locomotives.

It took some doing, but one day Etta gave me a catalog from a company in California called "Little Engines," which was run by a woman. Her husband founded the company, and after he died she took it over.

You could buy castings that were rough or fully machined. Not having a machine shop, I bought the finished parts. The advertisement in the catalog said, "Just bolt together." It took lots of time. The engine I decided to build was a 4-4-0—the engine that won the West—with four pilots, four drivers, but no trailing wheels.

Slowly the engine came together. I took the copper boiler to a great welder in town, and he brazed it together. Russ Homan's dad made a sheet-metal boiler cover. He was an artist with sheet metal and the boiler cover was a work of art.

I took the boiler home from the welder to my little workshop in our basement. I hooked it up to the garden hose and called up to Etta.

"I'm going to test the boiler for leaks. Do you want to watch?" I yelled up the stairs.

"Sure, I'll be down in a minute," she answered.

"This boiler will hold up to 200 pounds of pressure," I told Etta, as I turned on the water valve.

"How come there is water leaking out the bottom?" she asked.

The next thing I knew, water was leaking from all over the boiler. That was just one of my many disappointments.

As the engine was being built, we laid track around the swimming pool and made a cabana that looked like a railroad station with a ticket window. The track had several stops. The cherry tree was Cherry Valley. The apple tree was Applelation. The patio was Patio Junction. The willow tree was Willow Pass, and the pear tree was Pear Pass.

The engine was finally finished in 1971, and it ran around our swimming pool. With such a small firebox, it was very difficult to run the engine and tend the firebox at the same time. We had a going contest: Who could make the most trips around the track without stopping. My brother-in-law Hank was the winner. It was a great summer!

THE MAINE TWO-FOOTER

It was a big let-down when the little 4-4-0 went into service. Building the engine had been great for me. I would come home from the boat works, have dinner with the family, then go down to my little work shop until 9:30 p.m. While working on the engine I would forget all my problems at work. Not being a machinist, I had to put all my thoughts on what I was doing.

I decided to build a bigger engine. This was 1978. But this time I would do all the machine work, everything but the boiler. That is an art in itself. Our two-car garage was now going to be a one-car garage with a machine shop. The first job was to build a wall between the two garages and put in a heating system.

The second job was to find the machines. The first one we got was a very old belt-driven lathe that was still in good condition.

From the Cinnaminson Education Newsletter, 1973, Vol. 5, No. 3: "Fred McCarthy of Cinnaminson operates an exact replica of a late 19th century locomotive. The Camden and Amboy Railroad, one of the first in the nation, crossed the Taylor Farm for the first time in 1832. The locomotive, now displayed in the Smithsonian Institution, traveled on those tracks."

IT WON THE WEST—Model-maker Fred McCarthy stands next to the early-American 4-4-0 steam engine he built himself. The replica burns coal, requires drafting and looks and operates like the real thing. Its type "made the railroad what it is today" McCarthy explained, and his model measures two-feet high by six-feet long.

IT WON THE WEST — Model-maker Fred McCarthy stands next to the early-American 440 steam engine he built himself. The replica burns coal, requires drafting and looks and operates like the real thing. Its type "made the railroad what it is today," McCarthy explained, and his model measures two-feet high by six-feet long.

My neighbor, Jim Reilly, had a machine shop, and he had a $3,000 milling machine that was like new. He needed the space and sold it to me for $1,000. The next thing I knew, our one-car garage was full of machines.

I decided to build a Mogul type locomotive. The Mogul is a 2-6-0, which is twice the size of the 4-4-0 engine. Little Engine Company in California had all the castings for a 0-6-0 switch engine. All I had to do was add four wheels in the front of the engine and it would be a 2-6-0 mogul.

Making a live steam locomotive is a very time-consuming job. Some people work faster than others. It takes about 3,000 hours to build a Mogul. When you get into a big engine like a Northern 4-8-4, you're talking 7,000 hours, plus. For every engine that gets on the track, there are probably eight to 10 that never get finished.

When George Homan came on board at the boat works, I did not know where he would fit in. George was a master pattern maker. He'd served his four-year apprenticeship in Camden, NJ, and his father was the shop teacher at Collingswood Junior High School.

An idea struck me out of the blue. In Maine, they had 2'-gauge trains years ago. If we took a 2'-gauge locomotive and scaled it down to run on our 7 1/2" track, the engine would be one-third the size of a big engine. Boy, that would be some engine.

I talked to a few train builders at the New Jersey Live Steamers and got the same feedback. "The engine would be too heavy. Our rail wouldn't stand the weight. You're wasting your time." They condemned the idea without even thinking about it.

If the engine were built with cast iron, like the full-size engines, it would be too heavy for our rail. But if you made the engine out of good aluminum, it might work. Smokestack, connecting rods, bell stand, and domes—things like that could be made out of aluminum. That would take a lot of weight out of the engine, plus, the total weight would be distributed over 10 wheels. The Maine two-footers were 2-6-2.

It would work. I was sure of it.

I asked George Homan if he would like to make all the patterns for our Maine two-footer. If he started the job, he'd have to stay until all the patterns were finished. I didn't want to be stuck with half an engine. George said O.K., and we shook hands on it.

A magazine in England was running a series of drawings on how to build a Maine two-footer. This would be a big help in our project. The only problem was the engine had the looks of an English locomotive.

A NEW LIFE

Etta and I drove to Maine where some of the two-footers were in storage. Etta the photographer took pictures from all angles of the engine so we could make our engine look American.

We were pretty deep into the project when I realized that with my job running the boat works, I'd have to live 100 years to finish the engine. I would be in that group of guys who start and never finish things.

We found a man in Colorado who made live steam engines and steam boilers. After a lot of talking, we agreed on a time and cost to build our Maine two-footer. The price was $25,000, with monthly payments. George Homan would make the patterns, which would be sent to a foundry. The foundry would make the castings and the castings would be shipped to Colorado.

It looked like all our bases were covered.

THE COLORADO TRIP

Etta and I decided to go to Colorado and see what was going on with the Maine two-footer. The engine should have been finished and in our hands by then. The builder billed us at different stages of construction, and Etta would send him a check. The engine was paid for but no engine!

At the Colorado airport, I went up to a car rental booth and started to tell the young agent what I wanted to rent. Behind me, I heard Etta say in a very low voice, "Fred." As I turned around, I saw Etta passing out and ready to fall down on the concrete floor. She was only two steps away and I had enough time to grab her before she hit the floor.

I heard the young girl at the car rental booth say, "Next, please." There we were. I was sitting on the terminal floor, and Etta was lying on the floor with her head on my lap. People walking in both directions looked down on us as they passed. One lady stopped and said, "Is anyone helping you?"

"I don't know. This just happened," I said.

"If this was in Chicago you would have the medics in just minutes. Can I help you?" the woman asked.

"Thanks. I guess we will just have to wait and see," I said.

Forty minutes later, two paramedics showed up with their rolling stretcher. They said they were sorry it took so long getting there. The hospital was 25 miles away.

After taking Etta's vital signs, one of the men said, "Don't try to get up. You may be having a heart attack. All your signs are very low."

"I'm not having a heart attack," Etta said. We all got in the ambulance and started down the road to the hospital.

At the hospital they rolled Etta into the emergency room and started all kinds of tests. They found that Etta was O.K. For some reason, her blood count and blood pressure were very low. It could be from something she ate or the high altitude.

Etta rested for an hour after a couple of injections before we could leave the hospital. The only paperwork I had to give was Etta's name, address, and phone number. They didn't ask for any insurance.

We called the engine builder and he said he would meet us at our hotel at 2:00 p.m. in the lobby.

"Why can't we meet you at your shop?" we asked.

"I'll tell you when we meet," he said.

Our builder showed up at 2:15, and we walked over to the lounge and sat down in a booth. Now came all the reasons why the engine was not finished: His house burned down, and so on. He said he would have the engine in our yard in two months.

What could we say? Having a battle in the hotel would not solve anything. We said, "O.K., 60 days in our yard. If the engine is not there in 60 days, we'll be back." The meeting did not last long. He left, and we went to our hotel room.

The next day we took our rental car and drove around the perimeter of Colorado. We took the Colorado railroad up Pike's Peak. Living at sea level all our lives made it very difficult to breathe in the high altitude. On the third day, we started home.

We'd been home for two months when the phone rang. It was our engine builder. He said he would be at our house with the Maine two-footer in tow.

At last, all this work, time, and money were coming to an end.

From Maine to Virginia the track gauge is 7 1/4". That means if you took a ruler and measured between the rails at the top distance, it would be 7 1/4". In all the rest of the states in the U.S. the gauge is 7 1/2".

The Maine two-footer is a 7 1/2" gauge. The reason is, if we ever wanted to sell the engine, we would have a much bigger market.

When the engine finally came, I was a little disappointed. The engine itself was very good, but the piping and controls were very poor. It looked like just what it was: a "let's get it done quick" job.

A NEW LIFE

We made some repairs and finally got the Maine two-footer in great shape. I made two riding cars, which were over 10 feet long. The engine was put on the track in front of the house and ran through the Christmas trees. We had planted fir trees on our property, with the idea of selling them at Christmas time.

We had a few kinks to work out at first, but nothing serious. The engine was a dream to run. Two people could sit on the tender. The tender carried enough hard coal to last all day.

Did you hear that?

Hard coal.

Even full-size engines could not burn hard coal!

The two-footer was fantastic. We could run from 11:00 a.m. to 5:00 p.m. and only take on water twice a day. The hard coal was much cleaner than soft coal. At the end of the day you were not covered with coal soot.

The engine was so simple to run that anyone could run the train after one turn around the loop.

The good old boys were still around who said the weight of this engine would destroy the roadbed. After two and a half Christmas seasons, we did next to nothing to the track.

THE BIG TRAIN

In 1971, I volunteered as a fireman on the Black River & Western Railroad every other Saturday. This was like a childhood dream come true. It was a full-size steam locomotive that made excursion trips from Ringoes, NJ, to Flemington, NJ, on Saturdays and Sundays. The round trip was about 21 miles.

The day went something like this: Up at 5:00 a.m., get dressed and jump into the car. The trip from Cinnaminson to Ringoes took a little less than one hour. About 6:00 a.m., start wood fire in engine's firebox. Check engine over, and oil and grease the engine. When the wood fire was burning good, add a little coal. After the coal started to burn, add a little more until you have a good coal fire that is making steam.

Before the crew shut the engine down on Sunday, they would fill the tender with coal and water to be ready for the following Saturday.

The train would make several round trips every Saturday and Sunday with a short layover at each end of the line. Each round trip, the engine would burn almost one ton of coal and 1,000 gallons of water.

When the engine was working, the firebox was 2,500 degrees Fahrenheit. If the fireman let the grates fill up with ashes, the grates would not get the air to keep them cool, and those big cast-iron grates would melt. Without the grates, the engine could not run.

Keeping the water level in the boiler was another one of the fireman's jobs. If the water level got too low, the crown sheet would melt and the boiler would blow up. In the old days, it was not uncommon for a boiler to blow up and kill everyone nearby.

The fireman had to keep the firebox covered with coal. The coal had to be even. You couldn't have a pile of coal in one area and a hole in another. The firebox had to be even from one side to the other side and from back to front. As you can see, the engineer and the fireman had to work as a team.

When my son Freddy was 12 years old, I asked him one Friday night if he'd like to spend the day with me on the Black River & Western.

"Sure, I'd like to go," he said.

"You'll have to get up at 5:00 a.m.," I told him.

"That's O.K. with me."

When we got out of the car and walked over to the cold engine, Freddy said, "Boy, that engine is really big. I didn't think they were that big."

"Climb up into the cab and see how really big the engine is," I said.

Freddy was really a big help getting the engine ready for a day's work. I didn't know our engineer that day. It was the first and last time that ever I worked with him. He thought he was the best engineer in the world. For want of a name, I'll call him Joe.

The first layover was in Flemington. He said to Freddy in a sarcastic way, "Well, son, do you think you could run this engine back to Ringoes?"

Freddy thought for a short time and said, "Yeah, I think I could."

Joe looked at Freddy, "Are you sure you could run this engine? You know there's a lot to running a steam locomotive."

"Yeah, I know there's a lot to it, but I think I could do it," Freddy said.

"Well, let's see what you know about a steam locomotive," Joe said as he got out of the engineer's seat. He pointed to the throttle and said to Freddy, "What's this?"

"The throttle," Freddy said.

"What's this?"

"The Johnson bar. That makes the engine go back and forward."

"What's this valve?"

"That's the injector valve. That puts water into the boiler."

"What's this?"

"That's the sight glass. That tells you the water level in the boiler. There are two of them. One for the engineer and one for the fireman"

"What's this valve?"

"That is the blow-down valve. It lets you lower the water level in the boiler."

"What's this valve?"

"That's the blower valve. It keeps a draft on the firebox when the engine is stopped like it is now. Without a blower valve, the fire would go out."

Now our great engineer had a little different attitude.

"Son, how did you learn all about a steam locomotive?"

"I run my dad's engine," Freddy said.

"Where is your dad's engine?" Joe asked Freddy.

"It runs around our swimming pool in our back yard."

The day ended up being really fun. Freddy and I were very tired by the time we got back to Cinnaminson that evening.

THE STATE OF NEW JERSEY UNDERMINES SANTA CLAUS

The year was 1990 and we were in our second year of running the Maine two-footer at Christmas time. The railbed needed a little work. It hadn't been maintained for several months. Etta ordered 27 tons, one truckload of small stone. Charley Kastanek, an old friend, would help me work on the track and roadbed.

It was getting close to Christmas tree season, and we had to get ready by Black Friday, the day after Thanksgiving. We called our tree-selling operation the Train Tree Plantation. It took a couple of weeks to get the track back to normal. I'm very sorry I went by the book. It said to make the ties 12 inches long. It would have been much better if the ties were 18 inches long. This would make the roadbed look more like a two-foot gauge railroad, and be more stable. We used only half the stone. This gave us about 12 tons for another day.

The day we opened was great. The weather was bright and sunny, and the temperature was in the low 70s. All the helpers showed up. We had the same people for years.

The cars would drive in the entrance road. When they reached the parking lot, Patty Passerelli would say, "Merry Christmas, thanks for coming!"

Then she'd give them a map of the farm and say, "If you have any questions just ask any helper you see. Merry Christmas."

When they reached the parking lot, our good neighbor, Russell Serafini would show them where to park their vehicles. Russ would stand in such a way that they had to park close to the next car or run over him.

When they reached the Gingerbread House, they were given a handsaw to cut down the tree they'd picked out. Some people would look for hours.

After they cut down their tree, a wagon pulled by a tractor would take them back to the Gingerbread House to get their tree baled. My friends and relatives, Mark DiBartolomeo, Leo Quinones, Horace Ciccotelli, Mr. Bracchi, and Jack Wedell, ran the trees through the baler

The Maine two-footer ran from noon until 5:00. My son Freddy and I were the engineers.

In the Gingerbread House you could buy coffee, hot chocolate, donuts, and other items. This was run by Claire Wedell; her husband, Jack, drifted around and picked up any loose ends.

There were no charges for riding the wagon or the railroad. This got a little out of hand near the end. Every time I turned around, I kept seeing this eight or 10-year old boy. When we got back to the Gingerbread House, I turned around and asked him how many rides he'd taken on the train. He didn't know. "Where are your parents?" I asked him. "Oh, they went to the mall," he said.

After the trees were tied down on the car or truck, the people drove to the payout station. Etta's sisters, Marie and Gloria, or Etta's niece, Marietta, would take the money and give everyone a candy cane or apple, then wish them a Merry Christmas before they drove out the truck exit.

On sunny days, it was a lot of laughs and fun. On cold and rainy or snowy days, it was very muddy and not much fun.

Etta was a great person to work for. She served donuts and coffee in the morning, and a hot lunch at noontime. Everyone was given a Train Tree jacket. If you didn't have gloves or boots, Etta would give you some. And if you wanted to stay for a big dinner, come on in!

One Saturday, a nice young man walked up to me and said, I'm from the State of New Jersey's Department of Labor. I have an order signed by Robert Charcik that says you must shut down your railroad until you do one of three things: 1. Get amusement park insurance. 2. Get bonded. 3. Send $150,000 to our escrow account.

"This is not an amusement park. I'm giving free rides on my train to anyone who asks," I said.

"I'm sorry, sir. I'm just the server. I did not make up this order. Mr. Charcik did."

"We are only open four weekends a year, and you drop this on us the first weekend of the year. Don't you people have anything else to do?" I said, then turned around and walked away.

I went into the house and called Farm Family Insurance Company. I told the agent my problem.

"We don't write amusement park insurance, Mr. McCarthy. But I can tell you that amusement park insurance is a lot more than your farm insurance. I'd think twice before you make the move." I thanked him and hung up the phone.

The next step was to get bonded. This took three to four weeks. Christmas would be over then. What a mess. Those clowns up in Trenton had nothing else to do but think up crazy things. Before sending out an order, they should look into the situation.

Amusement parks charge for their rides. We did not charge for our train rides. I finally got mad. I told our broker to wire the state $150,000. You won't believe this! The state would not accept the money.

Somehow, Channel 11 in New York City heard about our problem. The station sent Brenda Flanagan out to do the story. She did a great job. First, she showed the viewer the engine, calling it "the engine that could, but can't." Then she interviewed me and made it look like I was crying.

Can you believe this? Brenda then went to Trenton and interviewed the department head who had started this mess. "Mr. Rubenstein, why did you refuse to accept Mr. McCarthy's money?" Brenda asked.

"It was our decision not to accept Mr. McCarthy's money," he said, not giving her any reason.

When Brenda Flanagan got done with Mr. Rubenstein, he looked like a real ass.

The engine has been sitting in the workshop for 19 years now without turning a wheel, thanks to good old New Jersey and the clowns in the Department of Labor.

Freddy as First Engineer on the 4-4-0   At Train Tree Plantation, 1987

Aerial view of Train Tree Plantation, Lumberton, NJ, 1980

The "24" train, a 1/3 scale live steam locomotive. The train carried up to 100 people at Chrismastime.

With Jackie Wedell on the "24" at Train Tree Plantation, 1989

Michele Quinones (left), and Marietta DiBartolomeo, our nieces, with Santa, 1989

We All Make Mistakes

JANUARY 24, 2009

Today Etta and I live in Jupiter, FL, eight months of the year, from October to June. The rest of the year we spend on our farm in Lumberton. In Jupiter, we have a small condo on the Intracoastal Waterway (ICW). From our fourth-floor patio, we watch the boats—from small rowboats to a large tugboat with a 600-foot barge in tow—going up and down the Waterway.

I woke up this morning at 5:00 a.m. and could not get back to sleep. My mind wandered from one thing to another. I started to think about my parents.

My father's name was Fredric Hamilton McCarthy. I am a junior. What did I really know about him? Or my mother, Genevieve McGrady? How did they meet one another, and where? What was the trouble between the two families? Why did my mother never see her father again after she was married? Did she just get married to get away from her stepmother?

The questions go on and on, and we will never know the real truth of the matter.

What I do know is that my mother's father, Joseph John McGrady, was born in Ireland in 1864 and died in 1951 when he was 87. He was not a poor man, but why wasn't he more helpful to his children, all 16 of them (seven by my grandmother and nine by his second wife)? My mother's mother died when she was very young. After her death, her father went back to Ireland and married a woman half his age.

The new wife, over a period of time, pushed the first wife's family out of the house. The four boys died in different parts of the country and my Aunt Dee Dee was the only one to go back to the house on rare occasions. My Aunt Marie and my mother never set foot in the house again.

When the old man died, the second wife took care of the money. He died very early one morning but the doctor, a friend of the family, did not sign the death certificate until after noon that day. This gave her time to empty out the safety deposit boxes and bank accounts.

The summer I got out of the Navy after World War II ended, I came up with a plan. I was living with my parents, and I told my mother that I was going to Baltimore to see one of my shipmates for a week. Instead I was going to drive to Chicago to meet my grandfather, whom I'd never seen.

I had the car packed with a few things and was ready to go. My mother walked me to the front porch and told me to be careful. After a little pause, she said, "I know you're going to see your grandfather. I wish you wouldn't." With that she turned and walked into the house. When my mom asked you not to do something, you just didn't do it.

When my grandfather died in 1951, I was surprised when my mother asked me to drive her to the funeral in Chicago. I had a new four-door Ford Victory and my mom, dad, and I drove it to Chicago. What a funeral! I had never seen anything like it and probably never will again. All the big shots of the Catholic Church were there—the cardinals and bishops. The choir was made up of 100 priests. There were flowers everywhere. Funeral cars were lined up as far as you could see.

Afterwards, we went to an apartment where we were introduced to uncles and aunts, most of them old enough to be my parents. It was a boring time, and I was unimpressed with the whole bunch. I thought that the whole family had just been waiting for the old man to die for his money. Now they were too old to enjoy it. One of my biggest regrets was that I didn't go against my mother's wishes and visit my grandfather when I'd planned, five years before he passed on. That's called hindsight.

With our prize-winning marlin (551 lbs, 12.5' long with a 60" girth) in San Juan, Puerto Rico, 1960

At the Cinnaminson house, 1970

Our silver wedding anniversary, 1979

En route to Florida with the *Mystic Lady*, in St. Michaels's, MD, 1990

Afterword

Gratitude

There are three things that have made my life so great.

My loving Mother, Father and brother Bob. Our family stuck together and looked out for each other.

My marriage—I was blessed with the most loving, caring, beautiful woman in the world. Without Etta, I would not be where I am today. In our 55 plus years of marriage, we have had only one spat and that was in the first month of our marriage.

And I feel very strongly that I was guided and watched over by The Big Boss upstairs.

Made in the USA
Charleston, SC
03 February 2010